ARCHITECTURE

art or profession?

To our mothers
LOTTIE LUBBOCK
& PAT PARADINE

ARCHITECTURE

art or profession?

Three hundred years of architectural education in Britain

MARK CRINSON
& JULES LUBBOCK

The Prince of Wales's Institute of Architecture

Manchester University Press
Manchester and New York

distributed exclusively in the USA and Canada by St. Martin's Press

ST. JAMES'S PALACE

The Royal Commission for the Exhibition of 1851, established by
my great-great-great-grandfather, Prince Albert, has, since its
inception, promoted new educational initiatives in the Arts and
Sciences. I am therefore delighted that the Royal Commission and
my own Institute of Architecture have come together to promote
the research for this new book. My own interest in architectural
education dates back some years to when I first realized the need
for a different kind of training for architects if any lasting
improvement was to be brought about in the built environment.
An essential first step, however, was to find out how the present
system had evolved, since no overall history of the subject then
existed. I am glad to say that this trenchantly-argued and well-
researched book now answers that need. Jules Lubbock and Mark
Crinson are to be congratulated on producing a much-needed work
of comprehensive research.

The most striking discovery for me was to be able to trace the
tendency for architectural education to become ever more narrowly
specialized and remote from the concerns of the public at large,
from the other building disciplines and from the process of
making buildings, as architecture became a profession in its own
right. Excessive specialization is not unique to this field.
But that is no justification for doing nothing to rectify the
situation.

In the early days those who designed buildings and planned towns
were drawn from an astonishing array of backgrounds - among them
astronomers, carpenters, bricklayers, dramatists, painters and
country gentlemen. This seems to have given them and their
buildings a certain breadth of vision. Even in the Victorian
period Pugin, Ruskin and their followers in the Arts and Crafts
Movement tried to keep the door open to a catholic approach. It
is interesting to find that several of the leading modernists
were similarly inspired: Walter Gropius wanted students to have
practical experience, and others wanted architects, engineers and
surveyors to start their professional education with a foundation
course in environmental studies - something my Institute has now
implemented. Sadly, many of these initiatives were squeezed out
by the drive for uniformity.

In devising courses of a more holistic nature, my Institute has been inspired by these imaginative ideas which had sadly failed to take root in the past. I very much hope that all the building disciplines, not just architecture, will be encouraged by reading this book to reverse the present trend towards over-specialization and uniformity, and to introduce a greater variety of courses with more cross-fertilization.

More, however, is at issue than improvements in the education of professionals. It is my firm conviction that each one of us is a builder both at heart and in practice. It is essential that professionals should not pre-empt this function. The creation of sympathetic and enjoyable surroundings depends upon all of us seeing that they are an extension of our own sense of pride and belonging, and upon all of us feeling that we can work to that end.

Copyright © Mark Crinson and Jules Lubbock 1994

Published by Manchester University Press
Oxford Road, Manchester M13 9NR, UK
and Room 400, 175 Fifth Avenue, New York, NY 10010, USA

Distributed exclusively in the USA and Canada
by St. Martin's Press, Inc., 175 Fifth Avenue, New York,
NY 10010, USA

British Library Cataloguing-in-Publication Data
A catalogue record for this book is available from the British Library

Library of Congress Cataloging-in-Publication Data
Crinson, Mark.
    Architecture—art or profession? : Three hundred years of architectural education in
Britain / Mark Crinson and Jules Lubbock.
        p.   cm.
    Includes bibliographical references.
    ISBN 0-7190-4171-6.—ISBN 0-7190-4172-4 (pbk.)
    1. Architecture—Study and teaching—Great Britain.   I. Lubbock, Jules.   II. Title.
NA2185.C75   1994
720'.7'041—dc20   93-49014

ISBN 0 7190 4171 6 *hardback*
ISBN 0 7190 4172 4 *paperback*

Designed in Adobe Minion
by Max Nettleton FCSD
Typeset by Servis Filmsetting Ltd, Manchester
Printed in Great Britain
by Redwood Books, Trowbridge

CONTENTS

FIGURES

ACKNOWLEDGEMENTS

Our greatest debt is to the Royal Commission for the Exhibition of 1851, without whose generous financial support this work could not have been undertaken. We are also grateful to the Prince of Wales's Institute of Architecture for a grant to assist with the publication of this work. Christopher Alexander, Gavin Stamp and Robert Thorne offered telling commentary on earlier versions. The research of Brian Hanson and Alan Powers, the authors of two important unpublished Ph.D. dissertations, showed us some of the routes by which this hazardous terrain might be crossed. A host of other people suffered our questions, offered advice or gave of their resources: Adrian Allan, Tony Barber, Neil Bingham, Peter Burton, Peter Carter, Jonathan Cater, Christopher Cross, Ben Farmer, Sebastian de Ferranti, Rebecca Foote, Patrick Hannay, Brian Hanson (again), Peter Gibbs Kennet, Angela Mace, Jim McKinnon, Andrew MacMillan, Byron Mikellides, Steven Morant, James Paul, Lord Rothschild, John Simpson, John Nelson Tarn and David Vickery. Katherine Reeve of Manchester University Press has picked us up and dusted us down, skilfully assisted by Hannah Freeman and Richard Wilson. Lastly, we would especially like to thank those architects, teachers and administrators who generously gave us their hospitality, personal recollections and wisdom during long interviews: Douglas Jones, William Tatton Brown, the late Percy Johnson-Marshall, Sir Leslie Martin, Elizabeth Layton, Reginald Cave, William Allen and Edward Mills. The views expressed here are, of course, ours alone.

ABBREVIATIONS

AA	Architectural Association, London
AASTA	Association of Architects, Surveyors and Technical Assistants
A&BN	*Architect and Building News*
ABT	Association of Building Technicians
AD	*Architectural Design*
AJ	*Architects' Journal*
AR	*Architectural Review*
CIAM	Congrès Internationaux d'Architecture Moderne
MARS Group	Modern Architectural Research Group
RIBA	Royal Institute of British Architects.
RIBAJ	*Royal Institute of British Architects Journal*
SATO	Service Arts and Technicians' Organization

INTRODUCTION

One of the major forces shaping the built environment since the end of the Second World War, perhaps the most important, has been the system of professional education through which all qualified architects have to pass. This may seem a surprising statement; many people would emphasise the influence of leading modern architects like Le Corbusier, Mies van der Rohe and their successors; others would identify the planning system or property developers, but the effect of the architecture schools has been neglected, perhaps because they are places of which few people other than qualified architects have either knowledge or experience.

This book, the first to provide a general history of the subject in Britain, sets out to show how the influence of architectural education has grown during the past three hundred years, and especially in the recent past. And it appears at a time when the place of the architectural profession within the building industry is changing with inevitable consequences for vocational education. A few moments' reflection will indicate the importance of the subject. For if towns and cities are shaped by buildings and buildings are designed by architects then their education (which in the UK is now compulsory, university-based and lasts seven long years) must be a major factor in the formation of the design philosophies which will see them through the course of their careers. Few of us, after all, would have the courage or determination to cast aside all we have learned with such difficulty and at such cost over so long a period of time, to rethink the basic principles of our profession and learn new skills from scratch.

But there is another way in which architecture schools have come to influence the built environment quite apart from their role in moulding the minds of the next generation. Following the example of the Bauhaus in the 1920s the leading international schools of architecture such as London's Architectural Association, Cambridge, Harvard, Yale or Berkeley have become the breeding grounds for new architectual imagery, experiment, styles, theories and fashions – a situation which has become more pronounced since around 1970, as we will explain in Chapter Four. Young teachers, at the beginnings of their own careers as architects and often before they have actually built anything, have used the schools to develop new ideas and even to form embryonic practices amongst their most talented students.

A final reason why the system of architectural education and professional qualification has assumed such importance is that over much of the post-war period the Royal Institute of British Architects (RIBA) has regarded it as one of the three pillars of the profession, the other two being public sector building, housing in particular, and the post-war British planning system. The system of architectural education therefore should be a subject of considerable interest to everyone interested in the built environment.

But is it in the first place really true that architects have so much power? Because their work is so visible they may seem more important than they really are, and hence the target for brickbats. After all, many different people and factors are involved in building: clients, landowners, developers, planning laws and regulations, engineers and other professions, builders, manufacturers and financiers, and last but not least the form of the existing town and its inhabitants into which all new buildings must fit whether badly or well. Architects like to call themselves the leaders of the building team, but are they really? Our answer is that architects were very powerful but only for a short period of time of about twenty-five years between the mid-1950s and the late 1970s. Architecture is basically a weak profession, very vulnerable to encroachment from the factors just referred to. The history of the way that the profession has organised the education and induction of its future members is in large part the study of how architects have tried to protect their function against such powerful forces. This book is therefore also an attempt to answer that question of how much power architects have over the built environment by looking at the way that their system of professional education and qualification has changed as they have adjusted their professional identity in an effort to strengthen it or to protect their position. Thus the history of architectural education is in large part the history of the profession. Debates over the content of the curriculum were debates over what the leaders of the profession believed that architects should be and how their functions differed from those of other professions, while the process of qualification concerned the question of how best to gain the most control within a hostile business environment.

We have chosen to examine architectural education in terms of historical change rather than in the form of a detailed study of present practice first because many of these practices only make sense in terms of structures that were devised often in the distant past and which have survived in the different conditions of the present. Second, because contrary to common understanding it is only very recently that architects have had any major responsibility for the appearance of buildings, let alone the shaping of the environment. This is a development that belongs only to the past hundred years. It may be helpful at this point to provide a broad outline of the book.

Before the mid-eighteenth century the vast majority of buildings were erected by builders with no pretensions to being designers. Architects, so-called, were only responsible for designing major monuments such as churches and palaces and since there was no profession as such they were trained in many different fields. Thus of the three founders of Italian Renaissance architecture Brunelleschi was a goldsmith by training, Alberti was a humanist scholar and Michelangelo was a painter and sculptor. Much the same was true in Britain. There was no established route for becoming an architect and the same was true for the other professions and crafts involved in building, all of which overlapped. Independent masters in the building crafts, employees in the Royal Works, workers in other professions such as painting, science or diplomacy and members of the landowning classes might all become architects as well as those who had served their pupillage with an architect – there were five different ways to become a designer of buildings. This is the situation that we describe in Chapter One, long antedating the establishment of a professional association, the RIBA, in 1834, or the arrival of compulsory qualifying examinations for membership in 1882.

The Industrial Revolution and the application of the means of industrial capitalism to the process of building after the 1780s changed all this. The large-scale building contractors and developers with their unified organisations and competitive tendering threatened to turn the architect into a cog within their machine. Furthermore, if any carpenter, jobbing builder or surveyor could become an architect simply by calling himself one and putting up a brass plate then those who had endured an expensive pupillage were defenceless. The professions mobilised themselves into their institutes – engineers in 1818 and architects in 1834. Four key measures were devised so that architects could protect their market against competition from all comers by controlling entry into their profession. Educational qualifications were the means to this end. The measures were

1 Compulsory examinations for membership of the RIBA in 1882.
2 The first full-time academic courses in 1895.
3 The RIBA Board of Architectural Education to oversee courses in 1904 and its Visiting Boards in 1922.
4 The Architects' Registration Acts of 1931 and 1938 to restrict the use of the name 'architect' to qualified people.

The development of this process forms the substance of Chapter Two and covers the crucial debates over whether architecture should be closer to the practical craft of building and the visual arts or to the more managerial professions, positions which correspond roughly to the battle of styles between Gothic and Arts and Crafts on the one hand and the classical style of the Beaux Arts on the other. By 1910 the latter had won the argument and control of the recently formed university schools of architecture.

Even so the qualified and registered architect remained a gentlemanly figure with a brass-plate practise specialising in private mansions, churches and major public and commercial buildings until well into the 1930s. As Sir John

Summerson pointed out in an article of 1942 on the post-war future of the architectural profession entitled 'Bread and Butter and Architecture' (Summerson 1942) the market in their services which they had succeeded in protecting by the end of the nineteenth century has been rapidly disappearing since the end of the First World War as a result of the slump, capital taxation and the decline of church-going. Architects could no longer afford to look down their noses at house building or commerce nor to leave town planning and the enforcement of by-laws and building regulations to surveyors and engineers.

The architects' response to this threat, resulting in the total reshaping of the profession and its system of education as well as the massive enlargement of their market and their sphere of influence, is the subject of Chapter Three. Their solution, hammered out by the Young Turks of the Architectural Association and Liverpool University's School of Architecture during the late 1930s was for a profession largely employed as salaried architects both within public sector architecture departments serving the Welfare State and within private practices to whom much public work was subcontracted. The leaders of the profession also pressed for a leading role in the formation and implementation of the new form of town and country planning and of other high-level policy matters affecting the building industry and the environment. The approach to education was modernist, in the broad sense of that word, and was imposed very effectively upon new entrants from the late 1950s onwards by virtue of the complete phasing out of pupillage in favour of an exclusively college-based education under the control of the RIBA.

This period marked the apogee of power for a basically very vulnerable profession. Architects headed the planning departments of the major British cities, and this gave the profession the power to reshape the cities along the lines thought out by Le Corbusier, amongst others, before the war. They could promote the kind of modernist architecture in which they believed even in the face of reluctant private developers who, before they were allowed to build, now needed permission, which was totally dependent upon the discretion of the architect-planners. The local authority architecture departments handled the huge quantity of the great post-war housing programmes upon whose success governments rose or fell, and this provided the architecture profession with its 'bread and butter'. The architecture schools meanwhile turned out the young designers who had been educated to take on these tasks, which were as much political and managerial as related to design. The image of the profession and the range of its involvement in building had been totally transformed both in fact and in the mind of the general public who came to believe, not without reason, that all buildings were designed by architects – a perception which enabled architects to enjoy great public esteem in the 1960s, but which has been at the root of the increasing unpopularity of architects ever since.

The formal college-based system of about thirty-six architecture schools had become the only route by which one could become legally entitled to practise as an 'architect' as a result of the Architects' Registration Acts, a privilege unique within the building professions. From the 1960s onwards the curriculum was firmly controlled by a central authority, the RIBA and its revamped Board of Architectural Education, seen by some of its leading members as a Ministry of Architecture in all but name. The curriculum was modernist and although not completely homogeneous the different shades of opinion were united in their common opposition to anything that could be accused of traditionalism, against which they were able to define themselves. Hence the classical Beaux-Arts curriculum – construction, lettering, Orders, measured drawing, composition and the study of typology and decorum, history, perspective, sciagraphy, sketching and studio design – was regarded as fixed and unchanging and thus unsuitable for providing students with an 'education for change' in the modern world.

It was none the less a surprise for us to discover, even as late as 1990 when one of the major changes had been a profound and widespread public disenchantment with the modernistic vision associated with the 'City of Towers', that all forms of traditionalism – whether in matters of style, practice or pedagogy – were excluded from British architecture schools (and everywhere else in the world) which none the less provided a home for new movements such as post-modernism, apparently at odds with modernism itself. We seek to explain this paradox in Chapter Four by borrowing from the history of science Thomas Kuhn's concept of the 'paradigm'. This sought to explain why when a new scientific theory displaced an old one it did so suddenly, not gradually, and then remained impregnable until it was suddenly displaced in its turn. Modernism after the 1930s was the new architectural paradigm which had gained majority adherence by the mid-1950s and around which the profession united to the exclusion of the old Beaux-Arts paradigm, but leaving itself free to develop in new directions often unforeseen by the modernist pioneers. And it was within the architecture schools that many of these new experiments were first conducted. The schools became a kind of architectural laboratory where Brutalism, non-plan, Archigram, post-modernism and deconstruction could all be fashioned without incurring the costs of actual building, often a decade or more before they appeared on the streets. That is how architecture schools have come to generate influential new styles and movements. And it is for all these reasons that architectural education has become so important.

But even as this book goes to press there are unequivocal signs of a further paradigm shift taking place in architecture as a result of changes in the planning system, the collapse of public sector employment, major changes in the construction industry, and the fact that the Government has even considered repealing the Architects' Registration Acts. Both architects and their education will change. We hope that this book will provide those people involved in reforming the architectural profession with a critical and historical perspective to enable them to steer their way towards a new system through an understanding of the reason why the existing system took the shape it did. In national politics historical knowledge and understanding is generally considered to be an essential qualification for politicians, and it seems reasonable to ask no less of those involved in legislating for the affairs of a very important profession within the nation's largest industrial sector.

The research upon which this book has been based was originally and very generously funded in 1989 by the Royal Commission for the Exhibition of 1851 for that very purpose, although none of us could then have foreseen the possible repeal of the Registration Acts. What could be seen at that time, however, was the existence of a 'hole in the market' in architectural education, namely the absence of any course where those who wished could study what might broadly be termed 'traditional' architecture, at a time when public distaste for modern architecture was very strong. There was also another 'hole in the market', namely the absence of any wide-ranging history of architects' education. In its unpublished form this book has already served the team which established the Prince of Wales's Institute of Architecture to formulate their aims and their curriculum in an effort to provide an education in traditional architecture. In the new circumstances we hope it will be of benefit to those who will have to reshape the whole field of the vocational education not only of architects but of all those who work in the building industry. Although our work had its origin in 'applied' history we hope none the less that it will prove to be a worthwhile contribution to the history of architecture in particular and to the study of vocational education and the process of professionalisation in general.

CHAPTER ONE

'From Wren's lodge to the neoclassical academy, 1660–1830

In the present, at a time of widespread specialisation and rigidly defined and regulated forms of professional training within the construction industry, the seventeenth and eighteenth centuries might seem both remarkably simple in some of their working relationships and chaotically diverse in their routes of entry, methods of training and even in the titles associated with certain tasks. Even to conceive of architects as the leaders of the building team mediating between client and contractor and controlling the design and executive aspects of building is to use a modern conception that fits uneasily with much seventeenth- and eighteenth-century practice. Wren, Hawksmoor, Vanbrugh, Paine, Robert Morris and Soane each experienced a very different form of induction into architecture, and each worked within different kinds of building organisation; and for every Hawksmoor or Morris there were hundreds of other figures calling themselves surveyors or master masons, carpenters or even undertakers, emerging briefly as the apparent designer of a building and then changing into speculators or engineers before perhaps disappearing again into the realms of craftsmen and builders. The social order may have been fixed but certainly the idea of the architect was not cemented into place within it.

It would be wrong, therefore, to look back at this period and to single out those aspects of it that best conform to our modern sense of the architect as those most worthy of attention. We start our history, therefore, not with Inigo Jones (1573–1652), the British prototype of the modern artist-architect and the promoter of an Augustan classicism, but with Sir Christopher Wren (1632–1723) and his more equivocal legacy. Both Wren and Jones were put in charge of the Royal Works, but it was only Wren who considered the Works not just as an organisation for erecting and maintaining buildings but also as a school of architecture and of building in its broader sense, wherein all manner of skills and aptitudes might be nurtured and developed – a potent version of the medieval building lodge, and one that has largely been lost to the modern world of building. As well as exploring this approach to education, discontinuous as it is from what followed it, we will also ask why Charles II and Wren did not take the opportunity of founding a Royal Academy of Architecture at the moment when it might have seemed most apt as a symbol of the restored monarchy. Both the King and his Surveyor admired French institutions and yet they did not imitate the French Academy of Architecture founded in 1671. To understand this we will consider the various forms of academy that did exist in Britain, the role of the Royal Society formalised in 1660 to promote experimental research, and of course the operation of the Royal Works itself.

Wren did not attempt to impose a unified system of training upon architecture; indeed the independence of and respect still held for craftsmen was such that the idea of a top-down imposition was almost inconceivable. Instead the period is characterised by the number and diversity of means or routes open to those who might become responsible for the design of buildings. Pupillage as a distinctively architectural form of training was a late addition to these routes and its appearance, together with the foundation of the Royal Academy in 1768, is usually taken to mark the emergence of the first model of professionalism in architecture. The force of this can easily be exaggerated but certainly we could see the RA as the establishment of a proper public arena for the arts and as the first institution upholding the architect as a cerebral figure distanced from the mechanical or manual aspects of building. This edifying idea of architecture, apparently aloof from the commercial world or the world of everyday skills, and even separate from the universities at this period, was however not the only possible conception of a national academy but instead represents the success of a particular confluence of interests at the end of the eighteenth century. Other possibilities are represented here in terms of the history of the idea of an academy over the preceding hundred years, including the notions advanced by Evelyn, Berkeley and Shaftesbury. Again we are as much interested in the discontinuities and contingencies of history as in its evolutionary patterns.

Why was there no Royal Academy of Architecture in England?

With the restoration of the monarchy in 1660, the Fire of London in 1666, and the appointment of Christopher Wren as Surveyor-General of the Royal Works in 1669, architecture in Britain reached a state of concentrated symbolic interest that it had rarely attained before. Returned from Paris, Charles II tried to recreate in new palaces at Greenwich and Winchester the images and attributes of royal power that he had seen in France at Versailles and the Louvre. The need to rebuild the City of London and especially St Paul's after the Great Fire produced conditions that revolutionised London's building industry (1). The building crafts had already been reformed under Inigo Jones's influence earlier

1 The rebuilding of St Paul's. Nineteenth-century engraving based on an original drawing

in the century so that by the 1660s their craftsmen were thoroughly acquainted with classical forms. Under Wren's control the Royal Works was forged into a large and relatively efficient organisation for architectural production.

Clearly then, great changes and opportunities confronted British architecture in the 1660s. But it is quite hard to picture how these affected the training of architects. The use of forms widespread on the continent since the Renaissance, and in particular the emulation of French achievements, would suggest that England might easily have copied the French Royal Academy of Painting and Sculpture (1648), a centralised body for reproducing and debating artistic practice to which architects were also admitted until they acquired their own Academy of Architecture in 1671. Yet no such body was formed in England until the foundation of the Royal Academy in 1768, and that was much less powerful in its architectural influence, a pale shadow of France's state-organised architectural education. Why was it that Britain had no academic system for architecture until the early twentieth century, and no centralised and exclusively academic education until the 1960s? That is a situation which needs to be emphasised and explained.

Wren certainly shared his sovereign's admiration of contemporary French architecture and its method of organisation. When he visited France in the summer of 1665 his business was 'to pry into Trades and Arts', to meet scientific and intellectual groups, and to write a work for the Royal Society called 'Observations on the Present State of Architecture, Arts, and Manufactures in

2 Construction of the east front of the Louvre, Paris: engraving by Sébastien Leclerc (1677)

France' (Downes 1988: 8). He was acting, in all probability, as an industrial spy and his intent was not just to meet France's leading practitioners, but also to bring back 'almost all France in Paper'. Whatever was attained, nothing survives. But a letter by Wren himself shows what he observed and what impressed him in France's architectural economy:

> I have buried myself in surveying the most esteem'd Fabricks of Paris, and the Country round; the Louvre for a while was my daily Object, where no less than a thousand hands are constantly employ'd in the Works; some in laying mighty Foundations, some in raising the Stories, Columns, Entablements, Etc with vast Stones, by great and useful Engines; others in Carving, Inlaying of Marbles, Plaistering, Painting, Gilding, Etc. Which altogether make a School of Architecture, the best probably, at this Day in Europe (2).[1]

Wren saw that the integration of the massive workforce engaged on the Louvre by the French Royal Building Administration was not simply a matter of practical efficiency but also an embodiment of theoretical knowledge in institutional form: 'An Academy of Painters, Sculptors, Architects, and the chief Artificers of the Louvre, meet every first and last Saturday of the Month', he observed (Wren 1710, Part 2: 261). Although he made no special mention of architectural training, he was clearly aware that the education of those with responsibility for the design and supervisory aspects of architecture was part and parcel of this system; the works were a school and people learnt on the job.

Obviously Wren would later have known about the separate French Academy of Architecture when it was formed in 1671 as a body to formulate theory and to regulate the standard of training for architects. Initially its educational facilities consisted only of lecture courses two days a week. By 1717 it had taken over much of the specialised training of architects in the skills and principles of design, although the students continued in their apprenticeships in the studios of individual masters. It was only when Jacques-François Blondel started his private school in 1743 that full-time architectural training was first offered. Like the original Italian academies of art, therefore, the French Academy of Architecture aimed at first to supplement the work that students did in their masters' workshops. It was only later that it began to place these workshops within the academy itself. However deeply impressed Wren was by his visit to France in 1665, there is no sign that he responded to the creation of a French Academy of Architecture in 1671 by calling for a similar one in England. Yet academies were not foreign to England.

Three kinds of academy had already been tried. The first was a body of learned men in the service of the King. In James I's reign the Order of the Garter was conceived as the basis for a Neoplatonic academy whose members would include Inigo Jones, Sir Henry Wotton and Ben Jonson (Pevsner 1940: 15; Rykwert. 1983: 131–3). Charles I was also interested in forming such an academy, but nothing came of this (Jenkins 1961: 65). The second form was that of the informal aristocratic academy, such as that run by Mary Sidney, second Countess of Pembroke, at her country house in Wilton. This included the poets Ben Jonson, John Donne and Samuel Daniel.

The third form of academy was a more independent and educational venture that aspired to a different kind of knowledge from that purveyed by the universities, the Inns of Court, or the Church, which was primarily humanistic, legal and theological. Indeed this alternative form of academy embodied the links which existed between science, dissent and educational reform in the first half of the seventeenth century, and was held in deep suspicion by those opposed to these interests. Francis Bacon had propounded a Solomonic College as both a scientific body and as a keeper of antiquities. More generally his ventures encouraged the setting up of institutions that would deal with the new sciences (then referred to as experimental philosophy) ignored by the universities, and would provide for an educated laity not limited to members of the upper classes. These ideas were carried into the second quarter of the seventeenth century by the Puritan pamphleteer Samuel Hartlib and the educational reformer John Comenius, who suggested a Pansophic College to teach all the new sciences (Hill 1972: 105). This, and Hartlib's later non-sectarian Invisible College (1645–48), as well as his attempts to replace lectures on law, divinity and rhetoric at Gresham College in London (actually established to teach modern subjects in both Latin and English, and controlled by merchants) with lectures on technology, all formed the groundwork for the Royal Society (Hill 1972: 107). In 1635, encouraged by Hartlib, Sir Francis Kynaston founded the

Museum Minervae in Covent Garden in order to teach neglected subjects to the nobility. Architecture was to be taught by the professor of geometry, together with arithmetic, algebra and fortification, and where appropriate the teaching was to be done through demonstration and experiment (Kynaston 1636: 4–5). Another private venture was the short-lived academy founded by Balthasar Gerbier in 1649. Gerbier was a friend of Hartlib's and his school was based partly on Kynaston's academy. It too was intended to provide an education in non-university subjects for young gentlemen. Parts of the curriculum dealt with drawing, carving, painting, perspective, fortifications and architecture; the last of which was described by Gerbier as 'as well for Building, as for Magnificent shewes, and secret motions of scenes' (Quoted in Power 1967: 30). It is not known if this would have equipped anyone actually to practise architecture, and anyway the academy folded within a year.

The work of these and other early seventeenth-century educational academies has to be understood against a background in which there was profound suspicion of mathematics and geometry as magical and possibly the work of the devil. The development of a mathematical approach to nature and the applied use of mathematics in technology, particularly for the theatre, was led by John Dee in the late sixteenth century and was deeply informed by Renaissance hermetic-cabalist traditions and alchemy. They were taken up in a safer form in Francis Bacon's science and Inigo Jones's revival of a Vitruvian interest in mathematical sciences and proportion (Yates 1986: 122–4). Jones had been inspired by Dee's Preface to the English translation of Euclid (1570) which argued that architecture should be included in the 'Artes Mathematical' and which used Vitruvius's inventory of the subjects necessary for the architect's education (republished in Yates 1969).

An academy of architecture, therefore, was certainly an option open to Charles II and to Wren. The lack of any strong interest in founding one was perhaps because they positively preferred the particular strengths of the Royal Works and the Royal Society, and believed that these provided an equivalent direction and training to that of the French system. Neither organisation, moreover, was saddled with the title 'academy', which still perhaps had esoteric and magical associations, quite apart from Papist and absolutist ones.

The Royal Society

It was on behalf of the Royal Society, of which he was a founding member, that Wren had undertaken much of his activity in France. According to its official history, the Royal Society had originally been a discussion group that had met at Wadham College, Oxford, in the years following the Civil War (Sprat 1667). Its meetings moved to London in 1658 and in 1660 Charles II granted it his patronage. It consisted of a number of intellectuals, scientists and dilettantes who met to pursue Baconian science and advance Bacon's 'Great Instauration', a state of pure and direct knowledge of nature and her powers, much in the spirit of the Comenian group already mentioned. From its first meetings at Wadham the Society had consciously sought to avoid political factions. Members came from both sides, Parliamentarian and Royalist, and they met together, at least according to the Society's later Royalist historians, to discuss the explicitly neutral and practical matter of 'natural knowledge' or 'experimental philosophy', while avoiding divisive topics such as philosophy, religion and the possibility of a reformed society. In the Baconian manner members compared their research, made experiments testing and verifying knowledge, and committed themselves to take no authority for granted.[2]

Like academies on the continent, the Royal Society patronised research, and like them it was part of a courtly apparatus of display. But in one major respect it was unlike those academies: it had no responsibilities for teaching, albeit by default, or for regulating a particular profession. Although it actively published, its operative model was the laboratory and the encouragement society, not the school. In the field of architecture, it was not, therefore, a body that set out to propagate architectural dicta and skills.

But the Royal Society did aspire to a mode of co-operative endeavour and it included several figures who practised architecture, Wren, Robert Hooke and William Winde amongst them. Such men probably saw their architectural activities as related to the Society's empirical philosophy. Several of its members submitted plans for the rebuilding of London in 1666. Furthermore the Society's interest in models and mechanisms was not far from the way that architectural problems were solved and we know that on some occasions, such as when Wren showed his model of the Sheldonian Theatre to the Society in 1663, it did discuss architectural matters (Downes 1988: 8).

The Royal Works

During his Surveyorship from 1615 to 1643 Inigo Jones had made the Royal Works into an organisation capable of erecting buildings such as his Banqueting House on Whitehall (1619–22) designed in a thoroughgoing Italian Renaissance manner. However, in accord with his sense of the architect's social and artistic status, Jones himself does not seem to have regarded the Works as a potential school for architects. In fact, Jones's intended successor, John Webb, was employed directly by Jones, not by the Crown.

After the Interregnum Wren revived the Royal Works when he was appointed Surveyor-General in 1669, forming around himself an integrated unit of designers, draughtsmen, clerks and craftsmen. Wren's Works may well have been based on his observation of the French Royal Building

3 Nicholas Hawksmoor: 'St Alhallowes church at Northampton', from topographical sketchbook (1680–83)

Administration that was being enlarged and reorganised by Louis XIV and his chief minister, Colbert, at this time (Rosenfeld 1977). Certainly this would accord with Wren's interest in contemporary French theory and architectural style. The axis between the Royal Works and the Royal Society, an axis balanced on Wren, was equivalent in some sense to the link between the French Academy and the Royal Building Works responsible for the Louvre.

Under Wren the organisation of the Works came to provide a flexible ladder of learning that could be scaled by an aspirant architect. The most famous example of this was Nicholas Hawksmoor, the son of a yeoman farmer who had been clerk to a plasterer before coming to London where he became Wren's personal clerk at the age of eighteen in 1678–79. Over the next fifteen years or so Hawksmoor took on a number of roles, working on many of the major projects of the Royal Works and sketching on his travels (3). His first official position was as Deputy Surveyor from 1683 to 1685 at the Palace at Winchester; he then became Clerk of Works at Kensington Palace in 1689 and worked as a draughtsman and clerk on the City churches and St Paul's during the 1690s. After this long apprenticeship, Hawksmoor produced his first designs in 1692 for the Writing School at Christ's Hospital, London (Downes 1979: 2). From

Wren Hawksmoor must have acquired his preference for empirical solutions and mathematical procedures over a respect for ancient authority; indeed, like Wren, Hawksmoor never abandoned the Gothic style as an option. The Works gave him a lengthy pupillage in the administrative, supervisory and drafting skills necessary to an official architect, but it did not compel him to adopt a safely anonymous style, rather the opposite.

Other architects progressed through the Works in a similar way during and after Wren's time. Thomas Ripley moved from carpenter to Labourer in Trust, Clerk of Works, Master Carpenter, Comptroller and Surveyor of the King's Private Roads. Henry Flitcroft worked up from joiner to Clerk of Works, Master Carpenter, Master Mason, Deputy Surveyor (for Ripley and Flitcroft see Colvin 1963–76, V: 88–9). William Dickenson was employed in the Works for some fifteen years as Clerk of Works, measurer, assistant and Deputy Surveyor, before he became an architect in his own right as one of the Surveyors to the Commissioners for Building Fifty New Churches in London (Colvin 1978). Later in the eighteenth century Kenton Couse and Stephen Wright were other architects 'bred up' in this way: Couse stayed in official service all his career but began taking private work some ten years after entering the Works as a Labourer in Trust; Wright entered at a higher stage as a Clerk of Works and then probably became an assistant to William Kent (Colvin 1978). Such patterns of training should not be seen as accidental and opportunistic lurches from one responsibility to another, but instead as progressive and flexible movements of varying and deepening experience in which there is evidence to show that older hands had responsibility for overseeing the training of new employees (Colvin 1978: 89). Thus, as in the French Royal Building Administration before 1671, the architect learnt design and structure through direct practical experience.

When Vanbrugh became Comptroller in 1702 the Royal Works had, with Wren and Hawksmoor, three major architects at its head all working in versions of a vivid baroque style; this conjunction of architects has itself been described as an unofficial academy of architecture (Colvin 1978: 13; Rykwert 1983: 151). But after Wren's dismissal in 1717, followed by Vanbrugh's death in 1726, the Works declined in influence.

In the Royal Works, as in the experimental philosophy of the Royal Society and in Wren's own approach to architecture, theoretical approaches to design were subordinated to an empirical understanding of building. To put it into the terms of contemporary French theory, this position was closer to that of the 'Moderns' than the 'Ancients'. Stated simply, the Ancients like François Blondel believed in the study of the authoritative and unsurpassed buildings of the classical past and in the use of absolute rules for proportions. The Moderns such as Claude Perrault felt that modern technology enabled them to surpass these monuments, and moreover that study of the past showed there were variable rules for proportions anyway. Similarly, Wren's approach insisted upon the interrelationship between the building industry and crafts and the executive powers of design and supervision, in contrast to the position of Inigo Jones. For Wren theory was born out of practicalities, and his approach was engrained in the very process of training.

The account given here of the importance of Wren's Royal Works for education sharply contradicts the common assertion that architectural education was changed by Inigo Jones's notion, based upon classical theory, of the architect as an artist-intellectual associated more with the King's court than with the guilds. John Bold has written, 'the idea of the modern architect was a development not from within the ranks of the building trades, with their stress on quotidian practicalities, but from within the realms of theory, supported by artistically enlightened patronage' (Bold 1989: 16; see also Wilton-Ely 1977). If any such architect existed in Jones's time the only example apart from Jones himself was John Webb, who is the basis for Bold's assertion. In practice, moreover, theory could not be so clearly separated from the building trades as Bold suggests and as Jones tried to make it. Dee's 'Preface to Euclid' of 1570, the text that first disseminated Renaissance principles of design and the Renaissance idea of the architect, was aimed at the artisan classes (hence its publication in English) who might improve their status through mathematical ability (Yates 1969). Ironically Jones himself came from this class and started his career as apprentice to a joiner, and his own rise may have owed much to Dee's text (Yates 1969: 82). In any case Jones does not seem to have envisaged the training of architects as one of the functions of the Royal Works over which he exerted autocratic control from 1615 to 1643.[3]

On the other hand the Royal Works under Wren's control produced many architects whose experience was formed in contact with the building crafts. Wren's Works was a form of quasi-medieval building lodge where the training certainly took place in the office, but also on site and working with and in the presence of the building crafts.

Moreover, in distinction to the traditional craft apprenticeship, the Works system was not restricted to one craft but enabled movement across the crafts and out of them. Unlike the Elizabethan prodigy houses, which were also schools of architecture in the sense of being training centres for local building skills, the Works was also a continuous and complex enterprise, providing work on many new and refurbished buildings.

We can conclude from all this that Wren eschewed an academy partly because of the presence of the Royal Society but also because he had a positive preference for the building lodge: the practical form of education at the Royal Works. Here he may well have been following Francis Bacon's utopian idea of a programme of co-operative action in the sciences, in which the work of craftsmen had an integral part to play (Hill 1972: 88). This relationship between Wren and Bacon contrasts with Inigo Jones's relation to John Dee. Dee posited a Neoplatonic idea of the architect as a mathematician in harmony with universal law and as a theoretician working in conjunction with the craftsman's mastery of materials (Hill 1972: 88; Rykwert 1983: 126). (This was misconstrued by Jones to mean that theory should become a means of mastery over the craftsman.) Meanwhile Wren, who inherited from both Jones and Dee a sense of the intellectual status of architecture with mathematical knowledge as its key, also had a Baconian vision of the Royal Works and it was this that held greater sway amongst the competing notions of the architect and his relation to the craftsman.

Routes into architecture

The Royal Works, however, were not the only place where architects were trained. John Evelyn, the diarist who was a close friend of Wren, a fellow founder of the Royal Society and a courtier, listed three types of architect in his 'Account of Architects' of 1664: 'Architectus Ingenio', 'Architectus Sumptuarium' and 'Architectus Manuarius' (or four types if we include the 'Architectus Verborum', or architectural writer; Evelyn 1664: 117). We have here a description of the people whom Evelyn regarded as responsible for architecture. The first of these is the ideal type described in the 'Account', whose best and probably only contemporary representative was Christopher Wren. A more common type is the architect-surveyor who is 'skilful in the Art of Building' and who 'Superintends and Presides' over the 'commonly illiterate Mechanick' (Evelyn 1664: 115, 117). 'Architectus Sumptuarium' is described as the client who pays for buildings. Finally, 'Architectus Manuarius' is the craftsman – whether a mason, joiner or carpenter – who actually carries out the building (Evelyn 1664: 117).

The variety of different types of architect listed by Evelyn also indicates the varying routes by which one could become an architect, the person endowed with responsibility for the design of buildings and the co-ordination of their construction, in the seventeenth and eighteenth centuries. There were in fact at least five methods of entry into architecture during this period: through the Royal Works, as a member of the educated upper classes, via the crafts, another profession, or by pupillage. This variety indicates that the practice of architecture was far from attaining the kind of professional cohesion already acquired by the church, law, the army and even medicine. The titles of 'architect', 'engineer' and 'surveyor' were not protected, were often synonymous, and sometimes combined with a number of other titles.

Something close to Evelyn's ideal type could be 'bred up' through the Royal Works, and this constitutes the first category. This type, whose training has already been described, was usually firmly acquainted with the crafts and had often started in them. He was experienced on the site and had acquired the administrative skills necessary to run an office.

The second category included those architects who were members of the nobility and gentry pursuing a humanist learning into the reaches of classical design by erecting their own buildings – Evelyn's 'Architectus Sumptuarium' (4). In the words of Roger North, who could himself be placed in this category, 'For a profest architect is proud, opiniative and troublesome, seldome at hand, and a head workman pretending to the designing part, is full of paultry vulgar contrivances; therefore be your owne architect, or sitt still' (Colvin 1978: 29). The concerns of a building's client and its designer obviously overlapped and the two functions can merge. The architectural interests of men like Sir Roger Pratt, John Chute, William Talman, and the Earls of Pembroke and Burlington might have been fostered by the Neoplatonic ideas of John Dee and the intellectual climate of the courts, as well as by the possession of the time and wealth to take continental tours and to buy or promote theoretical texts and handbooks on classical architecture. Most of them would have had an education in mathematics, drawing and surveying as a matter of course. Those few women who became involved in architecture at this period mostly entered through this route: one example is Lady Wilbraham, the designer of Weston Park, Staffordshire (1671), another is Elizabeth, Duchess of Beaufort, responsible for the buildings at Badminton (c.1650–80; Walker 1984, 1989). Such aristocratic designers would have been considerably aided by the degree of independence that could be expected of a highly-trained but socially-distinct work-force.

The third of these five routes was the category of master-craftsman, or in Evelyn's terms 'Architectus Manuarius', who had had a rigorous crafts training, often of seven or eight years, in masonry, bricklaying or carpentry and had often acquired design skills empirically. Well-known examples are Robert Mylne (5), Henry Holland and John Carr. In this form of training a body of knowledge was handed down from masters to apprentices. It would not be a large step, nor an unusual move, to use transmitted geometrical rules or construction details, for example, as the basis for generating entire buildings. In the eighteenth century the proliferating manuals and pattern-books on classical and Gothic architecture were largely bought by these craftsmen-architects, a category that also included surveyors, house agents and building merchants, who formed by far the majority of the 'profession', especially at the lower end of the market and outside London (Colvin 1978: 23–4; Jenkins 1961: 52–7). Even had they been interested – Wren after all did not travel except once, to France – most of them could not afford to travel abroad (although Mylne is an exception). Nor did they have a grasp of the higher reaches of theory that Dee advocated as a bridge between architects and builders, but they certainly had access to the tangible products of theory (6) and they could mimic its effects. Occasionally, as in the case of the brothers Robert and Roger Morris, they could advance themselves through aristocratic patronage not just to the position of architect but also, in Robert's case, to the writing of architectural theory. By the early nineteenth century, with the increasing distinction between architects and builders, master craftsmen with ambition tended to become entrepreneurs.

4 John Chute: staircase at The Vyne, Hampshire (c.1760–70)

A fourth type of architect were those who were also professionals in other fields, whether painters (Jones and Kent), diplomatists (Gerbier), playwright/soldiers (Vanbrugh; 7), or scientists (Hooke and Wren). These professionals, like the aristocratic architects, were amateurs in architecture both in the sense that they maintained other strong interests and that they had no formal training for it. Many of the artist-architects owed their involvement in architecture to the Renaissance belief that the arts of painting, sculpture and architecture were simply three branches of the same art of design (*disegno*) and that transfer across them was therefore easy (Wilkinson 1977: 134). Often, as in the case of Jones, Wren and Hugh May, these other professionals attained formal architectural status through their appointment to a higher post at the Royal Works. Like the gentlemen-architects their relation to classicism was significant in allowing their entry into architecture and then later in enabling them to consolidate their hold on part of the market. To gain a reasonably thorough knowledge of classicism early in this period required at least knowledge of foreign languages and preferably foreign travel, and these were rarely available to craftsmen.

In effect the delegation of duties in the Works became the model on which the fifth category, pupillage to a specialist architect, was based, because

5 Robert Mylne: Stationers' Hall, London (1800)

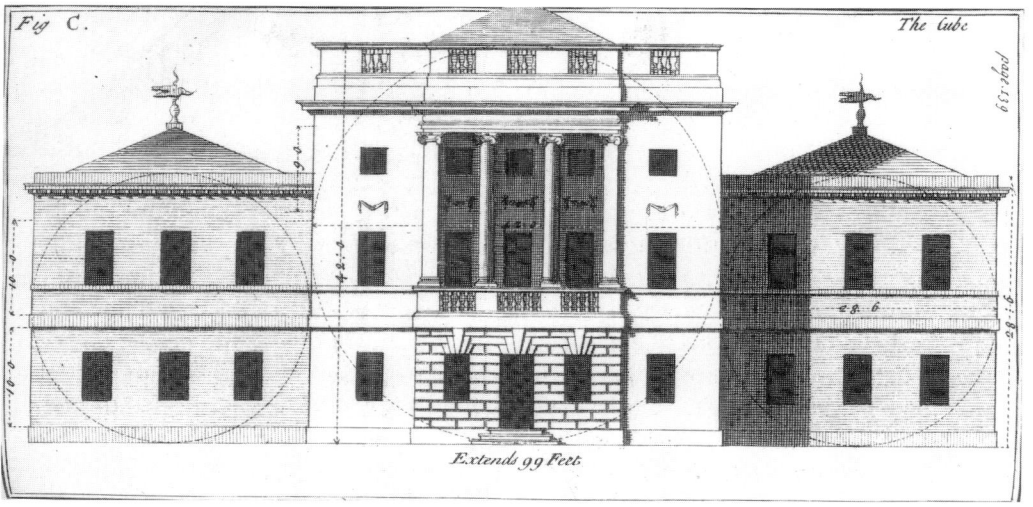

6 Robert Morris: elevation of a Villa showing proportional system

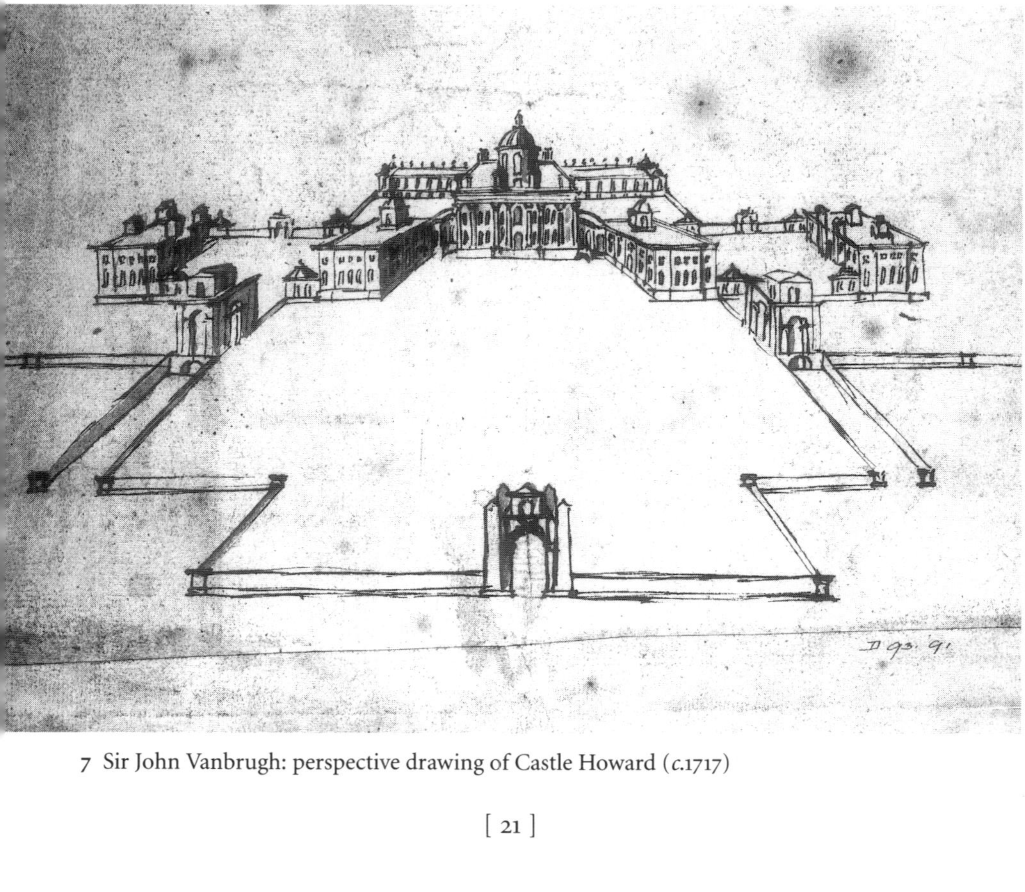

7 Sir John Vanbrugh: perspective drawing of Castle Howard (*c*.1717)

pupillage depended on a well-organised office through whose hierarchy and division of labour an aspirant architect could be developed. This form of training increasingly came to dominate and we shall describe it at greater length.

Pupillage

Pupillage first became a common form of architectural training in the eighteenth century. It is significant that architectural pupillage arose when apprenticeship in general, and particularly in London, was declining, yet after it had become common for members of the middle classes to put their sons, and occasionally their daughters, through an apprenticeship (Earle 1989: 85–6). Thus the growth of a defined form of pupillage, particularly as it initially developed in London, may have been in response to both these developments. It was for this middle-class market that Robert Campbell was catering when he included architecture in his *London Tradesman* (1747), a guidebook for the middle classes in choosing a business for their offspring. Yet Campbell could not point at that date to a distinct means to acquire architectural knowledge. He recommended a liberal education and travel, and stressed the need to know the secrets of the building trades as well as artistic principles, but could only indicate these needs: 'Though I scarce know of any in *England*', he wrote, 'who have had an Education regularly designed for the Profession, Bricklayers, Carpenters, etc. all commence Architects'.[4] When pupillage developed as a distinct form of training for architecture, it was thus linked with the particular needs of the middle classes, one of which was the desire to make a clear distinction of responsibility and division of labour between the architect and other builders.

Previously John Webb was the best-known case of an architect trained in an architect's office – in Webb's case that of his uncle Inigo Jones. Webb was employed by Jones from 1628 onwards and was groomed to take over the post of Surveyor-General. He acted as Jones's draughtsman for the rebuilding of St Paul's and must have aided the implementation of other designs by Jones. He also received instruction in Jones's architectural theory, especially a grounding in Italian classicism and Jones's notion of architecture as a liberal art based on the realisation of the Platonic Idea (Bold 1989: 14–16).

The Jones–Webb relationship, however, was an exception in the seventeenth century. It is not usually thought to have been until James Paine (1717–89) and then Sir Robert Taylor (1714–88) in the mid-eighteenth century that the practice of taking on pupils as a continuous aspect of office life was first established. James Paine stated that the architect should be 'bred an architect' (Binney 1984), although he was himself the son of a carpenter who had worked up through the building trade. Paine took on eight apprentices between 1756 and 1785, each of whom was articled specifically to train as an architect. Taylor had

8 John Nash: nos. 17 Bloomsbury Square and 68–71 Great Russell Street, London (1777–78)

at least seven pupils at different times including S. P. Cockerell (*c.* 1770) and John Nash (*c.* 1770s; **8**). He did not accept premiums but had his pupils bound by indentures. Through these indentures Taylor agreed to give his pupils a form of training in return for a set fee. Taylor did not speculate in building, and consequently the relatively large number of apprentice/pupils whom he took on learnt office practice quite separately from the practices of the developer or builder (Leach 1988: 170).

However, although the precise chronology is unclear, there is evidence to modify the common view, as expressed for instance by Howard Colvin, that Taylor led the way (Colvin 1978: 30). It is clear from these dates for instance that Paine in effect took his first pupils in 1756, well before Taylor, but Sir William Chambers followed only two years later. It was not until 1768 that Taylor began to take pupils, the same year that Soane became George Dance's pupil and that the Royal Academy was founded. This suggests a pattern of relationships and some serious thinking about the nature of the profession and the requisite qualifications amongst Taylor, Paine, Dance, Chambers and perhaps others during the 1750s and 1760s prior to the founding of the Royal Academy. Thus the emergence of pupillage was not entirely fortuitous: it does seem to have arisen as a result of some conscious thought on the part of a group of leading practitioners of the mid- to late-eighteenth century in London, rather than on the initiative of any single figure.

It is likely not only that pupillage was fashioned in order to promote a coherent professional identity, but also that it was intended from the first to be coupled with formal drawing lessons in an academy. There was a close connection between the establishment of pupillage by Taylor and Paine and the St Martin's Lane Academy founded by Hogarth in 1735 to teach drawing to artists and designers, which was the first British art school. Paine had studied drawing there but Taylor probably had links with it, through his apprenticeship to Henry Cheere, an ornamental sculptor closely affiliated with the St Martin's set (Girouard 1966: 188). Both Cheere and Paine were amongst those members who campaigned for the establishment of a Royal Academy.

By 1789 pupillage may have accounted for over a third of all forms of architectural training and by 1819 it had risen to nearly two thirds. Entry via a crafts apprenticeship or other occupations correspondingly declined to little more than a tenth of all architects by 1820.[5] After the mid-eighteenth century it became common practice for London architects to take on one or more pupils or apprentices. Although they were often used interchangeably, the two categories could be differentiated along the lines that while the pupil paid for his instruction, the apprentice, in the manner of the medieval craftsman, exchanged his labour for instruction. Consequently the status of the pupil was like that of an articled clerk, and that of the architectural apprentice like that of an assistant. In practice the type and quality of training received probably depended less on differences of status and more on the nature of the architect's office. In the worst offices pupils might be set repetitive tasks or even domestic chores. In the late eighteenth century, as the system settled down, premiums varied wildly from £10 to £210 (Crook 1969: 64–5). Ideally, during his five or six years training the pupil would learn methods of draughtsmanship and the techniques of office practice. With the formation of the Royal Academy in 1768 the pupil could attend evening lectures, perhaps show his designs and have access to a library. Ideally again, he would want to complete his education and find future clients by travelling abroad and creating his own body of sketches and measured drawings of classical and modern buildings in Italy, Greece and the Levant. Campbell felt that travel was the best way to gain the taste necessary for judging architectural proportions (R. Campbell 1747: 156). By his mid-twenties the young architect would be equipped for practice and would join a partnership or form a small office of his own by screwing his brass plate to his door.

This ideal training was rarely formulated in print. One exception is the description in *An Essay on the Qualifications and Duties of an Architect*, an anonymous pamphlet of 1773 probably written by James Peacock who worked in the office of George Dance (Du Prey 1982: 27–8). Here the prospective architect is from a middle-class family and has had a good general education until the age of fifteen. He is then articled to an architect. In his first year or two he learns to measure and improves his drawing. Then he is taught to design and to draw plans, sections and elevations; he is instructed in mechanics, hydraulics and perspective, improves his French and finally travels abroad. During his tour he draws and measures classical monuments, 'studies their Proportions, searches into their Antiquity, explores the Materials of which they are composed, and the Manner in which they are put together, and makes every Observation that is likely to prove of the least Utility'. He then compares these buildings with modern ones and 'improves upon both in his own Designs'. When he returns home he is well prepared in the studiousness and probity required to become an architect (reprinted in Kaye 1960: 48–50).

What this training left out, as its author admitted, was any knowledge of the practical side of building and its materials, tools, skills and surveyance. Knowledge of these matters would have to be parcelled out, just as Peacock seems to have taken on the surveying duties in George Dance's office; otherwise the strictly architectural elements of training, such as drawing and designing, would be diluted. This, then, was a kind of academic education on tour and inside the office, without direct contact with the building trades, and thus it was very different to the system under Wren in the Royal Works.

It is doubtful if any architect actually received the education prescribed in this pamphlet, although George Dance's office may have been the model. John Soane's education approached it. He supplemented the office practice he received under Dance and Holland with attendance at the Royal Academy, and then made a tour abroad as their Gold Medallist from 1777 to 1780. Furthermore Soane's father had been a bricklayer and it seems that Soane developed a familiarity with craftsmen's work while he was still a clerk for Holland (Du Prey 1982: 1–32).

Soane's own pupils, however, received an education that came as near as any to approximating to that described in the 1773 *Essay*. Pupils spent between three and seven years in Soane's office, paying premiums that rose with Soane's fame from £50 to 175 guineas, and working a twelve-hour day six days a week with six weeks holiday (Bolton n.d.: 12–19). George Basevi, for example, joined a number of pupils in Soane's office in 1811 after a brief trial period. He soon learnt a set of drawing techniques including a carefully graduated series of studies of the Orders and mouldings, often from examples in his master's own collection. He began to attend the Royal Academy in 1813 for a few evenings a week (and sometimes, with permission, for whole days) at the same time as he was measuring masons' work, copying designs, making working drawings, doing quarterly accounts or squaring dimensions in Soane's office. In 1816 he set off for a three-year tour of Italy and France, and during this time he attended the Academy of St. Luke in Rome (9; Bolton n.d.: 3–8). Basevi was probably amongst the best equipped of Soane's thirty pupils but amongst them his experience was not exceptional. A particularly interesting method that was peculiar to the office was to send pupils in pairs to make drawings of work in progress (10). This compelled the pupils to analyse the 'mechanics of building' closely and to evolve a suitable recording method (M. Richardson 1990: 52; Bolton n.d.: 3). The combination of pupillage from a conscientious master with access to the Royal Academy meant that these pupils could gain a sound training and keep up with scholarship and fashion which the craftsman-architect could often only hear of at second hand.

In their Articles of Agreement Soane undertook to teach his pupils the 'Art, Profession, and Business of an architect' (M. Richardson 1990: 52). Nowhere, however, was there mention of craft, nor was there evidence of familiarity with the crafts within Soane's system of pupillage. This point needs to be stressed. Soane's ideal was of an architect who was a poetic designer, an intellectual and a manager imbued with high ethics, who could lead by virtue of his very distance from mechanical work. Soane's lectures at the Royal Academy (11), for example, were not on matters like construction, but on aesthetics. This ideal was quite unlike that of Sir William Chambers who was in some respects Wren's successor. Although Chambers shared Soane's desire for a higher status for the architect, he wanted his position to be based on a comprehensive and sensitive understanding of every aspect of building work (Hanson 1987). Soane designed buildings like the Bank Stock Office (1792) which are characterised by poetic lighting effects achieved as celebrations of abstract intellect and carried out in a personal style governing every detail. By contrast Chambers's Somerset House (1775–80; 12) was envisaged as a great collaborative venture of all the arts and crafts, a display of learning using the techniques and forms already familiar to the work-force. Which of these ideals could survive, co-operate with, or indeed resist changes in the building industry, became one of the most significant questions to face nineteenth-century architectural training.

To sum up: although there is no direct evidence it seems likely that pupillage developed as a system of training within the offices of several leading London-based architects with official duties in the few decades following the breakdown of Wren's Royal Works. At first it evolved informally but soon a formal structure of instruction coupled with part-time attendance at an academy and foreign travel was formulated which by 1800 had become the predominant route into the profession, certainly for London-based architects. Although the academy, therefore, had some part to play it was a role distinctly subsidiary to office work. None the less several schemes for a more ambitious kind of academy were formulated in the century preceding the foundation of the Royal Academy in 1768 and we shall turn to these now.

9 George Basevi: topographical drawing made in Italy, probably a view of Praeneste (1817)

10 Henry Parke: progress drawing of work on Soane's Old Dividend or Four Per Cent Office, Bank of England (1818)

The academy in the late seventeenth and eighteenth centuries

The complexity of ideas about architectural training in the Restoration can be further unravelled if we turn back again to the writing of John Evelyn, who shared many of Wren's views on architecture. Yet Evelyn was one of several members of the Royal Society who were interested in forming an English academy of architecture.[6] Evelyn was expertly acquainted with architecture and town planning. In 1662 he had served on a committee for improving London's public works. He wrote a pamphlet on smoke pollution and its implications for what we now call zoning. Furthermore he had an

11 Anon. (office of Sir John Soane): comparative sections through the Pantheon at Rome and the Rotunda of the Bank of England, made to be used as a lecture illustration for Sir John Soane (*c.*1820)

12 Robert Chantrell: Somerset House (1775–80) by Sir William Chambers. A drawing by a
pupil of Sir John Soane made to be used as a lecture illustration for Soane (1813)

encyclopaedic grasp of economic practices which he planned to employ by
writing histories of all the trades and crafts – well illustrated by his *Sculptura*,
a history of engraving and sculpture – and he held a kind of open brief from
the King to stimulate the economy with his trenchant proposals.

In his *Sculptura* (1662), Evelyn identified drawing as the basis of sculpture
and architecture (Evelyn 1662: 104). It was a necessity, but Evelyn believed it
could only really be promoted through the kind of academies that had been
founded in Italy from the latter half of the mid-sixteenth century, where artists
had

> Books of *Drawings* of all the old, and Renowned *Masters, Rounds, Busts, Relievos* and
> entire Figures, cast off from the best of the Antique *Statues* and Monuments, *Greek*
> and *Roman*; There was to be seen . . . likewise divers rare and excellent *Statues*, both
> of *brass and marble*; *Modells* and divers fragments of *Bases, Colomns, Capitals,*
> *Freezes, Cornishes* and other pieces moulded from the most authentique remains of
> the antient famous buildings, besides a universal collection of *Medaills*, things
> Artificial and natural. (Evelyn 1662: 113, 116–17)

Evelyn's translation of Fréart de Chambray's *Parallel of Architecture Ancient
and Modern* (1664) made the language of classical forms and theoretical thinking on classical architecture more easily available in England. In this sense it

[29]

was like the first translations of Serlio (1611), Vignola (1655), Palladio (1663), Scamozzi (1667) and others. But Evelyn's book was more than just a translation. It was a collection of essays including Fréart's work, Alberti's 'Treatise on Statues', Evelyn's own 'Account of Architects', and in later editions Sir Henry Wotton's 'The Elements of Architecture'. It holds a particularly interesting position both as a tool of training and as a polemic for Evelyn's own views on architectural education, and is therefore worth considering at length.

The book was intended both for 'mechanics' and for 'politer students of this magnificent art'; it was both a handbook on the forms of classical architecture and an introduction to its theory.[7] In his own essay Evelyn claimed a high social and intellectual status for the architect. As Dee had done in his Preface, Evelyn repeated Vitruvius's account of the ideal qualities necessary to an architect. Apart from his native docility and ingeniousness, the architect must be literate and have drawing skills; he must know something of geometry, optics, arithmetic (both for proportions and for doing accounts) and be well read in history and philosophy (to understand nature); and he must be acquainted with music (for acoustics), medicine (to gauge environmental conditions), the law, and astrology (to ensure good fortune) (Evelyn 1664: 116; Vitruvius, *De Architectura*, 1.1).

In his 'Account', Evelyn argued that architecture should be taught in the universities. His viewpoint differed markedly from Inigo Jones's notion of architecture as a liberal art dependent on 'Invention' rather than a mechanical art (Bold 1989: 14). Evelyn's approach sprang from the notion that architecture was another branch of experimental philosophy; it was the epitome of the mathematical sciences, demanding a thorough knowledge of the 'lineary arts'. His ideas were closer to those of the pre-Restoration promoters of academies who had expressed their dissatisfaction with the restrictions of the universities:

> Great pitty I say it is, that amongst the *Professors* of *Humanity* (as they call it) there should not be some *Lectures* and *Schools* endow'd and furnish'd with *Books, Instruments, Plots, Types* and *Modells* of the most excellent Fabricks both in *Civil* and *Military Architecture*, where these most noble and necessary *Arts* might be taught in the *English* and Vulgar Tongue, reviv'd to their proper, and genuine significations. (Evelyn 1664: 118)

Without explicitly alluding to an academy or calling for one in name, Evelyn hoped that part of the new Whitehall Palace might be given over for the use of artists and architects for their 'ease and encouragement' (Evelyn 1664: 118). This is clearly a reference to the 'stately apartments' granted by Italian princes as homes for academies (Evelyn 1662: 113). Evelyn was asking for a training, status and responsibility unheard of before in English artistic and architectural practice. But it was one which he had been able to observe as it was set up in 1648 by Lebrun for the French Royal Academy in Paris during Evelyn's stay there.

Evelyn's programme of university education was clearly a way to produce more of his ideal architect. The problem however in reproducing someone like Christopher Wren was that he had had no formal training in architecture. Wren had acquired an education in the classics and then studied mathematics and science at Wadham College before becoming Professor of Astronomy and a leading practitioner of the new experimental philosophy. With a grounding in engineering and the making of functioning models, Wren taught himself the additional knowledge he needed for architecture through observation, reading and a short visit, not to Rome, but to Paris. Wren's background was not unusual. Robert Hooke, a fellow Royal Society member, had a similar scientific training, as had such continental contemporaries as Claude Perrault and Guarino Guarini.

Evelyn's ideal was of a wide-based academic education, separated from the building trade, that could produce architects of the calibre of Wren, who of course had not had such a training himself. This ideal was informed by notions of the role of an academy based on information about the various French academies. Evelyn's idea was rare at his time and was not to be carried out in Britain for over two centuries. As we have seen, England after the Restoration had a collection of bodies that went some way to fulfilling the role of an academy: the Royal Works, the Royal Society and the various courts in country houses. These produced all three of the architects described by Evelyn.

The idea of an official academy was set off again in the early eighteenth century and this time it gathered momentum. Circumstances had changed considerably since the Restoration. The revived interest in Inigo Jones's work may account for the need felt by many architects to travel abroad, especially to Italy, as a way of learning about the architecture of classical antiquity and its revival since the Renaissance. William Kent, Thomas Archer and William Talman all travelled to Italy and James Gibbs studied at the Academy of St Luke in the early years of the eighteenth century. When in 1758 Robert Mylne won a prize at the Academy of St Luke, the practice of joining an Italian academy had become commonplace. Most of the neoclassical generation did likewise: George Dance the Younger, Nathaniel Dance, Robert Adam, William Chambers and James Wyatt.[8] It is quite probable then that this widespread experience of academic education in Italy contributed to the campaign for an official English academy.

However, the call now was to a different kind of authority than that advocated and embodied by the long-lived Surveyor-General. After Wren's retirement from the Works in 1717, the importance of the Works declined and the Surveyor's position was taken over by political placemen and administrators until it was reorganised by a series of reforms in 1761, 1782, 1815 and 1832 (Jenkins 1961: 111–12). To some extent the eclipse of the Works was applauded by those who preferred a formal national academy. For example, the Earl of

Shaftesbury's advocacy of an academy in 1712 was made explicitly against the control that Wren held over the production of public buildings. Shaftesbury was for the Ancients and against Moderns like Wren. 'Without a *Publick Voice*, knowingly guided and directed', he argued, 'there is nothing which can raise a true Ambition in the Artist' (Shaftesbury 1732: 402). The guidance would come from the kind of academies, for painting, sculpture or architecture, that Shaftesbury envied in France and that the 'supine Un-concernedness' of the English Court had barely considered (Shaftesbury 1732: 406).

Similar in its aims, Bishop Berkeley's *An Essay Towards Preventing the Ruine of Great Britain* (1721) was written as a call to civil responsibility after the financial disaster of the South Sea Bubble. Like Evelyn after the Restoration (see his *Tyrannus*, London, 1661), Berkeley advocated a return to sumptuary laws to discourage private luxury, and like his predecessor he recognised the role of architecture and the fine arts in restoring the 'Discourse of Public Spirit'. A scheme of public works would bring social cohesion and help to restore the economy (Berkeley 1721: 20). To accompany this Berkeley recommended the establishment of an 'Academy of ingenious Men' who would write a history of Great Britain and 'make Discourses proper to inspire Men with a Zeal for the Public' and these would aid the improvement of English usage (Berkeley 1721: 20). Although he did not call specifically for an academy of architecture, it is important that Berkeley saw the encouragement of public works as closely linked to the founding of an academy, even if the latter was to be primarily of a literary nature. Both were to be important arms of civil society and part of the apparatus of display that would ensure 'Concord and Union' while discouraging party allegiances.

Berkeley's views on the promotion of the arts by the state brought him to the attention of the Earl of Burlington and his circle (Luce 1949: 82–3), a group known to architectural history as the Palladian movement, concerned with reviving Inigo Jones's vision of an Italianate architecture in the service of a Whig faction and of fixing this culturally through major public commissions and new state institutions. Burlington was one of the principal sponsors of the Royal Academy of Music in 1719, and at the same time he created his own informal academy at Burlington House, with Colen Campbell, William Kent and G. B. Guelfi representing the arts of architecture, painting and sculpture, and with Handel, Pope and Swift occasionally representing the other arts. Soon he also acquired a collection of drawings by Jones, Webb and Palladio. Burlington's informal academy was part of his reordering of cultural power and imagery, involving the promotion of architectural publication – which, save for Evelyn, Wren's circle had largely ignored – and the patronage of architecture. By playing down the role of the Works and the architectural prestige of its Surveyor, Burlington could influence the style in the Works while arbitrating taste from within his own 'academy' with its close connection to the court. The architects whose careers Burlington fostered in the Royal Works, Kent, Flitcroft and John Vardy, were all directed along Palladian lines. Burlington's own informal academy was little if at all concerned with training, certainly not in the formal sense of the transmission and development of knowledge and skills. By implication it was, however, concerned with classical education through books, discussion and travel. Similarly it was little interested in breaking the distinction between the upper-class 'virtuoso' and the subsidiary and dependent 'mechanic' (Rykwert 1983: 257–8 n. 416).

Burlington's circle was often opposed by a group of artists and architects that developed in the 1730s and 1740s around the St Martin's Lane Academy and the nearby Old Slaughter's Coffee House, who espoused the naturalistic fancy of the rococo style imported from France and traced their descent from the baroque as manifested in the works of Thornhill, Vanbrugh and Wren. The St Martin's Lane Academy was a reprise of an academy of painting run by Godfrey Kneller from 1711 to 1717 and then reopened with more ambitious if thwarted intentions by James Thornhill in 1724. The academy that opened in 1735 was based on Thornhill's collection of casts and was mainly devoted to providing figure drawing classes for ornamental designers, painters, sculptors and the occasional architect (13). Here an extraordinary association of leading designers, Hogarth, Hubert Gravelot (who also ran a drawing school of his own), Isaac Ware and others taught and discussed the new continental fashion for rococo, and these members were responsible for the buildings and decorations at Vauxhall Gardens (1742–50). James Paine, who worked under one of James Gibbs's clerks of work, attended St Martin's and gained a considerable reputation for his figure and ornamental drawing (Girouard 1966: 190). Like Wren's Royal Works in the Restoration, the circle had many scientific connections, yet its importance for architectural education lies in its guild-like sense of mutual protection and promotion (Paulson 1971, I: 371), its combination of both applied and fine arts centred on the practice of figure drawing, and the manner in which it embodied stylistic diversity in opposition to the authoritative Italian classicism often known as Palladianism that was espoused by Burlington's academy and that dominated the Royal Works by this time. By contrast the St Martin's Lane group was patronised by Frederick, Prince of Wales, the centre of political opposition to George II.

An eclectic individuality based on empirical learning characterised the work of Hogarth's circle and must have been imbued at the St Martin's Lane Academy. The group wanted to raise the status of British architects and artists through a more formalised training and this was why, despite Hogarth's personal opposition, they supported the establishment of a national academy that had been gathering impetus in the writing of John Gwynn (another member of St Martin's) and others who proposed a 'Public Academy' as the proper place for the teaching of drawing, perspective and geometry, with an elite of artists

13 Anon.: a life class, possibly at St Martin's Lane Academy (c.1760)

and architects as officers (Gwynn 1749). When the Society of Dilettanti, of whom Burlington had been a member, took up the cause many of the St Martin's Lane group joined with its members on the committee formed in 1755 to consider a national academy (Girouard 1966; Pevsner 1940: 183–4).

The coming together of Burlingtonian and rococo tendencies in the formation of the Royal Academy seemed to represent the melding in a national institution of the often conflicting ideas of an academy as a school or as a body of cultural arbitrators. The access to social elevation that the St Martin's Lane circle had seen in formal training was now apparently to be linked to the maintenance of a permanent cultural elite. In effect, though, the second outweighed the first; Burlington and the Society of Dilettanti's notion of an academy gained precedence.

The Royal Academy was finally formed when William Chambers, who had studied in J. F. Blondel's architectural school in Paris, used his influence with the King to assist its foundation in 1768 (Jenkins 1961: 105). Chambers thus ensured that he and other neoclassicists like Reynolds dominated the new institution.

Together with its annual exhibitions and elite group of Royal Academicians, the institution made some provision for architectural education, particularly

14 Stephen Burchell: drawing of classical fragment in the collection of Sir John Soane,
    probably done while Burchell was a student at the Royal Academy (1825)

through its shared facilities for drawing from other drawings, casts (of which
those of architectural fragments were particularly useful; 14), and from the life
model (little used by architectural students). However, although its prime
mover was Chambers, the fact that only four of the thirty-six founder members
were architects may account for the relative modesty of this provision.
Architectural students attended lectures on perspective and a professor of
architecture was appointed to read six annual public lectures on the history and
theory of architecture.[9] These were repeated year after year without change by
the first professor, Thomas Sandby, totally neglected when George Dance was
appointed in 1798, but assiduously delivered after Soane succeeded him in 1806.
A library was created to which architects could have access in the evenings.
Furthermore, medals were periodically distributed as prizes for architectural
drawings. The Silver Medal was awarded for 'the best accurate figured drawings of some noted building in London' (Royal Academy 1797: 35). To win the
Gold Medal students had to make an original design and attend on a set day to
sketch a given subject in five hours. On winning the Gold Medal students were
granted a scholarship to stay in Rome for three years (Du Prey 1982: 55–85).
    Thus the Royal Academy provided the kind of theoretical resources that

might not be available elsewhere and located them in a setting that would be conducive to the reception of ideas if not actually encouraging their dissemination and debate. The Royal Academy had neither the facilities nor the motivation to equal the role of its French counterparts, which gave an intense and inclusive instruction designed to train recruits for royal or military service. It cannot be seen as an engine of educational debate, and it was certainly not a national school of design, but within its limited compass it did supplement the training received in London offices. For Gwynn and for Chambers it was intended to foster a combination of intellectual and practical accomplishment, the second of which was understood specifically as the ability to draw: an acceptable acquirement for the gentleman-architect, and one that was thought sufficient to encourage bonds of respect and clear communication with the building trades.[10]

Conclusion

Wren had considered the idea of an academy without explicitly calling for an academy of architecture. This may have been because he recognised that when the Royal Works functioned effectively it was both a school and a building works. When the Royal Works declined after Wren was sacked, a vacuum was created and the call for an academy returned to fill it. But when eventually established the Royal Academy offered only supplementary facilities to the system of pupillage which was now predominant.

What emerges from any consideration of training during this period is that there was no single route of entry into the profession nor was there any form of education specifically for architecture until the growth of pupillage in the mid-eighteenth century. It can also be said that if at the beginning of the period buildings were designed by men who could have built them and often did, by its end they were increasingly designed by men who had no training in the building crafts. Accordingly the social origin of architects changed from the great variety that existed in the seventeenth and early eighteenth centuries to the predominantly middle-class backgrounds of late eighteenth- and nineteenth-century architects.[11] With this change, of course, the social status of the architect was raised, codes of practice were established and professional ethics began to be sketched out. The building professions became separated and the surveyors and civil engineers began to define their own training and work more distinctly (Jenkins 1961: 107–9).

Each of the forms of induction into architecture during this period underwent some form of change or development. Broadly, however, it could be said that what can be characterised as the building lodge held sway over the early part of the period, exemplified by the Royal Works and by the guilds and their building workshops, but not by the larger purely architectural offices that developed later, where architects took on pupils and trained them in a strictly professional expertise. These lodges were complemented to some extent by the informal and formal academies that became more popular in the eighteenth century, as well as by the publication of architectural theory. It was only towards the end of the period that this balance of medieval and modern methods, and in effect therefore of crafts practice and design, began to be seriously disturbed with the growth of specialisation, and notably in architecture with the overwhelming rise of pupillage. With the latter, not only did access to the designer's role in architecture become socially limited, but also, and perhaps even more importantly, the opportunity to work in close co-operation with the crafts was severely restricted.

Notes

1 This letter was later published in *Parentalia*, see Wren 1710, Part 2: 261.
2 Sprat 1667: 28, 47–8. As Hill and Yates have pointed out, Sprat's account plays down the Comenian origins of the Royal Society, as well as its earlier internationalist aspirations (Hill 1972: 128; Yates 1986: 171–92).
3 During Jones's time Francis Carter was one of the few men brought up in the Works who can be classified as an architect (Colvin 1963–76, III 133–7).
4 R. Campbell 1747: 157–8. When Campbell described these building crafts he stressed with each of them the skill of drawing, the need to know geometry, and the ability to design.
5 Kaye 1960: 47 n. 32. Kaye's figures are patchy, first due to their reliance on the *Dictionary of National Biography*, and second due to the high number of architects, nearly a third, for which there are no details in 1789.
6 Thomas Sprat wanted an academy to standardise language, probably along the model of Richelieu's French Academy set up in 1635 (Sprat 1667: 41–3).
7 Letter of 1690 quoted in Welcher 1972: 62; Evelyn 1664: 113.
8 For accounts of these experiences see especially Jenkins 1961: 96–9; Du Prey 1982: 109–93. Jenkins also points out Paine and Gwynn's criticism of these travels (Jenkins 1961: 99–100).
9 The lectures were 'calculated to form the taste of the Students; to instruct them in the laws and principles of composition; to point out to them the beauties or faults of celebrated productions; to fit them for an unprejudiced study of books on the Art, and for a critical examination of structures' (Royal Academy 1797: 22).
10 See Hanson 1987: Ch. 1. Indicative of these bonds was the list of subscribers to Chambers's *A Treatise on Civil Architecture* (1759), including glaziers, engravers, carpenters, painters and sculptors.
11 Kaye 1960: 47 n. 32. Kaye probably underplays these changes since his data is extracted from the *Dictionary of National Biography*.

CHAPTER TWO

The design of professionalism and its resistance, 1834–1938

If the seventeenth and eighteenth centuries can be characterised by the variety of routes of entry into architecture, the later period can be seen as one of successive arguments and debates leading to the eventual triumph of a professionalised vision of the architect that was both narrowly focused and extraordinarily powerful. At every attempt to define and defend this notion of the architect, resistance to it and alternative visions can be found. Architectural training and its associated institutions was the most common area of struggle, but the issue of professionalisation also relates to broader changes in the construction industry and the planning of cities and towns.

The period opens with the establishment of the first professional institute for architects in 1834. This consolidated eighteenth-century developments but also provided a springboard for modernisation; specifically, demarcating the role of the architect within the specialised ranks of the building industry with the aim of protecting it from competition and encroachment. This led towards the RIBA's regulation of entry into the profession, the institution of formal qualifications based upon education, the augmentation of pupillage and then the shift to college-based training during the course of a century. A group of satellite institutions were set up to carry this through: departments at University College and King's College, London, the Architectural Association, and eventually the full-time university departments starting with Liverpool. Other institutions, such as the Government Schools of Design and the Royal Academy, were established or reformed during the period to help with the great reorganisation of labour and training. The leading protagonists of this movement within the architectural sphere were men like T. L. Donaldson, Robert Kerr, Richard Phené Spiers, Charles Reilly, A. E. Richardson and Reginald Blomfield. Few of them are outstanding as architects, but all were good organisers and persuasive polemicists, most were well-travelled and internationally connected, and many were charismatic teachers. The styles they advocated ranged from the frankly eclectic, through the neo-baroque and neo-Georgian, to a strict classical copyism.

The resistance to this movement towards professionalisation arose as an early disenchantment with the Royal Academy and a suspicion of the RIBA as institutional representations of, and perhaps even as means of exploiting, the rise of industrialised methods in building. The question that A. W. N. Pugin, Alfred Bartholomew, Joseph Hansom, John Ruskin, William Lethaby and members of the Arts and Crafts movement all raised was whether these changes were inevitable, as natural as the shifting of rock formations, or whether in fact they were brought about by and served the interests of certain groups. In their various ways all these resisters wished to re-establish continuity with craft traditions and building lore, to heal the division between design and building and to return in some form or other to the building lodge, both as the way in which building and architecture were practised and as the framework in which people learnt to exercise their craft or profession. Several of them were protean figures who spread their ideas in a number of different formats and contexts, aiming them as much or more to those outside the new profession as to those inside it. Their influence within architecture has thus often been amorphous or partial, interpreted in terms of a particular style rather than as a matter of philosophies and practices, patterns of response and belief, all running through an integrated vision of society.

Training and the battle of the styles

It is important at the beginning briefly to consider how developing concepts of architectural training related to that most commonly discussed aspect of Victorian architecture, the debate about style. Broadly it could be said that where the Gothic Revival looked to already established means of training to provide its architects (although Pugin favoured locally-based schools), those who were interested in classical styles increasingly came to look towards academic education to provide them with allies, assistants and successors. Several of the Gothic Revivalists, notably Pugin and Ruskin, saw the great medieval monuments as having been designed by pious monks and built by joyous craftsmen. What theory there was in the English Gothic Revival was neither formulaically understood nor seen as best suited to transmission in an academy. In fact the characteristic Victorian tussle over commissions often called the 'battle of the styles' was, like the eighteenth-century dispute between neo-Palladian and rococo tastes, hardly possible in a centralised national education system like that of France. Viollet-le-Duc's case is exemplary. Although he was appointed Professor of Art and Aesthetics at the Ecole des Beaux Arts in 1863, his reputation as an arch-critic of the academy meant that he was received with enormous hostility, forcing him to resign within five months. By contrast, in the 1850s, August Reichensperger, the most influential Gothic Revival theorist in Germany, argued that it was the relative freedom from bureaucratic control and academic training that had allowed the English Gothic Revival to flourish to such good effect (Lewis 1989: 186).

In England Gothic was learnt by painstaking touring, drawing and measuring, and restoration work, and most of the Revival's architects were pupil-trained, with a fair element of autodidacticism. Their architecture was imitative, 'developed' or idiosyncratic, and its ecclesiological dimensions were to do with planning for liturgical programmes – certain notions of hierarchical spatial organisation or church furnishings for example – rather than a set of procedures for composition; they were often the domain of architectural theologians rather than architectural theorists. Composition, understood as the control exerted by one mind using a set of design strategies, was inimical to Gothic Revivalists who used more empirical techniques and for secular buildings often planned in a robustly functionalist manner. The contrast with the French system can be seen in the most typical drawing techniques: in Britain the perspective was the primary means to convey a sense of the building, while in France orthographic drawings were preferred, together with stereographic and geometric methods. Gothic Revival buildings served public programmes through a combination of historical association, utilitarian flexibility and a pragmatic use of engineering techniques. Later the Arts and Crafts architects retained some of these *ad hoc* approaches, to which they added a view of vernacular building and craft traditions as the generative basis of architecture.

It was perfectly possible to learn classicism similarly, as Soane, C. R. Cockerell, Sir Charles Barry, Inigo Jones or indeed Brunelleschi had learnt it, through pupillage, travelling and painstaking archaeological investigation. And, as we have shown, the building lodge flourished in Wren's Royal Works. But increasingly, from the mid-Victorian period onwards, travel seems to have become less important and classicism came to be regarded as a style whose grammar had to be learnt and applied in dialogue with a set of rules. There is thus an important distinction to be made between the notion of 'secret' lore and *ad hoc* practice passed down within the lodge which pervaded the history of Gothic architecture, and the much more public knowledge of the Orders. Accordingly in their pedagogical aspects, and certainly in the later nineteenth century, Gothic tended towards the lodge where classicism tended towards the academy. The Houses of Parliament, the Oxford Museum, and Cologne Cathedral were all seen by Gothicists from time to time as projects where architects might be nurtured within a vigorous artisan community (Lewis 1989: 186), although the Germans went much further with this than the British. Gothic Revivalists of the Puginian or Ecclesiological kind were somewhat distrustful of these organic working communities, while those like George Gilbert Scott and John Ruskin were more interested in them.

On the other side, the academy was the place where classical theory, graphic skills and the procedures of composition would be learnt (Robert Macleod

1971: 100). The architecture of University College, where one of the first architectural schools was set up, was Greek Revival and the most fervent supporters of academicism were men like Donaldson, Tite and Knowles, all of them classicists of various kinds. Furthermore, many of the men who set up the RIBA saw it as an institute promoting classicism (Papworth 1835–36: 112). But, as we shall see, in the last decades of the century to be a classicist was not necessarily to want academic education. For example, while Richard Norman Shaw and his followers, several of whom worked in eclectic varieties of classicism, could accept the role of an academy as a group of learned men, they were opposed to a bureaucratically-run academic system on the lines of the Ecole.

The foundation of the RIBA

This period opens with the formation of the Institute of British Architects in 1834, the culmination of a series of societies that had been established in the previous forty years to advance the interests of architects. These included the Architects' Club (1791), the London Architectural Society (1806), the Architectural Society (1831),[1] as well as the informal get-togethers between leading London architects such as Taylor and Chambers. The new Institute immediately became a focus for efforts then being made to define the practice of architects as distinct from that of other workers in the building industry. At that time the skills of designing, measuring, surveying and making specifications could belong to the architect, the surveyor, the builder or any one of a number of designations. At the same time the architect's function and status were also put in question by the new large general contractors who could control both design and finance, either bypassing the architect or employing him as a cog in their own machine of divided labour. The new Institute, therefore, would attempt to establish the status and specific role of its members and to do this it had to have some influence upon architectural training. But this concern with training was very much a secondary objective (unlike the case of the Architectural Society, for instance, whose primary aim had been to improve architectural education and, ultimately, to set up a 'British School of Architecture'; Colvin 1978: 28).

The Royal Charter, granted in 1837, defined the Institute's educational responsibilities in a broad manner: it was to be 'an Institution for the general advancement of Civil Architecture, and for promoting and facilitating the acquirement of the knowledge of the various arts and sciences connected therewith' (RIBA 1971: 3). There was no indication of the preferred means of gaining this knowledge, although an occasional class of student members was set up in 1838 with a few medals, sporadic lectures, and access to the RIBA's cast collection. It was to be nearly a hundred years, however, before the Institute took on much of the regulation of education and this was to happen within university and college architectural schools, in preference to training within offices. This change towards greater academicism and towards centralisation of education went hand in hand with the development of architects as specialists in design and in certain other aspects of building production, working under legally binding contracts. As J. B. Papworth, one of the founders of the RIBA, wrote in 1835,

> Architecture embraces the whole art of designing in all the means which its study can supply, in composition, proportion, ornaments of every kind, light, shade and colour. He, therefore, who delegates his power over any of these in the building which he erects, as considering them inferior in his art, is not fully embued with the true spirit. (Papworth 1835–36: 113)

Particular skills such as drawing, design and supervision, the ability to select and creatively recombine elements and to delve into the higher reaches of mathematics and geometry, were all claimed as belonging specifically to the architect in a province set apart form the work of the artisan. Design itself became subject to rationalised procedures and aesthetic or historical theories distanced from matters of craft and construction, and so to some extent did the means by which design was learnt.

Industry and architecture

The variety of methods of entry into architecture that existed in the eighteenth century was not reformed and rationalised out of existence, as happened in France. This variety even survived vestigially until well into the twentieth century. But the cause of their eclipse in Britain was clear; it was the development of industrial capitalism, and especially the replacement of small manufacturing production by large-scale industry with its factory system and division of labour. The rapid expansion of the building industry both immediately before and after the Napoleonic Wars encouraged organisational change similar to that which was taking place in other industries, resulting in major adjustments in the social division of labour and in great industrial conflict (for comparative tables of annual growth rates see Crafts 1983: 180, 185).

This change to larger-scale industrial production meant that forms of knowledge and the ways by which they were transmitted also changed. Knowledge of crafts had been controlled by master-craftsmen and transmitted virtually unaltered from generation to generation. We have seen how in the seventeenth and early eighteenth centuries the majority of architects either had crafts backgrounds or acquired a crafts training under the master craftsmen who had multiplied after the Great Fire. Clearly, if there were to be changes in the role of the crafts they would have important implications for architects and architecture. Early in the nineteenth century several of the new large-scale general contractors, such as Thomas Cubitt, assembled waged workmen, all the crafts and sometimes an architectural office into one organisation so that buildings could be subject to the process of manufacture. Others would submit estimates for a work and then subcontract out parts of it on a competitive basis, choosing the cheapest. Thus although small firms continued to dominate, there was an increasing gap between them and the large contractors upon whom they depended for subcontracts and who were the active agents for change in the industry. Changes did not come about by the introduction of new machinery, of which there was little in the building trade at this time, but by the reorganisation of work brought about by these general contractors (Price 1980: 19–34). The new workshops were like building factories in which a greatly expanded scale of operations and the minute separation of functions entailed less responsibility or scope for the individual artisan, a dependence on detailed instructions, and hence a decay of traditional skills. The big firms had little interest in the maintenance of craft standards and security of work; what they were after was profit and the accumulation of capital, and contractors often had little previous knowledge of building. By the mid-1820s the system of lump-sum competitive tenders had become generally accepted for large developments and the general contractor was firmly established.[2]

These contractors not only threatened the independence of master builders, but also that of the burgeoning professional sections of the industry. The new division of labour threatened the intermediary role of architects who seemed to be becoming merely design specialists within the system. The executive functions of surveying, design and structural engineering were separated out as professional associations like the RIBA grew up to protect these specialisms by defining distinct fields of expertise. The Surveyors' Club had been formed in 1792, the Institute of Civil Engineers in 1818 and the Surveyors' Institute in 1868, all claiming to oversee the status and integrity of their members' specialism regardless of market needs, and all part of the growing subclass of professional men in Victorian Britain. It was with these groups, and particularly the engineers, that architects felt the most rivalry, and changes in training can be seen as attempts to keep up with or excel the other professions, rather than to unify or merge with them.

Architects had to deal more with the legal aspects of their work and, in line with the new streamlined 'contracts in gross', to provide more detailed drawings, fuller specifications, and more scrupulous supervision.[3] Previously arrangements had been looser and only in special larger buildings, such as St Paul's Cathedral, would a range of wooden models, moulds and templates be used to communicate specifications from the office to the craftsmen. All of the new developments had consequences for architectural training, not least amongst which was the severing of the architect from the building craftsman. This was the premise behind Soane's system of pupillage with its use of the

artisan as an instrument for the architect's artistic intellectualism and idiosyncratic individuality, but it was a fatal blow at Sir William Chambers's ideal
of the co-operative relationship between the architect-leader and his semi-
independent craftsmen (Hanson 1987).

However, it would be wrong to portray these developments in architectural
practice purely as a defensive reaction to the circumstances of 'restless and
competitive anarchy' within the industry (Price 1980: 25). There was also a
unique opportunity here for establishing the architect's professional credentials. Hence, for example, some architects like John Nash and Robert Smirke,
as well as James Wyatt at the Royal Works, took quickly and enthusiastically to
the new system, for it actually helped to consolidate the architect's developing
role as an expert 'man of taste', someone set apart from the dirty business of
construction, from commerce, from the more mechanical professions and
from the lay public. Furthermore the use of detailed specifications and working
drawings which laid out methods of construction as well as the finished
appearance was in part a response to the loss of craft skills, but it also further
contributed to this decline, separating design from execution, enhancing the
distinct role of the architect and removing much of the craftsmen's freedom to
contribute to the design of a building (Port 1967: 101). Architects could secure
their power and professional self-definition by controlling those aspects of
specifically architectural production under the new conditions, by adopting
some of the restrictive practices of the guild, and in the process deskilling the
building trades. The formation of the RIBA and its growing ambitions can be
seen then as a direct exploitation of these industrial developments for the
benefit of one section of the construction industry. It is possible to envisage a
different scenario in which industrialisation would be accompanied by investment in developing all the building skills. But in Britain, at least, this was not
to be. We must now examine the means by which these changes were brought
to bear, and we will find that they necessitated a powerful enhancement of the
architect's metier through emphasising and limiting the methods and institutions appropriate for his training. First, however, we will see how pupillage
retained some aspects of eighteenth-century diversity.

Pupillage

Pupillage, established in the mid-eighteenth century, had become the most
common but by no means the only form of architectural training by the end
of the century. Its importance was maintained throughout the nineteenth
century, although its form, conditions and length were never universally
defined. Like the present system of degree and diploma, pupillage was not
however regarded as sufficient training in itself, and it was often followed by
travelling and by working as a draughtsman or assistant. Usually pupillage

started at fifteen or sixteen, although occasionally it could commence at twenty-one after a university education; this might also entail a class difference and different architectural aspirations. Pupils were often expected to have a background in languages and some knowledge of mathematics, geometry and drawing. Their pupillage could last anything from three to seven years, although it was usually five or six. Generally speaking articles merely stated that the pupil was to learn the 'art or profession of an architect'. What was understood by this was that the pupil would be trained in architectural drawing, measuring, site work and the general running of the office, though there were often variations on this.[4] In 1890 the RIBA issued a model form for articles, stipulating that permission should be granted for pupils to attend lectures and classes in order to prepare for the RIBA examinations, but this does not seem to have applied to outlying areas, where such classes may not have been available.[5] Pupillage could be good or bad, since the system was largely unregulated and depended a great deal on the qualities of the pupil master. Architects could exploit the system by taking the premium and simply using their pupils as assistants. Inevitably the bad examples were seized on to represent the entire practice by those utilitarian educational reformers who favoured academic education.

In Dickens's *Martin Chuzzlewit* (1844) the fictional training of the hero provided a paradigmatic example of bad pupillage (15). Pecksniff's attitude to Chuzzlewit and his other pupils demonstrates this graphically:

> His genius lay in ensnaring parents and guardians, and pocketing premiums. A young gentleman's premium being paid, and the young gentleman come to Mr Pecksniff's house, Mr Pecksniff borrowed his case of mathematical instruments (If silver-mounted or otherwise valuable); entreated him, from that moment, to consider himself one of the family; complimented him highly on his parents or guardians, as the case might be; and turned him loose in a spacious room on the two-pair front; where, in the company of certain drawing-boards, parallel rulers, very stiff-legged compasses, and two, or perhaps three, other young gentlemen, he improved himself, for three or five years, according to his articles, in making elevations of Salisbury Cathedral from every possible point of sight; and in constructing in the air a vast quantity of Castles, Houses of Parliament, and other Public Buildings (Dickens 1844: Chapter Two).

For other matters Pecksniff would hand over to his servant/assistant:

> Thomas Pinch will instruct you in the art of surveying the back garden, or in ascertaining the dead level of the road between this house and the fingerpost, or in any other practical and pleasing pursuit. There are a cart-load of loose bricks, and a score or two of old flower-pots, in the back yard. If you could pile them up, my dear Martin, into any form which would remind me on my return – say of St Peter's at Rome, or the Mosque of St Sophia at Constantinople – it would be at once improving to you and agreeable to my feelings (Dickens 1844: Chapter Six).

15 Phiz (Hablot K. Browne): 'Mr. Pinch and the New Pupil on a Social Occasion'

Although there was much pompous pretence in Pecksniff, little was delivered: his establishment was nothing more than an expensive lodging house. Should they actually design anything Pecksniff's pupils found that the master would make a few unnecessary additions and claim the work as his own. However, Dickens's early radical faith in progress and dislike of privilege, hypocrisy and untested institutions, was here, in the devastating caricature of the pupil-master, providing fuel for the more scientifically-minded radicalism (to which Dickens himself did not subscribe) already being brought to architectural education by the Benthamites and utilitarians, a movement whose architectural adherents were committed to academic education under the rubric of the RIBA.[6] The fictional Pecksniff seems to have been an extreme example of the negligent pupil-master: a compound of vices rarely approximated even by the surviving records of bad pupillage (Saint 1983: 54–6). However, this form of apprenticeship was clearly open to the kind of exploitation anatomised by Dickens.

But some commentators saw that a better form of pupillage was possible. In a lecture delivered in 1847 at the London Architectural Society, Robert

Sandeman directed the pupil-master to oversee a progressive development of the pupil's abilities. In the first year there would be drawing instruction by stages and directed reading, 'keeping the Poetry of the Art from [the pupil]'. The second year would have a variety of office work with as much drawing to scale as possible. The third year would concentrate on visiting and reporting on works and assistance in surveys, giving liberty for the pupil to follow up sciences and practice perspectives. In the fourth year the pupil would be chief assistant at every survey or levelling and would develop elevation drawings, perspectives and colouring. In the final year the pupil would be given designs to proportion and execute, he would take out quantities, level, survey and make calculations (Sandeman 1847). Such a pupillage would prepare the architect for the non-designing tasks that actually took up most of the time in a typical nineteenth-century practice.

For potential architects with aspirations towards the prestigious activity of design, pupillage was at its best when there was access to complementary classes at the Royal Academy or in the many provincial architectural clubs and associations such as those at Glasgow, Edinburgh, Newcastle, Manchester and Birmingham, which gave prizes and ran occasional classes (Powers 1982: 26). These provincial practices were further aided by the growth of professional periodicals from the 1830s onwards.

Although small offices could often provide sound experience in building and office practice, nevertheless the best experience of pupillage was generally felt where the office was like an atelier or in the larger offices where budding architects could undertake a variety of graduated tasks on a number of types of commission. We have already seen how assiduously Soane had directed his pupils' training. Later in the century the offices of Sir George Gilbert Scott, Ernest George and Richard Norman Shaw are good examples of these large, multifarious offices. Scott's and Shaw's offices in particular produced a number of notable architects: under Scott, for example, were trained G. E. Street, G. F. Bodley, Rowand Anderson, T. G. Jackson, E. R. Robson, J. J. Stevenson, William White and Scott's sons John Oldrid Scott and George Gilbert Scott. Scott himself had benefited from a sound pupillage under James Edmeston with access to a good library, sketching trips, attendance at a drawing school and then a period of employment with a large contracting firm before working as a clerk of works (Scott 1879: 55–77). Scott may not have shown as much personal interest in his pupils' development as Soane, but the hierarchy within his office – one of the largest in Europe at this time – and especially the role taken by the salaried assistants provided an excellent framework for tuition, and there was an open and uninhibited practice of criticism and an efficient parcelling out of responsibilities (T. G. Jackson 1950: 58–61). Not for nothing was it known as the 'Spring Gardens Academy'.

Amongst the pupils of Shaw were many of the future leaders of the Arts and

Crafts movement: men like Ernest Newton, Edward Prior, Mervyn Macartney, Gerald Horsley, Sydney Barnsley and others, while William Lethaby and Robert Weir Schulz were assistants. Many of these men went on to form the Art Workers' Guild which fostered vernacular methods of building and supported the pupillage system. In Shaw's office they were given several weeks' trial period before any articles were signed. Then they were usually articled for three to five years on premiums between £100 and £300. Their first tasks were to learn how to measure up buildings and how to draw the very fine plans and elevations for which Shaw's office was renowned. Based as they were in London, Shaw encouraged his pupils to attend the RA School and the AA Class of Design. They were gradually granted various liaison and site responsibilities and freedom to design small jobs and even sometimes to collaborate on larger buildings. The final stage of pupillage was to be made clerk of works. At the end of their time Shaw helped most of his pupils by giving them 'setting-up' commissions. The offices of Shaw and Scott, amongst others, clearly demonstrate that pupillage did not have to be Pecksniffian. Indeed, that caricature can be more than balanced by the image of a well-organised office as a kind of nursery of talent.

Gradually pupillage became a route that women could take into the profession. By the 1870s several women were working as pupils and several were accepted in the offices of Arts and Crafts architects, notably Beatrice Phillips, who was a pupil of E. W. Godwin and several women who studied with C. F. A. Voysey, but their acceptance as professional designers was more difficult. In 1898 Ethel Charles, who had been articled to Ernest George, became the first female member of the RIBA (Walker 1989: 96–9; Walker 1984). Only in the 1920s, however, did women first regularly enter the profession.

The reform of architectural training, 1830–60

We have seen how bad practices of pupillage were ridiculed by Dickens in the person of Pecksniff. By the time *Martin Chuzzlewit* was published in 1844 the elements of an alternative both to pupillage and to the teaching offered at the Royal Academy were already being assembled by radicals influenced by utilitarian ideology deriving from Jeremy Bentham; particularly by his idea of subjecting all institutions to rational analysis and reform aimed at achieving material progress and measured by the rigorous moral arithmetic of 'utility'. Utilitarian enterprises were underpinned by new notions of what constituted the art and the science of architecture. A different kind of division of labour seems to have been encouraged by this duality, and with it new debates about what was meant by each of these terms. Furthermore the utilitarians stoked and rearoused the issue of an architecture bound up with public administration. They thus also rekindled the question of a centralised profession, and their obsession with measurable expertise was the drive behind the evolution and refinement of a system of examinations. In a sense the RIBA and all that it stood for by the end of the century can be seen as Bentham's architectural monument.

The first new enterprises were based at two London colleges, King's and University College, and at the new Government Schools of Design. Set up by Jeremy Bentham in 1826, University College had already established a reputation for itself as the flagship of secular utilitarian education. The academic curriculum at King's (founded in 1828) and University College was wider than those of the older universities and was focused on scientific and professional education. Both colleges ran teaching hospitals and taught law. T. L. Donaldson, a prime mover in the establishment of the RIBA, was made Professor of Architecture at University College in 1841 and remained there until he was succeeded by T. H. Lewis in 1865. From 1840 civil engineering and architecture were taught at King's College, London under the direction of William Hosking, who held a chair in the 'Arts of Construction'.[8] Hosking was succeeded by Robert Kerr, from 1861 to 1890, although it was not until Banister Fletcher succeeded Kerr that design was introduced. Neither college aimed at a complete professional training, but instead to provide the foundation-stones for pupillage.

Donaldson was well acquainted with academic methods; he had spent much time in Paris and Rome, where he had become a member of the Academy of Saint Luke in 1822. He had attended Soane's Royal Academy lectures in the 1820s and he was a firm believer in the professional status of the architect. His work in this respect earned him the title 'father of the profession', although this title was also often given to Soane (*Building News*, 49, 7 August 1885: 204). Later Donaldson compiled an important professional guidebook, the *Handbook of Specifications* (1859). His aim at University College was to create a part-time, systematic elementary course of architectural education (16). To do this the syllabus was divided into 'Architecture as a Fine Art' and 'Architecture as a Science', although Donaldson believed that engineering and architecture were directed by the same scientific principles.[9] The reasoning here may have been that for architects to have a leadership role in the building process they needed at the elementary stage to know the principal elements of engineering, the field of their closest rivals. Thus University College had a basic first year curriculum that would serve both fields: mathematics, physics, chemistry, geology and drawing. Professors of mathematics, natural philosophy, chemistry, practical chemistry, civil engineering (the first in the country), architecture, mechanical principles of engineering and descriptive machinery would all contribute to the course, as well as a lecturer on geology and a teacher of drawing. Occasionally, in a schematic way, Donaldson would use a practical demonstration such as 'the introduction of a bricklayer and a hodful of bricks to demonstrate the construction of brickwalls' (Bellot 1929: 265). T. Roger Smith added

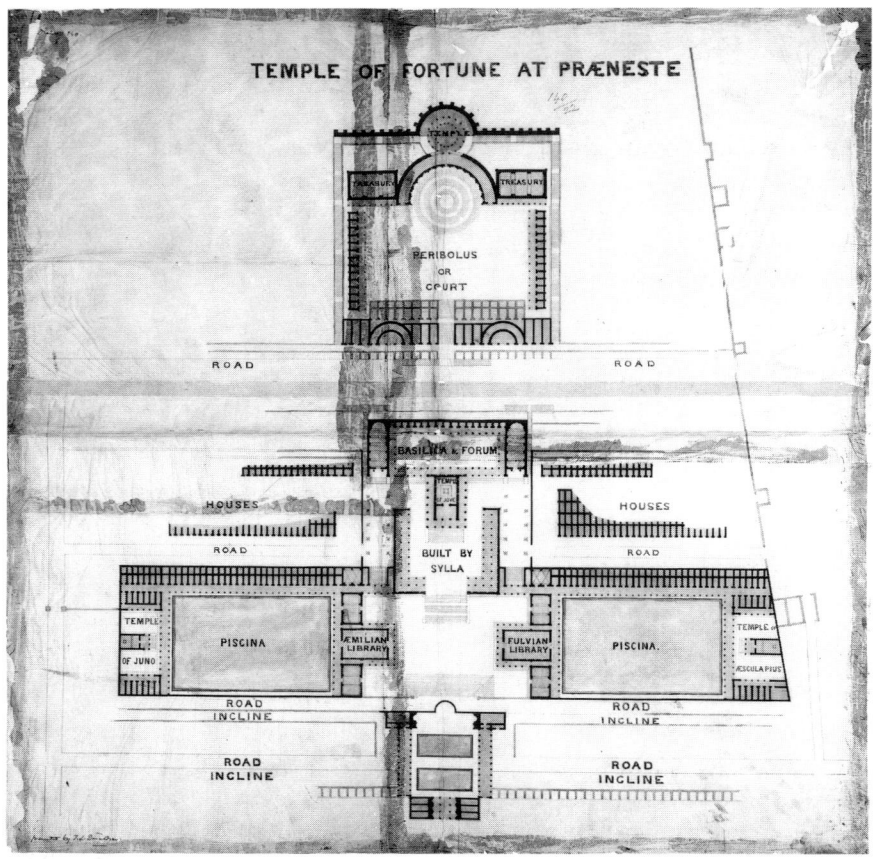

16 T. L. Donaldson: Temple of Fortune at Praeneste (lecture diagram, c.1842–65)

lectures on professional practice, and construction lectures were appended in 1892, but no design was taught until the twentieth century.

Resistance

A powerful resistance to these developments arose almost immediately. For example, the utilitarian ethos of King's College was attacked by A. W. N. Pugin in his book *Contrasts* (1836) with its plates juxtaposing Kings's Palladian front with the Gothic of Christ's College (Christ Church), Oxford, choosing a medieval, 'Catholic' image to contrast with a classical, 'Anglican' view of London University (17). The 'uncollegiate' University College designed by William Wilkins, with its 'pagan exterior' and 'useless dome and portico' was later criticised in Pugin's *True Principles of Pointed or Christian Architecture*

(Pugin 1841: 45). Elsewhere in *Contrasts* Pugin dismissed the notion that architecture could be taught according to 'the trammels of a system' within 'factories of learning'. In Pugin's view only 'the mere mechanical use of tools and the general principles of drawing' could be learnt through instruction, and he was dismissive both of pupillage as it then stood and of attendance at the Royal Academy. The pupil attending an office 'Lolls over his desk, draws the five orders, then pricks off plans, and, when his apprenticeship is nearly expired, he may, perhaps, be able to rule the lines of an elevation clearly and do a tolerably neat plan' (Pugin 1836: 34). At the Royal Academy

> He idles a little more time, copies a few more casts, makes another composition, and perhaps he gets a medal, perhaps not. At any rate it is time he set forth on his travels to classic shores; and thither, at vast expense, is he sent, and three of four more years of the most precious period of his life is spent in going over, for the thousandth time, the same set of measurements on the same set of cornices and columns (Pugin 1836: 34).

For Pugin the fundamental problem with architectural training was the dictatorship held over it by 'men of business'; both the architectural pupil-master and the general contractor. It was to the latter in particular that Pugin contrasted his vision of medieval architecture with craftsmen in a subordinate position following the rule of an architect designing according to the 'truth' of materials and construction and the convenience and propriety of their architectural disposition.

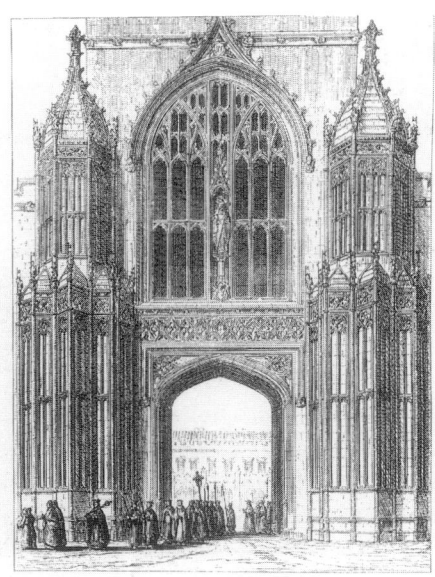

17 A. W. N. Pugin: 'Contrasted College Gateways' (1836)

Pugin's critical response to the effects of industrial capitalism on architecture was markedly different from that of pupil-masters like Soane who sought an intellectual position above the mêlée, and from that of the founders of the RIBA, many of whom were followers of Soane, who had reacted with a combination of acceptance and the hurried attempt to instal professional protection. It was different too from Pugin's own position before about 1840, when he was much more complicit with the system.

Pugin's criticisms of architectural training were repeated in his *Apology for the Revival of Christian Architecture* (1843), where he also presented his own alternative. Instead of 'a pagan journey . . . to form . . . small Doric men' (Pugin 1843: 20), Pugin wanted students to travel to Britain's own medieval monuments and natural landscape and resources, and to use these as 'a school for study and contemplation' (Pugin 1843: 21). The study of local vernacular would be promoted through local schools for local architects. When linked with a due religious knowledge and an acquaintance with 'the annals of his country', the student would be able to design according to 'Faith, customs and natural traditions' (Pugin 1843: 21; see also Pugin 1841: 30). To counteract the charge that this ignored the great changes taking place at the time, Pugin then attempted to detail the intimate links between the nineteenth century and the period of the past that he revered.

Another reaction, different from Pugin's and more in tune with the resistance by independent master craftsmen to the industrial threat, was the effort made by Robert Owen and the architect Joseph Hansom to set up a Grand National Guild of Builders in 1833. The idea was to resist the worst effects of industrialisation by binding construction workers together in a building community whose mouthpiece was eventually to be a new magazine, the *Builder*, started in 1842 and later taken over as part of the new professional press.[10] In 1842 Hansom also proposed a 'Builders' College', attached to his own practice, and intended to move constantly between the teaching of handicrafts and design skills, 'to fill up the vacuity in that section of art which lies between the mere constructor of buildings, and the architect and engineer'.[11] By healing specialist divisions Hansom hoped a new class of builder would emerge.

Hansom was also associated with Alfred Bartholomew, his successor as editor of the *Builder* in 1843 and the son of a watchmaker. Bartholomew organised a society with links to the Young England group, which included Disraeli and Lord John Manners, called 'The Freemasons of the Church' who had been planning a National Architectural College as early as 1831 with a similar remit to Hansom's. This College, in many respects a more academic version of Wren's Royal Works, was also an extraordinarily radical and ambitious idea. It would be an estate of the realm with control over public surveyorships and the power to regulate the whole of the building industry and thus heal the divisions within it. An architectural training in the College would take twenty years divided into four graduated parts working up from 'Mason' to 'Mathematical Master Mason' (Bartholomew 1846; *Builder*, 18 February 1843: 23–4). Bartholomew's aim was to create a building community that could hand down an orthodoxy of practice and knowledge (Hanson 1987: 113–17). However, like Hansom's short-lived attempt to set up a Builders' College, it came to nothing.[12]

None the less Pugin and Bartholomew shared this much with Donaldson and his fellow-thinkers, namely a belief in training in colleges closely bound up with the State. (Hansom stood apart from both groups in his advocacy of a privately-run building lodge encompassing academic work and practical instruction on site.) However, while Pugin and Bartholomew held to a nationalist medieval vision of architectural practice, with the architect and craftsman as guardians of 'old principles' within a harmonious social and economic hierarchy associated with the Tory paternalism of the Young England movement, Donaldson, like Bentham, believed in capitalist industrialism as a progressive force that demanded different economic associations and different forms of training. They wanted to produce a special kind of professional, knowledgeable in history and aesthetics just as much as in abstract but positivistic mathematics.[13]

Thus the welcome Pugin gave to the Government School of Design when it was first set up in 1837 was consistent with his general approach to professional education. He saw it as a chance to embody his ideas:

> A school of *national artists*, not mere imitators of any style, but men imbued with a thorough knowledge of the history, wants, climate and customs of our country; who would combine all the spirit of the mediaeval architects and the beauties of the old Christian artists, with the practical improvement of our times and our increased anatomical knowledge; we should then create a school founded on the old principles, and yet a true expression of our period (Letter to J. R. Herbert in the *Builder*, 2 August 1845: 367).

Of course this School of Design, and its related provincial schools, was not set up to teach architecture, but Pugin saw that it might train designers and craftsmen for architecture. The basis of this training, he hoped, would be the study of nature and its controlled disposition in design; what the Victorians called conventionalised ornament. He was disappointed. In practice he found the School 'perverted by copying . . . stale models' in a 'miserable system of adaptation of obsolete symbols and designs, appropriate only to times and people from whom they originated' (Letter to J. R. Herbert in the *Builder*, 2 August 1845: 367).

Other institutions

Independent of Pugin's viewpoint, the Government School of Design merits discussion in relation to architectural education. The School was like the

French Ecole Polytechnique, Napoleon's schools of drawing and design, or technical schools in Germany in so far as it was a state body which attempted to carry out the same systematised education through provincial offshoots (twenty-one of them by 1852). One of its Superintendents, William Dyce, had inspected German schools and wanted to make the School of Design into a *Gewerbeschule* (a technical as opposed to a design school, which was the next tier in Germany) with an attached *Werkstatt* (workshop), but this was never carried out (Macdonald 1970). The School's founders, many of whom were utilitarians and supporters of the Reform Act of 1832, wanted to break the monopoly over art education held by the Royal Academy. There were similar contemporaneous attempts to reform the Royal Society, the Royal Institution and the medical profession (see Roy Macleod 1983).

The Government School of Design was a means by which the reformed State sought to supply industry with designers and to impose a particular elevating notion of Good Design. Yet although it subsidised and interceded in the supply of specialists for industry, thereby helping to complete the displacement of the old workshop organisation, and although its first director (from 1836 to 1837) was the architect J. B. Papworth, whom we have already met as one of the founders of the RIBA,[14] the School of Design refused to have anything to do with a specifically architectural training because, so it said, 'it interferes with the right of private individuals' (*Builder* 1846: 465): in other words, such a training might affect the incomes of those architects who relied on the money they received from pupillage. Although it had a master for architecture, students seem to have done little beyond copying ornamental drawings (Pugin's 'obsolete designs') and some perspective and figure drawing. In the 1850s, however, the reformed Government Schools of Design began to teach architecture either as an art subject (decoration) to art teachers, or as a science subject to builders in the form of construction. This separation echoes Donaldson's curricular separation of architecture as an art and architecture as a science and it is similar to the way access to life drawing was used to separate the artist from the designer. In these dichotomies architecture was either engineering and building or art and decoration, and the effects of this false opposition continued to influence architectural education.

Although at their outset the Government Schools of Design may seem to have been peripheral to architectural training, they did grow in importance. With their national competitions they provided an often essential complement to pupillage in the provinces. Arthur Beresford Pite, for example, entered the South Kensington Schools of Design in 1876, and Edwin Lutyens took advantage of their facilities from 1885 to 1887, combining them with judicious travelling and sketching (18). In the 1890s the Schools of Design added architectural design to their curricula (Powers 1982: 25), and in the early twentieth century many of them opened architectural departments (at Canterbury, Hull,

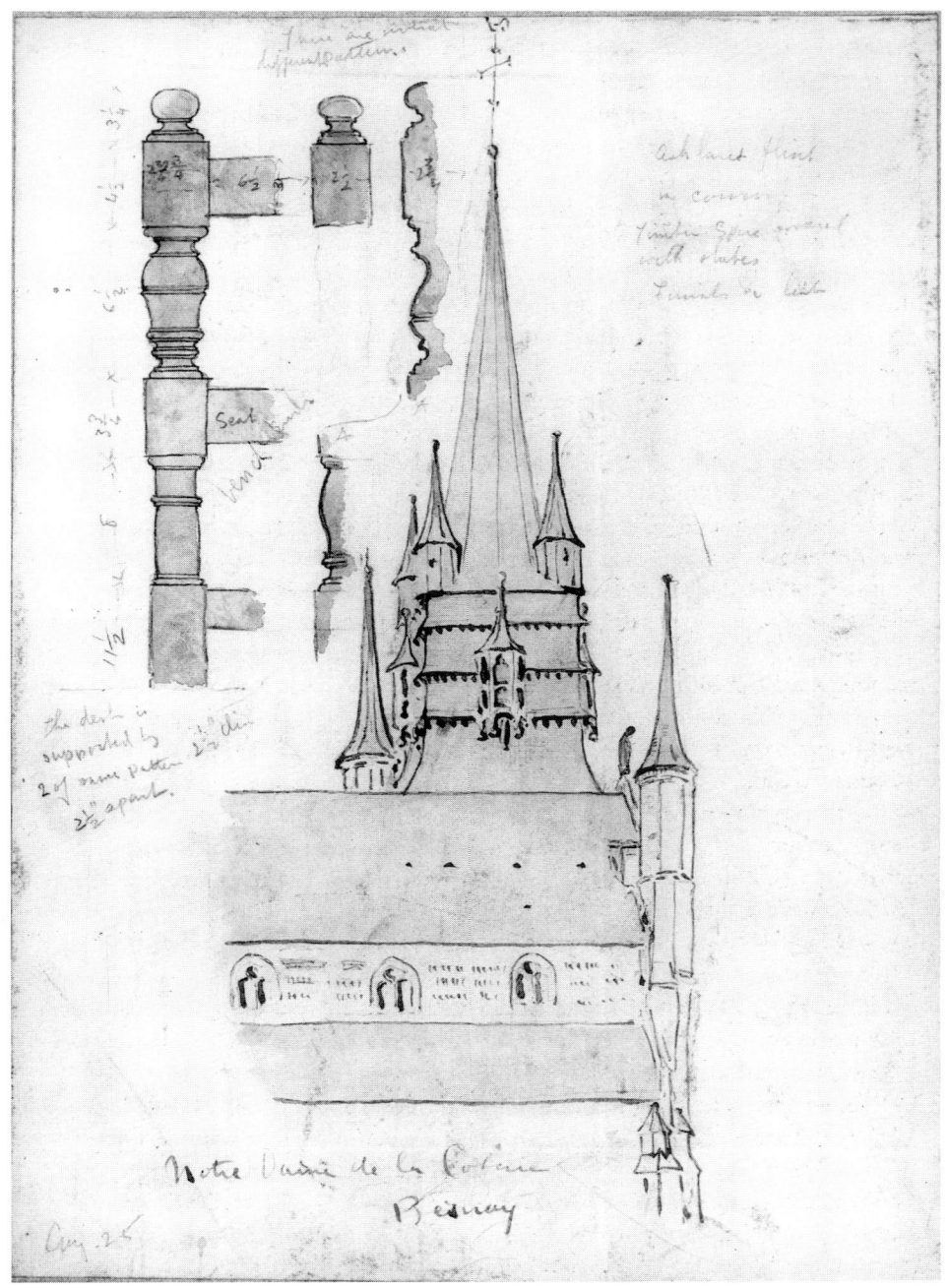

18 Edwin Lutyens: sheet of drawings made in Normandy (1885–87)

Birmingham and Heriot-Watt, for example) and many of these have survived to the present day within the recently (1991) chartered universities, formerly polytechnics. They demonstrate that some of the foundations for state education in architecture were in place before the so-called Beaux-Arts period of the 1900s, and long before the final setting up of what we will call the Official System in the 1960s.

However, perhaps the most important of these potential alternatives to pupillage was not a state body at all. In 1847 a school of design was opened up by the Association of Architectural Draughtsmen, joining various facilities that had been opened by the Association five years previously. This new body, the Architectural Association, was set up by architects as a way of augmenting their education in areas that pupillage and the Royal Academy did not supply. Amongst its founders was Robert Kerr, later to become Professor of Construction at King's, who, through letters to the *Builder*, had conducted a campaign against pupillage in the mid-1840s.[15] The most significant provision at the new AA was a design class. In this class weekly subjects were set for which drawings were prepared in students' spare time and brought in for criticism by other students, there being no instructors. An Elementary Design Class was started in 1869 and classes in modelling, watercolour, woodcarving and life drawing were tried during the 1860s. The AA came to foster an anti-pupillage attitude, seeking the use of examinations and diplomas to protect professional status and responding promptly and positively to the RIBA's moves in these directions. As we shall see later, it also came to play a significant role in fostering most of the theories that came to reform architectural education.

The movement towards examination and registration

The interest in using examinations and a system of registration had been growing in strength since the mid-nineteenth century. As we have shown, there had been close ties between influential members of the RIBA and the new architectural teaching at places like the AA and University College. The RIBA began seriously to consider adopting an examination system in the mid-1850s, following discussion of the issue at the AA. The issue was taken up in turn by James Knowles, Alfred Bailey, William Tite and then J. W. Papworth.

Knowles's 1853 AA prize essay on the subject of architectural education is often seen as the catalyst for this debate. Knowles argued that a diploma should be awarded following successful completion of an examination in architecture. It is quite clear from this essay that the examination issue was just as much, or more, about social status as it was about protecting the public. Knowles saw examinations as a way of giving the RIBA powers similar to those of the Inns of Court, the College of Physicians or Apothecaries' Hall. Thus examinations would help to preserve the term 'architect' from 'undertakers, carpenters and builders', especially if entry was restricted to 'scholars and gentlemen' to guard against malpractice (Knowles 1853: 10, 15). These ideas were passed by Alfred Bailey, President of the AA, to William Tite and soon J. W. Papworth read a paper to the RIBA arguing that a Board should be set up by the Institute in order to run examinations and issue diplomas (Summerson 1947: 11). The campaign for formal education may have been largely conducted by architects and pupils, but many of them had close connections or worked in accord with professional institutes and government agencies. J. W. Papworth, for example, had acted as Secretary to the Government School of Design when his father, J. B. Papworth, had been Director.

In 1860 J. W. Papworth chaired the RIBA Committee on Architectural Education, which included T. L. Donaldson. John Ruskin and the wealthy ecclesiologist and patron A. J. B. Beresford-Hope were invited to make contributions while architects like George Gilbert Scott were consulted on the merits of pupillage.[16]

As a result of this committee's deliberations a voluntary examination ('voluntary', that is, for membership of the RIBA) was started in 1863, modelled partially on those used at the Ecole des Beaux Arts and partially on those of other professions (See Appendix). Anticipating this examination the AA set up a Voluntary Examination Class in 1862 to prepare students in its factual requirements (Summerson 1947: 20), but otherwise the exam had little uptake, due to its voluntary nature and possibly to the opposition it faced from the provincial pupil-masters. It did, however, establish the RIBA in the role of examining body.

The question of professionalising architects through the use of examinations became a particularly fraught one in the 1860s. Ruskin's position on this issue took up some of Pugin's arguments of the 1830s and 1840s. In the 1850s Ruskin had been involved in the Architectural Museum, founded in 1851 by George Gilbert Scott on the basis of L. N. Cottingham's collection of medieval architectural specimens and casts (19). This was in large part a response to the perceived decline in building craftsmanship that had resulted from the increased division of labour and mechanical production of the industrial revolution, and may have been originally inspired by the Cologne building lodge (Hanson 1987: 216–22; Jenkins 1961: 171–2). The Museum became a centre for architectural debate and a school for carving and drawing architectural ornament. In 1857 it was swallowed up by the new South Kensington Museum. For Ruskin, however, the decline in building skills remained an important issue.

Ruskin identified the architect closely with the painter and sculptor. What elevated the work of all three was the way in which it embodied imagination stimulated by natural objects, particularly the landscape and the human body. This theory informed the lecture that he gave to the RIBA in 1865, where he

19 The Architectural Museum, Westminster

argued that there was no opposition between naturalism and invention. Engineers should have separate schools while architects should study with sculptors in the same university or school courses (Ruskin 1864–65: 146). As this seemed beyond hope the best that could be done would be to refine training by concentrating study on natural form and the way it was treated in the best examples – Ancient Greece, Renaissance Italy and Gothic Europe. The sequence of learning should be: first, drawing simply from nature; second, an enquiry into 'mythological significance'; and third, the study of how sculptors had treated natural objects. These suggestions were obviously not intended to offer a complete curriculum of architectural education, but Ruskin saw them as essential correctives: '[they] would yet be the directest method of resistance to those conditions of evil among which our youth are cast at the most critical period of their lives . . . We may not be able to produce architecture, but, at the least, we shall resist vice' (Ruskin 1864–65: 147).

Ruskin helped to polarise the debate, and the reactions that followed this lecture demonstrate the way in which architectural thinkers disposed themselves at this time. Ruskin's desire to separate engineering education from architectural education was one of his most controversial views. Simultaneously it struck at one of the key tenets held at University College and King's College, and also at the rising interest in the French system of architectural education and the Ecole Polytechnique.[17] Many of Ruskin's respondents referred to Baron Haussmann's contemporary replanning of Paris into a geometric web of wide boulevards. Donaldson, ever the eclectic, could agree with Ruskin's plea for union of architecture and sculpture and also admire Haussmann's work. However, George Edmund Street and John Pollard Seddon saw the contradiction between the education system that had produced Haussman's architects and that for which Ruskin argued. Matthew Digby Wyatt felt that what Ruskin wanted was already in place, while J. W. Papworth rejected his views almost entirely. But Ruskin's most fervent critic was Robert Kerr, as befitted a professor at King's College and one of the founders of the AA. Kerr contrasted professional responsibility with Ruskin's amateurism. Like an engineer the professional architect must be 'a servant of the public for the efficient design of buildings' (Ruskin 1864–65: 150). Using a doctrine of Pugin against Ruskin, Kerr saw art as playing a small part: 'Architecture, as an art, [is] the beautifying of that which is constructive; but, first and foremost, the subject must be constructive.' Beauty, for Kerr, was the 'finishing grace [of] a thorough knowledge of plan and building' (Ruskin 1864–65: 150). The engineers were to be kept at bay not by emphasising the artistry of the architect but by subsuming their knowledge into the comprehensive vision and control of the architect.

Ruskin's lecture formed part of the deliberations of the RIBA committee on 'Artistic Architectural Education' which was set up in 1864. Its final report (1869) may show Ruskin's influence in its recommendation that students should understand massing and organic form (Startup 1984: 18–22). However, Ruskin would have been fiercely opposed to the most important recommendation, which was for compulsory preliminary examinations with the RIBA controlling teaching. After starting on a voluntary basis in 1869, these examinations were eventually made an obligatory qualification for Associateship of the RIBA in 1882 (see Appendix). Their aim was to test technical competence and measurable skills, rather than quality of design. They were also intended to increase the membership of the RIBA and thus improve its control over architectural affairs. Membership of the RIBA was about a fifth of the total number of architects at this date; a proportion which had risen from less than a tenth in 1841 (Jenkins 1961: 211, n. 1). Crucially, the examinations tested knowledge of construction and of historic styles and tended to neglect practical building skills. Their effect was immediate in the case of the AA. Design subjects were set as exercises in specified styles, with planning made part of design rather than specification in 1885; construction was taught through lectures; and stereotomy was brought in by the Beaux-Arts educated Lawrence Harvey in 1886 (Powers 1982: 15).

With an established examination system as a compulsory qualification for

Associateship, it followed that more architectural schools would be required. In 1887 the RIBA held an International Conference in London at which several American lecturers spoke on architectural education within American universities (first established in the United States in 1869), and there were also accounts of the curricula at the Ecole des Beaux Arts and the Ecole Spéciale d'Architecture (Cates 1887). The conference thus set out to account for these academic systems in a favourable manner and the result was predictable:

> These systematic courses contrast forcibly with the custom of pupillage adopted in England, which ensures only some three years of office training . . . and leaves the student to acquire in a haphazard manner, without due guidance or encouragement . . . knowledge which is indispensable: he thus too often becomes only a sketcher or draughtsman, or a mere practical man without sound scientific knowledge (Cates 1887: 5).

In line with the resolutions made by the 1887 Conference the RIBA expanded its examinations from the sole preliminary examination into a three-tiered system: Preliminary, Intermediate and Final. The second two tiers of examination both succeeded probationary work known as Testimonies of Study: these were specified sheets of drawings and illustrated memoirs which had to be submitted before students could sit exams (see Appendix). Again, the AA were first to react, appointing teachers and completely reorganising their classes by 1892, and in the early 1890s many other architectural schools began to base their courses on these examinations, including in 1895 the first full-time course in architecture, established at Liverpool University. With the growth of a system of examination, so a requirement for registration in order to practise as an architect, as well as an apparatus of control and policy-making in education, seemed to be necessary.

The overall institutional picture of changes over the next fifty years requires a summary before we move into the debates around them. By the early 1900s the RIBA had devised a system of 'recognition', by which if the schools fulfilled certain conditions (see Appendix), their students could gain exemption from one or both of the RIBA Intermediate and Final examinations. Up until this point schools had generally based their syllabuses on the RIBA examinations, which their students had sat, but in 1902 the AA and Liverpool were recognised for exemption from the Intermediate examination. In 1904 the Board of Architectural Education was set up by the RIBA to devise a syllabus for the schools of architecture and to co-ordinate the various methods of training. The Board of Architectural Education's outline 'uniform scheme' was published in 1905 and, after some changes, by 1908 (coming into effect in 1913) Associateship depended upon taking a course in accordance with this scheme. Anyone, whether at a school of architecture or not, could still qualify by taking the

RIBA's own examinations. In 1923 this system was augmented when the RIBA set up Visiting Boards to inspect architectural schools every two years and advise on recognition. After three unsuccessful attempts in 1886, 1888 and 1891 the registration issue was eventually taken up by the RIBA in the 1920s, leading to the two Architects' Registration Acts in 1931 and 1938. These Acts also established the Architects' Registration Council (ARCUK) to keep a register of those architects who had successfully passed through the examination system and to provide legal protection over professional use of the title of 'architect'.

Registration: profession or art?

By the late 1880s the only missing link in the agenda proposed by Knowles in his 1853 Essay was registration. This will be discussed, *inter alia*, in the remainder of this chapter. What exactly was meant by registration? Basically it meant that only those people who had qualified as architects through professional examinations should have the right to use the title 'architect' in their professional practice. In some countries all buildings must actually be designed by a registered architect, but not in Britain. The purpose of registration in Britain was simply to obtain legal copyright over the use of the title, but not a legal monopoly of design. This was because Parliament, wary enough of granting copyright on the title of 'architect', was not prepared to go further. Registration, however, was a crucial part of the armoury of methods by which architects sought to protect themselves against their competitors and predators in the industry and the building professions.

Registration was not necessarily bound up with the creation of a formal educational system. In France it was imposed in the nineteenth century as a condition for working on *government* projects. In Britain the campaign for registration was largely conducted at this time by the Society of Architects established in 1884 and led by men whose names (H. R. Gough and G. A. T. Middleton were the leaders) are not well remembered by history; men who tended to be either on the surveying side of the profession or who dedicated much of their time to administrative matters, but who had influential links with those at the head of the RIBA: Charles Barry jun., John Whichcord and Sir Horace Jones (Powers 1982: 13). If in the late eighteenth century pupillage had been seen as a method of grooming for the profession, the campaigners for registration increasingly came to see it as insufficiently systematic or measurable. The question that split these campaigners at this time was whether registration should come before a firm examination system linked to academic education had been established. Consequently when the Society of Architects produced a Parliamentary Bill on the issue in 1888–89, the Bill was defeated mainly as a result of lobbying by the RIBA who saw registration as a step that should be taken only after improving and expanding education (Powers 1982: 34).

This disagreement over timing was minor compared to a larger schism amongst architects that was exposed by the registration issue. The conflict was between the interests of 'professional architects' and those of 'art-architects'; a conflict that expanded and deepened the rift discussed earlier between such men as Ruskin and Scott on the one hand and Kerr and Donaldson on the other. Thus a number of prominent architects, largely belonging to the art-architect camp, came into opposition with both the Society of Architects and the RIBA over the very question of professional education. On the occasion of the Registration Bill's reintroduction in 1891 a group of forty-four architects and twenty-four artists published a Memorial in the *Times*, declaring that architecture was not examinable and that registration would adversely separate architecture from the other arts (*The Times*, 3 March 1891; see also *The Times*, 7 February 1888). What particularly angered the opponents of the RIBA at this time was the way it wanted to exert its brief for education by condensing architecture into certain professional protocols. Furthermore, they were fearful lest examinations be used as a means to test the ability to design.

The collection of essays put together by Norman Shaw and T. G. Jackson (who had both signed the Memorial) entitled *Architecture: A Profession or an Art?* (1892) is the best-known expression of this opposition. The Memorialists, as these writers came to be known, were fundamentally concerned with the neglect of what they called 'art' in contemporary educational developments, especially because of the influence of examinations which were said to be incapable of determining architectural worth and to encourage cramming, imitation, and learning limited to books. It was felt that 'art', by which was understood both the faculty of design and the ability to foster the building crafts, could not be encompassed by such a system, even though it included a paper on design.[18] It was the crafts side of this understanding of art that distinguished the Memorialists from RIBA professionals whose understanding of architecture as an art was based on the idea of the architect as the source of all aesthetic decisions, the fount of fine art expression: the Soanian type. The Memorialists expected the problems of professional competence, public trust and the protection of the public against bad building – the ostensible reason for professional examinations which they saw as a pretext in the campaign for legal registration rather than its real purpose – to be handled by local by-laws and building acts. They argued that only such acts could protect the public against buildings not designed by architects, buildings which formed the vast majority at that time (perhaps 90 per cent) and which were ignored by the profession's policy. This justification for examinations was thus rejected, exposing the real intent of the advocates of registration as the promotion of a caste system with protected professional status and, most damagingly in the view of the Memorialists, a rigid separation of functions and abilities.

There were, however, various interests and emphases amongst the Memorialists. The group included teachers such as Leonard Stokes and Arthur Beresford Pite, who were also at that time against examinations. It included older architects like Shaw and Jackson who had been close followers of the Gothic Revivalists, and a younger group including Lethaby and Prior, who were part of the Arts and Crafts movement. Some of them, like the stained-glass designer John Clayton, were interested in a Renaissance tradition of the unity of the arts achieved through a Beaux-Arts system, while others were Gothicists and Ruskinians believing in an essential link with the building crafts through personal experience (T. G. Jackson), close co-operation (J. J. Belcher), or, like William Chambers, through the sympathetic sovereign-architect enabling the work of craftsmen (R. N. Shaw). The implicit contradictions in the group required another ten or twenty years fully to emerge.

William Lethaby's contribution to the collection was an essay on 'The Builder's Art and the Craftsman' that called for the rejoining of the intellectual and manual aspects of architecture. Training had been reduced, according to Lethaby, to rote-learning from books of facts about old buildings and historical styles, with design as 'the "scholarly" rearrangement of drawn representations of these "features" in a new *drawing*' (Shaw and Jackson 1892: 151–2). But the best design used to be based on an insight into these processes, 'it was the *imaginative* foresight which came of the designer's experience of his former results' (Shaw and Jackson 1892: 153). Architecture had always been the co-ordination of crafts to enable expression and experiment; a 'craftsman's Drama' (Shaw and Jackson 1892: 151). Delight would arise with the fit construction of buildings rendered by traditional skills using local materials. The fundamental problem was that the crafts had become divorced from the process of design, and design had lost its direct contact with real processes and materials; design had become doctrinaire and workmanship servile. Examinations, drawing methods of mechanical precision and professionalism would not help to revive building crafts, indeed, they were part of the reason for the demise of these crafts. Instead the process of learning architecture must involve prying into materials, a working understanding of the crafts, and a close and intense knowledge of buildings, so that conception and execution could be reunited.

Lethaby's criticism of the contemporary production of architecture was Ruskinian in its inspiration and diagnosis. The division of labour and the narrow interests of the profession had separated the work of the hand from that of the mind. Lethaby's cure was directed at architectural students, but he also believed that building craftsmen might eventually become architects. He did not, at least at this period, follow Ruskin in wanting to give artisans an increased role in determining the finished form of their work; the architect was 'to remain ruler in the kingdom of the crafts' (Shaw and Jackson 1892: 151).[19] In other words, Lethaby admired architects whose understanding of the crafts and personal control of every detail only tightened their authority over architectural production. The Ruskinian notion of the building as a record of the spirit expressed in the work had been adapted in architecture as the expression of the personality of the architect alone. Thus Lethaby's cure, at least at this time, was actually less inspired directly by Ruskin than by later architects' revision (and distortion) of Ruskin's ideas.

The Memorialists were united with Lethaby by their vehement antagonism to the purely office-bound architect, by their desire to keep the bonds with craftsmen and artists as close as possible and by their sense that the latter was threatened by the new examinations and the campaign for registration. The Memorialists were also united in their doubts about pupillage (because it was so much a part, as we have seen, of the apparatus of the gentlemanly, brass-plate profession) and their desire to have architectural education in the schools. Here they were supported by several members of an emerging Beaux-Arts camp in Britain who saw schools as institutions where design would be the most important objective; design, that is to say, seen as based on a body of theoretical knowledge, and the crucial arm of the executive powers of architects. But most of the Memorialists, Jackson and Lethaby most prominently, saw school training as a way of reconstituting the elements of a building lodge, in which the activities of design and building would be integrated and the skills of construction would be foremost. They saw lodge-like institutions, whether in schools or in architectural practice, as one way to counter the kind of specialisation that registration would further advance. Their position was similar to that of William Chambers in the eighteenth century and not unlike that of Wren, the subject of revived interest at this time (20). They did not want professionalism to be used to limit entry into architecture or to separate designers from a sympathetic understanding of the crafts.

The campaigns for examinations, academic education and registration were regarded by their supporters as necessary responses to the continuing changes in the building industry, and thus as inevitable extensions of those needs that had led to the establishment of the RIBA in 1834. Pupillage alone, however, had rarely if ever been regarded as sufficient training for the responsibilities of an architect. The question was whether the manifold growth of building types, engineering technologies, mechanical services, methods of contracting and building regulations during the nineteenth century required a complete change in architectural training in order to cope with them. For most of the Memorialists at this time the answer was 'not a complete change, but an augmentation of existing training'. For the RIBA's bureaucrats and for the increasing number of supporters of a Beaux-Arts system, the answer was 'Yes, a complete change.'

20 John Seymour Lucas: 'St. Paul's – The King's Visit to Wren' (1888)

Arts and Crafts architectural education during the 1890s and 1900s

It is important to understand how the Memorialists, and more widely the Arts and Crafts Movement, attempted to put their ideas on training into action. Broadly, and put at its most idealistic, it could be said that the Arts and Crafts Movement, following Ruskin, attempted to recuperate the practices and skills that had been dissipated or destroyed by the Industrial Revolution and to locate the architect in the camp of the sculptor and painter, rather than in that of the engineer and contractor.

The Movement gained its greatest period of influence on architectural training during the 1890s. In that decade the Memorialists acquired control of several architectural schools, notably at Liverpool, the AA, Birmingham and

[65]

the new schools set up by the London County Council, and attempted to model them to accord with their ideas, one of which was to resist registration and, as far as possible, examinations, another of which was to draw together the various building crafts in a creative combination. The results were, inevitably, experimental compromises. The curriculum established by the RIBA examinations held sway and all the major schools ran courses that were aimed at satisfying their needs, but many did not regard them as the final end of education. The examinations as they stood in the late 1880s seemed to concentrate on the presentation of designs; little attention was paid to perspective drawings, to construction (no full-size details), or to the first-hand or hands-on study of building crafts and materials (*Builder* 1891: 460; and see Appendix). The last two were concerns held particularly dear by the Arts and Crafts Movement.

The London County Council was the ideal arena for putting Arts and Crafts ideals into practice. It had the power to integrate architecture into building training because of its large Architects' Department devoted to the Arts and Crafts ideal of collaboration, although this advantage was not exploited in practice.

Lethaby could begin to put the ideas he had expressed in 1892 into effect when in 1894 he was appointed Art Inspector to the London County Council's Technical Education Board (21). Sidney Webb, who ran the Board, wanted to improve the competitiveness of London's economy as part of his Fabian social democratic vision of modernised national efficiency and extended state control (Swenarton 1989: 96–7). The immediate problem for Webb's Board was how, with the decline of apprenticeship, to provide skills training for London's manufacturing and building trades. Hubert Llewellyn Smith, another follower of Ruskin, had produced a *Report on Technical Education* for the LCC in 1892, in which he stigmatised the inadequacy of training facilities and deficiencies in the teaching of design and modelling, and called for an approach to training that would include giving workmen a grasp of the principles underlying their trade, in order to counteract the extreme subdivision of production (Swenarton 1989: 108–10). He advocated LCC intervention and specifically suggested a new school of architecture and the building trades in London because of the neglect of architectural training. Llewellyn Smith shared the Memorialists' concern that training within any trade would only reflect the existing conditions of that trade, and that schools had to be changed in order to improve both the trade and the training. But existing art schools taught hardly any workmen and they also mirrored industry's division of responsibilities; they would thus have to be reformed to include crafts and professions and incorporated in a London-wide system of vocational schools. The Technical Education Board was set up and Lethaby was made Art Inspector on Llewellyn Smith's recommendation.

21 Gilbert Bayes: portrait plaque of W. R. Lethaby (1923)

Lethaby soon produced 'Architecture and the Allied Arts' (1895), a blue-print for a new 'central higher polytechnic' independent of existing voca-tional frameworks (see *LCC Technical Education Board Minutes*, 3, 1895). It would be 'higher' because other polytechnics such as those at Chelsea and Regent Street would provide workshop-based training for architects' pupils, and then the 'central higher polytechnic' would train these pupils together with craft students. The model here was the German polytechnic system with its two-tiered technical and design schools. The nucleus of this central school would be a course in 'practical architecture' held in workshops common to architects and art-workmen, to which the other courses would be related. Thus building construction and design would be taught in close relation to technical training in masonry, carpentry and other trades, and students would have to specialise in one ornamental craft. The workshop learning, then, was at the centre and around it were arrayed instruction in manipulative, constructive and graphic skills. Drawing would not be specifically architectural drawing, but drawing from nature and solid geometry (Rubens 1986: 205). According to lectures that he gave in 1895 Lethaby saw this programme as part of a larger strategy in which the contracting system was abolished, building unions took on a guild-like control of quality, and an expressive architecture was based on the simplest form of constructional rationalism (Lethaby 1895: 334–5).

On Lethaby's suggestion the Central School of Arts and Crafts was set up in 1896 and Lethaby himself was made part-time Director. He shared the post with George Frampton until he became sole Principal in 1902. The Central School was set up explicitly to provide for 'apprentices, pupils and workmen engaged in, or connected with, artistic handicrafts the best instruction in art and design as applied to their particular industries' (*LCC Technical Education Board Gazette*, 2, September 1896: 159). Thus craft was both a valuable tradition and a necessary measure of value that should be tied in with industrial production rather than isolated and therefore crushed by it. Unlike the Department of Science and Art art schools (as the reformed Schools of Design had been known since the 1850s), the Central School would not have examinations and would not admit amateurs, and its emphasis would be placed squarely on instruction in the crafts learnt mainly through the direct handling of tools in the workshop. This last was, as we have seen with his ideal course, a key tenet of Lethaby's approach. It was also crucial that craftsmen should perceive the links between their own and other crafts. Lethaby regarded drawing not so much as a skill in itself as a means of recording, seeing and articulating thoughts, which might be closely related to the practice of craftwork through the study of natural forms (Gronberg 1984: 18).

So how did all this relate to architectural training? The important thing to note is that Lethaby did not see architecture as necessitating a rigidly distinct form of training, but he did regard it as a domain encompassing many of the crafts. In effect this meant that craft exercises, although important, remained subsidiary to classes in architectural design. Building and architecture, therefore, formed the initial core of classes at the Central School, together with such related trades as modelling and ornament, stone working and leadwork. The thirty-seven architects formed the second largest group of students. The architecture class was oriented towards rationalist notions (in the French tradition of Viollet-le-Duc and Choisy) through which the practices of the builder and the architect, it was hoped, could be drawn together. As Halsey Ricardo, the head of architecture, explained: 'We approach the subject entirely from the builder's point of view; that is to say, we base our designs on necessity . . . We don't profess to study beauty of form and decoration as such; whatever beauty we may gain is such as springs naturally out of utility' (Wood 1897: 243–4). Lethaby later gave a specific example of this:

> The actual practice of stone-cutting [is] specially contrived to bring home to the mind of the student the group of facts connected with the finding of forms by successive reductions in the squared quarry-block . . . taken together with a course of solid geometry, [this] should lead to the almost intuitive knowledge which is necessary as a groundwork for design (Lethaby 1904: 160).

Architecture at the Central School was taught as design, craft and construction. Construction was taught in weekly lectures, while masonry and leadwork were learnt on one evening a week. Design was taught two evenings a week, and students could attend drawing classes where nature was studied as the basis for ornament (Swenarton 1989: 117). Because the students were part-time, the Central's courses were both supplementary and to some extent experimental. Nevertheless, there seems to have been little new social mixing across the hierarchy of building functionaries at the Central.

Even Lethaby realised that the Central School could not in itself provide a radical reorientation in architectural training. By 1899 he was speculating on the benefits of a school exclusively for building (as opposed to the Technical Education Board's other nine polytechnics), where all of the building trades, including architecture, could gain a knowledge of building as a whole (Powers 1984: 50). In 1901 he laid out his ideas to the RIBA: building schools would revive the functions of medieval workshops, where the art of building was developed by the continuous experiments of masons and carpenters; the building trades unions needed to assume the function of the old guilds and take responsibility for training; and construction would be learnt by model demonstrations and mechanically, following the lead of Wren, Viollet and Choisy (Lethaby 1901: 385–94. Lethaby's audience was sceptical). In 1904 the LCC opened the Brixton School of Building, which was seen by Lethaby as a basic technical polytechnic, on a German model, rather than as a higher polytechnic like the Central School.

The idea at Brixton was to train all practitioners of building trades, including architects, under the same roof and with the emphasis on workshop instruction. A building was acquired with a large hall (converted from swimming baths) which could be used as a laboratory or as a space in which practical construction exercises could be collaboratively erected (**22**). Beside this there were building trade workshops and studios, and above these were placed the architectural drawing offices and workshops (Swenarton 1989: 121–3). There was also a component for 'experimental research of an educational type in connection with builders' materials and composite structures' (Rubens 1986: 213). The architecture department was opened in 1906 and run by Arthur Beresford Pite, who was also professor of architecture at the Royal College of Art and who seems to have encouraged his Brixton pupils to attend design classes there. At the RCA Pite ran a two-tier system: the first a basic pre-professional training in all the arts and crafts, the second a specialised architectural training. In both design was firmly based upon an understanding of traditional construction.[20]

At Brixton emphasis was placed on the 'practical combination of the studies in the several trades and branches as required by a master builder, foreman or architect' (*RIBA Kalendar*, 1910–11: 262). As in the case of the Central School, RIBA exemption was withheld from Brixton, and so after 1910 the course seems to have attempted to follow the general requirements of the RIBA exams (Powers 1982: 64). But characteristic features remained. David Vickery, a student at Brixton from 1939 to 1942, has attested to its vigour even at this late date:

> There was one intake annually into a professional 'building' course. The term 'building' was taken to cover all those professional disciplines the exercise of which resulted in a finished building. Thus, in any one year could be found a half a dozen students intending to be architects, a few intended to be structural engineers and

22 Brixton School of Building: construction exercise (1911)

others who were to be either quantity or land surveyors or just plain builders. The assumption was based on the idea that whatever one's intended profession, some 70 or 80 per cent of the required knowledge of building would be common . . . every week three hours was spent in workshops. Each craft was practised for about six weeks so that, by the end of a thirty-six week year, every student had spent a significant amount of time in every shop.

Those who decided to become architects spent one or two days per week in the studio:

It left one able to design a small building, to size the pipes for the heating system, to design the beams and columns, to write the specification within the current building regulations, to take of the quantities and to be able to discuss the construction process in an informed way with the craftsmen executing the work (D. Vickery, pers. comm.).

What little that remained of the Lethaby-inspired experiment at Brixton was finally dismantled in the 1960s and early 1970s by the standardising ardour of the modern Official System.

Returning to the early years of the century, some of the experiences of the Central School also rubbed off on Regent Street Polytechnic, which started architectural evening classes in the late 1890s to accompany its large building construction department. However, it was Regent Street's combination of practical instruction with classical expression (producing architects like Vincent Harris, A. E. Richardson and Alfred Bossom) that was most closely to mirror developments in the RIBA's educational policy.

Some similarities can be found at Liverpool and the AA. The Arts and Crafts vision dominated Liverpool University School of Architecture when it was set up in 1895 and provided the first full-time architecture course (designed as a two-year prelude to pupillage). Its Director, F. M. Simpson, was a Memorialist who saw the advantage of a university-based course as a chance to broaden the disciplines related to architecture (Simpson 1895). Liverpool gave an extensive crafts training to its first-year students based on the notion that the architect 'should be a master builder . . . able to guide and direct the workmen under him' (Simpson 1896), and by 1901 a full-time degree course had been started. In 1895 the AA set up a School of Design and Handicraft. The AA, whose committee by this time was dominated by Arts and Crafts supporters, also arranged for its students to study crafts at the Carpenters' Company Trades Training School at Great Titchfield Street and workshop demonstrations at the LCC Central School (23).[21]

Elsewhere Birmingham School of Art had strong Lethabitic leanings in the early 1900s, and both at the Glasgow School of Art and at the Edinburgh School of Applied Art architecture and building students were often taught together (for these schools see Powers 1984 a: 56–7). Classicism was not inimical to these

23 Hubert N. C. Curtis: 'A Club Boat House', AA fourth-year project (1911)

schools, indeed it was very visible at Regent Street and Glasgow, and encouraged by Pite at Brixton. 'Free Style' united the Memorialists as an ideal of stylistic freedom and unity with the crafts. This eclecticism might sometimes enable strategic alliances with Beaux-Arts supporters, except on the issues of examination and registration. It also opened the way for significant conversions, most notably in the cases of C. H. Reilly at Liverpool and Reginald Blomfield, who had come to oppose the fundamental Memorialist principle of craft training by 1905.

Disputes on education, 1900–10

In general the period from 1900 to 1910 saw a continuous battle between the Memorialists and the advocates of a French Beaux-Arts system, especially concerning influence within the RIBA. The background for this battle was a declining interest in the Arts and Crafts ideals; craft work at the AA, for instance, had declined by 1898 and its School of Design and Handicraft was closed in 1912, while at Liverpool the Memorialist Simpson was replaced in 1904 by C. H. Reilly, a converted classicist (**24**).

24 Augustus John: portrait of Charles Herbert Reilly

In the early years of the century, however, Lethaby was directly involved with formulating RIBA policy on architectural education. He and a number of other members of the Art Workers' Guild and fellow Memorialists (Blomfield, Champneys, Macartney and Ricardo), prepared a discussion document for the RIBA in 1903. Pupillage was attacked for its unreliability and neglect of a grounding in construction. Instead they proposed a common basic training in building methods, a preliminary course before office work, and then an advanced course (Rubens 1986: 214).

When the Board of Architectural Education was set up in 1904 to devise a syllabus or scheme for the schools of architecture and to have it adapted by them, many of the Memorialists, including Lethaby, were appointed to it (*Architectural Review* 1904: 18). It was intended initially that the Board would not be controlled by the RIBA, but the Memorialists had by now given up their absolute opposition to examinations and set themselves to 'humanise' the RIBA exams (Blomfield 1911: 767). The notion of training in schools was accepted, but factions immediately appeared over the question of a new syllabus and the kind of links that schools could make with practice.

In the first Board of Architectural Education report after it was set up in 1904, Lethaby suggested a two-year course followed by two years of evening classes while in pupillage the syllabus was to be 'Governed by the principle that construction is the basis of architecture' and history was to be taught, in the mode of Auguste Choisy, on this basis (Powers 1984a: 62). History and design were thus to be understood in relation to construction, while in the RIBA exams they were kept separate from it. A typical Lethaby proposal was the use of workshop or laboratory training. This had a twofold aim: to enable demonstration rather than handling of materials, and to encourage experimental work or research in building methods. It was therefore essentially different from proposals made earlier by various Board members, either for study of buildings in progress, or for the use of building yards and engineering schools (Startup 1984: 36). But Lethaby was defeated on this.

The Lethabitic notions in this first report were a major threat to the professional and artistic ideas of the architect held by the other members of the Board of Architectural Education Committee. Supporters of the French method of training wanted a systematic teaching of design and a clearer professional hierarchy with architects at the top. To establish and forward these aims entailed academic education. The final report on the syllabus, published in 1905, recognised the engineering and practical aspects of architecture (although Lethaby's desire for laboratory demonstrations of materials was blocked) but, without specifying style, placed the emphasis squarely on an academic education in design. There were to be two years in the schools followed by two in an architect's office, with a thesis as the culminating task. The syllabus was divided into five subjects: materials, construction, architectural drawing, design ('evolved . . . out of constructional necessities') and history of architecture (explaining evolution through 'constructional, material and social conditions') (*RIBA Kalendar* 1905–6: x–xi).

This syllabus has been seen as an Arts and Crafts creation that only subsequently became overtaken by a new classical revival (Brandon-Jones 1984). A closer examination shows that it was already a catch-all capable of providing for the other main camp represented on the Board, those who supported a Beaux-Arts system. This can be seen in the attitude to drawing and design. Where design in the introductory course was geared to the solution of constructional problems, in the advanced course abstract ideas of scale, proportion, spacing and disposition were introduced. The latter is very like the combination of pure architectural form and classical principles that Blomfield came to advocate most influentially in his book *The Mistress Art* (1908) and that Geoffrey Scott argued for in his *Architecture of Humanism* (1914). In architectural drawing the introductory course dealt with working drawings, geometry, freehand drawing and measuring, while the advanced course took these skills to a higher level and gave some encouragement to drawing from the antique and from life. In fact the compromise nature of the scheme is evident in its key statement: '[training should] be governed by the principle that construction is the basis of architecture, and its correlative principle that architecture is the interpretation of construction into forms of aesthetic value' (*RIBA Kalendar* 1905–6: x). The style of those forms was deliberately left unspecified. Here, as elsewhere, Lethaby hoped for a common orthodoxy of practice rooted in the traditions of construction that he saw as best manifested in the eighteenth century (Lethaby 1904: 159–61).

Although Lethaby remained on the Board, the publication of this syllabus in 1905 marks the rise to dominance of more conventionally academic notions of training. This brought to fruition a training in detail inspired by the Beaux Arts but in general following the RIBA utilitarian line, that clearly envisaged the architect as an intellectual who learnt design autonomously in the academy and communicated with the building work-force largely through his drawings. These ideas dominated the Board after 1910, biasing it against attempts to integrate design and the crafts of building construction. Lethaby's schools continued meanwhile to exist on the margins of this architectural establishment, although Lethaby himself resigned from the Central School in 1911. He continued to advocate a common basic technical training, often citing the German schools as good examples, but other aspects of his position changed at about this time. From this moment he developed a belief in engineering and mathematics as well as building expe-rience as the essential components of architectural training, rehabilitating Wren as the ideal architect steeped in mathematics and science, and down-grading the vision of unified building crafts that was behind the Central School.[22]

In effect the coexisting variety of practices that had characterised architec-tural education over the previous two hundred years had, during the decades immediately before and after the turn of the century, splintered into their separate and now antagonistic parts. In 1910 some of these positions had begun to cohere around Beaux-Arts principles of teaching; in effect Blomfield and Reilly (both recent converts to the Beaux-Arts) came to dominate over Lethaby and Jackson. The next twenty years was their time of greatest influence.

The year 1910 marked a watershed both in the educational policy of the RIBA and, more importantly, in the profession's view of itself and its place in the world of building. The efforts of Pugin, Ruskin and their successors to maintain or restore some kind of lodge-like integration between builders, craftsmen and designers had failed. The leaders of the architectural profession now saw themselves as constituting a profession of architectural designers whose form-giving function naturally placed them in charge of the building team. Education should therefore be academic, in universities alongside that of lawyers and doctors, and the curriculum should be grounded in the archi-tectural classics, historical knowledge, drawing and mathematics.

The Beaux-Arts approach to architectural education

It is now time to retrace our steps a little and ask how training was approached by advocates of the French Beaux-Arts system. As we have seen, in the seventeenth and eighteenth centuries the French Academy of Architecture was one arm of a centralised, absolutist power. J. F. Blondel's ideal had been for students to apply theory directly, and this became a more realisable aim as the bonds between the Academy's lectures and its ateliers became closer. An exemplary method was laid down by J. N. L. Durand at the Ecole Polytechnique, established for engineers in 1795, where structure and design were regarded as inseparable, and composition evolved additively and symmetrically according to the set units of graph paper and the resolution of a limited number of functional variables. Polytechnique students placed their faith in mathematical reason and positivism, employing the new methods of descriptive geometry devised by A. F. Frézier and Gaspard Monge, and treating style merely as decorative clothing. Some aspects of this approach were also installed in the Ecole des Beaux Arts when it was established in 1819, following reforms of the Academy during the Revolution.

French architectural education as it was honed in the nineteenth century became a centralised state-run system based on competitions and closely linked to the government's building offices.[23] In Paris and the provinces students worked in ateliers in order to prepare for the entrance examination of the Ecole des Beaux Arts: this included a twelve hour test on architectural composition and modelling tests of eight hours. Sixty successful students (out of four to five hundred) entered the second class of the Ecole in which time was devoted equally to lectures and to studio work. In the studio as many as eighteen different *concours* (competitions) would be set: these could be for *esquisses* (sketches), larger rendered projects, construction studies of the Orders, history of architecture, drawings of the human figure, ornament and antique casts. After fulfilling these obligations they could move into the first class. In this class training was focused on between ten and twenty teaching ateliers where students, under the guidance of a *patron* (a prominent architect and teacher), worked largely on more complex projects for the regular competitions administered by the Ecole. All other subjects were taught by lectures at the Ecole and were now subsidiary to these studio projects. For large projects the student was expected quickly to devise a ruling idea, expressed in a small-scale *esquisse* and worked out *en loge*, a period when students were strictly confined and isolated, thus preserving the product of individual creation. The *esquisse* would then be elaborated over a longer period of time and the finished project would be expected to deploy recognised building elements according to accepted rules of composition. A set number of mentions in competitions enabled a student to sit the diploma test, the entrance into official government work that was

[76]

instituted in 1887. The apex of the system, and the most prestigious competition, was the Prix de Rome, and success in this would enable students to round off their training by studying in Italy for four or five years. Employment as a State architect followed.

The Ecole des Beaux Arts had an immense effect upon American architectural training in the late nineteenth century, first through personal experience and then later through a deliberate emulation of the French system. Over five hundred Americans studied at the Ecole between 1846 and 1968, with many others attending Parisian ateliers. In 1893 a campaign was launched to promote uniform French standards across all American schools, and in 1903 the Beaux-Arts Society initiated a Paris Prize. The design theories of Julien Gaudet and others were initially transmitted directly through Beaux-Arts trained teachers like Paul Cret at the University of Pennsylvania. Curiously, despite the shared language and the International Conference of 1887, not much seems to have been known in England about the specific character of this American variety of the Beaux-Arts tradition until after 1909.

In England, as we have seen, the Ecole's evolving ideas and practices had little impact on architectural education until the last decades of the century. When they first came to be used in the late nineteenth century, they were not directly connected to calls for an apparatus of institutional regulation, because this regulatory control had already begun to be pieced together. But it was to be given an important added impetus by the Beaux-Arts ideology of design.

The growth of interest in the French system can be quite simply characterised and positioned in relation to the growth of apparatuses of control in architectural education. As we have seen, there was a rising interest in the idea of an academy for architecture throughout the eighteenth century, an interest not satisfied either by the formation of the Royal Academy in 1768 or the establishment of the RIBA in 1834. Gradually in the nineteenth century a few members of the profession became interested in or gained experience in French or German schools, notably the Scots William Playfair and Thomas Hamilton, but also Cuthbert Broderick and James Elmes. Other figures like T. L. Donaldson (who had visited the Ecole in 1817), Robert Kerr and Arthur Cates campaigned for some of the benefits of the French system. It increasingly became the view of such men that the Royal Academy was a pale shadow of what was offered in France; it gave few lectures, its facilities were poor and it offered only one architectural student the chance to study abroad every three years. At the Ecole there were two lectures a week, two fine libraries, and students were sent to Rome every year and maintained there for five years.[24]

In 1856 Charles Barry, C. R. Cockerell and Philip Hardwick attempted to reform architecture at the Royal Academy School by making it into a two-year course intended to follow the elementary courses at University and King's Colleges and the Government School of Design.[25] But the proposal was not taken up and it was not until 1870 that the RA started a drawing school specifically for architects. In that year the post of Professor of Architecture at the Royal Academy was filled by a Beaux-Arts student and devotee, Richard Phené Spiers. Thus a key educational position was occupied by a man who had experienced full-time education in architectural design. Spiers started a seven-year part-time course closely geared to the RIBA Preliminary examination, but his attempt to emulate the Beaux-Arts curriculum were frustrated by the part-time attendance and the variety of styles that his students practised.[26] Despite Spiers's aspirations and his contacts with Paris, there were a number of Gothicists like Street, Shaw and Waterhouse who played an important role at the Royal Academy, acting as Visitors setting subjects and judging the results. Spiers's influence was, however, more widely spread through his books, especially *Architectural Drawing* (1887) and *The Orders of Architecture* (1890), which were specifically aimed at students taking the RIBA Intermediate examination and the AA's Elementary classes.[27] Spiers was not alone. We have seen how a serious debate on the French system had started in the 1860s, and this was redoubled by the 1880s, especially in a series of papers read by White, Spiers and others at the RIBA in 1884 and at the more international conference in 1887.[28] An interest in Renaissance architecture had become a strong feature of the Arts and Crafts Movement, best epitomised by Reginald Blomfield's *Renaissance Architecture in England* (1897). Often this interest was directly translated into classical theory, in Blomfield's case especially. But the most important development was that full-time academic courses began to be established in the 1890s.

Other elements of the French system were already being put in place. A system of prizes had been developing in order to foster presentation skills, refine responses to briefs and display student work for public consumption. They covered many shades of Victorian eclecticism; amongst them were the Soane Medallion (dating from the earliest years of the RIBA) for contemporary subjects (**25**), the Tite Prize (from 1876) for Italianate designs, the Pugin Studentship (from 1865) for medieval buildings in Britain, the Owen Jones Studentship (from 1887) for ornament and coloured decoration and the Godwin Bursary (from 1881) to study contemporary architecture abroad. At the end of the century there were ten such awards, while by 1930 their number had more than doubled (Allibone 1986). In the 1880s ateliers began to appear (*Architect* 1887: 279). In 1887, as we have seen, the RIBA made Associateship dependent on a three-tiered examination system, and in the 1890s and 1900s certain schools modelled themselves on the French curriculum. The next spurt of activity came around 1910 when Beaux-Arts advocates renewed their pressure for a central school, for facilities in Rome and for the opening of teaching ateliers in London. Although an atelier had been open from 1887 to 1891, the first of a new and more substantial trend was opened in 1913 under Arthur

25 L. S. Balfour: 'An Institute of Architects', Soane Medallion entry (1895–96)

26 William Holford (Liverpool student and Rome Prize winner): Piazza del Popolo (*c.*1932)

Davis's tuition, with several others following in the 1920s (Powers 1982: 29–30, 224). The central school notion, of course, was not new; Donaldson is said to have seen the RIBA originally as a school and the idea was supported by Knowles and Kerr, and advocated later by William White in 1884 and T. G. Jackson in the 1890s (for Donaldson see White 1885: 13; Knowles 1853: 18; Kerr 1846: 205). But again in 1910, although several influential educators agreed on its importance, it still could not be established (Powers 1982: 213–15). However, the British School at Rome was finally set up in 1912 with funds from the Royal Commission for the Exhibition of 1851. A variant of the French method of competition was used with a subject design fulfilled over a set period, followed by an *en loge* design. Successful students made drawings and surveys in Rome (**26**), culminating in a large *envoi* (L. Campbell 1989).

At the same time as the rise of these Beaux-Arts approaches and techniques a series of reforms were devised in the form of examination and inspection, that eventually, as we have seen, would place architectural education predominantly under the control of a central institution, the RIBA, with its own regulating body, the Board of Architectural Education.

Thus a professional association gained significant control over architectural education, arguing that to gain entry into its ranks it had to oversee the form and standards of training. Furthermore it gained this control just as Beaux-Arts supporters were taking over positions of power within the architectural firmament. To help implement their power Visiting Boards were introduced in 1923 as a usually informal arm of this system, without the power to appoint external examiners to each school. Reilly, who was the first chairman, claimed that the idea came from a similar device in the medical profession (Reilly 1938: 117). Initially these Boards would visit schools every two years. Even at this date, however, the Memorialists still had sufficient influence on the Visiting Board to insist on six months practical work (on a building site or working for a firm) and to oppose too much emphasis on drawing skills (Startup 1984: 65–8).

According to the Beaux-Arts view, study in schools was considered more professional the more elevated it was from hands-on building; it had to have less emphasis therefore on construction. Building was seen as commercial; professionalism was seen as a combination of distance from and regulation of this commercial practice, and the key to both of these was the control of design. Thus in 1911 when they had taken over the Board of Architectural Education (Blomfield had been made chair in 1910), the Beaux-Arts supporters introduced more design into the syllabus with thesis subjects set by Reilly (Powers 1982: 108). Reilly pressed for the Board to adopt Liverpool methods wholesale: to advocate more measured drawings (**27**), orthographic Testimonies of Study

27 W. Nasby Adams: University Library, Cambridge (by Stephen Wright, 1754–58) measured drawing by a Liverpool student (1907)

shaded in the French manner and compositional exercises as well as an atelier system and a school in Rome (Powers 1982: 114–15). In the same year Reginald Blomfield announced that Testimonies of Study and a new final thesis would account for nearly half of the total marks obtainable in the RIBA exams (Blomfield 1911). Other Reilly proposals came in, as we have seen, almost as quickly.

Arts and Crafts educational policy was hopelessly compromised in the eyes of these Francophiles, and those Arts and Crafts schools that survived, such as the LCC schools at Brixton and the Central School, were 'the subject of ribald comment' and had their exemption withheld by the Board of Architectural Education (D. Vickery, pers. comm.). To reconcile design with building was to compromise professional and academic integrity by infecting the autonomy of design with the commercial pragmatics of the construction industry. Instead the new model was to be the kind of curriculum established at Liverpool by C.H. Reilly, with its emphasis on the systematic studio-led teaching of design based on classical principles; easier to teach and supposedly easier to assess. Furthermore, pupillage, in this French-tinted vision, could never adequately convey these principles: education had to be within the academy; ateliers would replace pupillage, becoming the hub of the educational wheel.

The Beaux Arts took over most schools in the first twenty years of the century, just as various forms of classicism took over architectural practice, and a new network of contacts with French and American schools was established. Under Reilly's galvanishing direction from 1904 Liverpool became the most influential British Beaux-Arts school, expanding its intake from a dozen students in 1904 to 200 by 1909. At first Reilly attempted simply to advance an English classicism based on the Greek Revival and Cockerell and supported by Blomfield's theory. By attracting Patrick Abercrombie to teach at Liverpool from 1907 and making S. D. Adshead head of a new Civic Design department from 1909, Reilly linked the school to leading developments in the field of town planning, a crucial move for the future development of modern architecture in Britain. Following his 1909 visit to the States, Reilly installed a Beaux-Arts system with American-style jury criticisms and with arrangements with American offices to take fourth-year students for periods of six months (Reilly 1938: 122; see also Liverpool Architectural School 1910–20; Budden 1932; Stephenson 1992). Soon students from all over the British Empire were flocking to Liverpool, returning after five years to design huge axial buildings for the public works departments of Egypt (28), South Africa and other colonies.

Liverpool's studio teaching took up more than half the syllabus, increasing with each year until it took up nearly all the time in the fifth year. It was aimed at achieving a visual logic that related proportion to both functional and geometric hierarchy; a logic clothed in classical vestments but one which could

[82]

28 Mahmoud Riad: combined bus and railway terminal station for Alexandria, layout
plan – fifth-year thesis design (1931)

also help form a cumulative knowledge (Reilly 1914: 12). Following the set problems, design ideas were worked out in six-hour *esquisses*, subjected to formal criticism, and then elaborated in vast drawings on which junior students were allowed to help in exchange for picking up methods of draughtsmanship.[29] In the first year fantastic programmes were set as a stimulus to the imagination: a Palace for Kubla Khan, a State Bed for a Musical Comedy Queen, a Barge on the Grand Canal for Mussolini (Reilly 1938: 209). The programmes became more complex through the school, until students reached the climax of competing for the Rome Prize, and this formed the model for the long and complex design thesis that terminated most Beaux-Arts courses in Britain.

As Alan Powers has pointed out, however, Liverpool was preceded in this direction by Glasgow. At Glasgow, following its native classical tradition and the several Beaux-Arts trained Glaswegians, there were French teachers like M. Girardon and, from 1904, the French architect Eugène Bourdon became head of the school. Glasgow's systematic education, involving the development of *partis* and the elabortion of *esquisses*, probably came closer to the Parisian system than any other British school (Powers 1982: 156–64; 1984: 56–9).

Glasgow became the first school to open its doors to female students in 1905, although at University College they had long been admitted to the preparatory course. Manchester University followed in 1909, and the AA in 1917. Despite its tardiness, however, the AA quickly established itself as the most attractive venue for women students.

In terms of style and pedagogy the AA had been moving towards classical approaches in the first years of the century, abandoning what Reilly called its 'cowsheds and pig-styes approach' (Reilly 1938: 122). This was substantiated when the Beaux-Arts educated Howard Robertson made the evening school into an atelier in 1914. In the 1920s, as Robertson became one of the most active Beaux-Arts theorists in Britain and Robert Atkinson, the Director of Education, made an RIBA-sponsored tour of American schools, the AA was opened up to the influence of the French and American systems. Meanwhile, University College acquired a Department of Town Planning in 1914, appointed the classicist A. E. Richardson as head in 1918 and opened its first atelier in 1920 (Bellot 1929).

At the International Congress on Architectural Education held in London in 1924 a kind of Beaux-Arts League of Nations ruled the stage. The Congress was a forum for gauging the spread of the Beaux-Arts model and assessing its national variations; it was found, for instance, that in Italy schools were rapidly expanding, in the USA the system was in the hands of university schools, and in Britain a non-centralised system with four different types of institution (technical schools, schools of art, independent professional schools and universities) was spreading. Over-optimistically, one Beaux-Arts supporter wrote that the Congress was 'the scene of the official obsequies of Victorian pupil-lage'.[30] Arts and Crafts supporters like Pite and C. R. Ashbee could only make brave noises by now largely lacking in institutional weight while Lethaby sent a letter.[31] This then was the height of Beaux-Arts influence in Britain, when the RIBA and most of the architectural schools were in general accord with French and American approaches; in other words, a time when the RIBA had at last established some of the mechanisms necessary for overseeing and regulating the training of architects, and when the schools had adopted those methods – dominated by elaborate studio projects – that could instruct students to design in the Grand Manner.

Yet although the Germans had no representatives at the Congress, it was a contemporary German method at the Bauhaus, obliquely referred to by Lethaby, that now became the most catalytic and yet most mythical source of change for modern British architectural education. Ironically, as we shall discover in the next chapter, German education, which had been intermittently considered throughout the nineteenth century and openly envied with the imperial rivalry of the turn of the century, only became a viable model in the years of that country's national defeat.

Victory of registration

The RIBA finally launched its own campaign for registration in 1927, after amalgamation with the Society of Architects in 1924 and in the face of civil engineers, other building professions and architects who were not RIBA members. In the USA, where an academic system had developed much more quickly than in Britain, the State of Illinois had passed a registration law for architects in 1897, the first of a flood. The RIBA had adopted a registration policy in 1905, and successive international congresses between 1900 and 1911 had supported registration.

In Britain, when a Registration Act was passed in 1931 granting the RIBA responsibility for architectural training, the government also attempted to limit RIBA control through the separate Architects' Registration Council which alone had the power to bestow the title 'Registered Architect'. However, ARCUK, although ostensibly made independent through its lay electorate, was soon reformed by a second Registration Act in 1938 (now restricting use of the title 'Architect') so that the majority of its representatives had to be architects. Thus the registration body, ARCUK, came under the firm hand of the RIBA – a situation that has continued until the present day.[32] The control of practice was henceforward also bound up with the control of education, effectively meaning that discussions of the institutions and practices of education were limited to those already within the profession. Registration effectively promoted a wide and steady mainstream of professional practice. If an architect

[85]

refused to register, as in the case of Sir Ninian Comper, he could deliberately distance his practice from the dominant architectural culture. Most others, however, were forced into conformity. Registration was thus the culmination of the process of professionalisation that had been inaugurated by the formation of the RIBA in 1834. It was finally completed by Beaux-Arts administrators who saw design skills as the crucial aspect of the fully buttressed profession. Nevertheless there remained a ragbag of institutions and methods of entry that was not finally sorted out until the 1960s.

Conclusion

The importation of Beaux-Arts methods was not a brief, aberrant foreign intrusion into British architecture, but part of a longer development that had started in parallel with changes brought about by the Industrial Revolution. Between them, the RIBA, the RA and the AA had already formed the satellite bodies of a kind of unofficial academy. Although private and independent bodies, they could circulate influential visions of the profession and thus also of its means of entry and education. None of them, of course, administered state control over education in the way that the Ecole in Paris did; none of them was quite such a centrifugal force. But they were amongst the myriad authorities, both public and private, that helped to professionalise and specialise the production of architecture, if still in a less centrist way than in France.

The opposition to this movement to order and regulate training in line with new economic relations started in the 1830s with Hansom, Pugin, Bartholomew and others. In the second half of the century efforts were made by Ruskin and the Memorialists to orchestrate this opposition. Yet on one level all that this opposition succeeded in doing was to increase the distinctions, already made by mainstream thinkers, between notions of art and science within architectural education. Little effort was made to advance the claims of pupillage as a coherent alternative to academic education, nor to create continuing models of the building lodge as an alternative to general contracting. For want of anything better, it was felt that academic education had to be the framework for a reformed architectural education. This at least accorded with the views of those who upheld the notion of an architectural profession with a clear position within the building industry and with power to control entry into its own ranks. A Beaux-Arts system fitted well with the aims of these professionals and could easily infiltrate a situation that was already sympathetic to academic education.

Notes

1 Jenkins 1961: 112–17. Kaye mentions other forerunners (Kaye 1960: 63). Kaye's sociological book is still the best account of the rise of professionalism within architecture, and of the relation between this and a free market economy.

2 Jenkins 1961: 199–200. For a contemporary account of skills decay see Noble 1836: 27.

3 Jenkins 1961: 201–2, 205. For contracts in gross see Port 1967.

4 R. H. Haslam's agreement of 1895 with C. F. A. Voysey stipulates that he would 'learn the art profession and business of an architect and the art of pattern designing'; accordingly he also agreed to protect Voysey's copyrights (RIBA Archives HaR/1). By contrast William Butterfield's 1831 articles to Thomas Arber give no details at all on what Butterfield might expect to learn (RIBA Archives BuWi/1).

5 *RIBA Kalendar*, 1890; Robert Williams's Articles of 1902 in the possession of Douglas Jones. Perhaps by compensation Williams's master agreed to allow him access to all 'estimates, calculations, drawings, plans and specifications'. There is also no mention of this in G. T. Smith's articles to the Aberdeen architects William Smith and William Kelly. Smith, however, took the RIBA preliminary exam in 1895 and became an RA student in 1898 (*Licentiate Nomination Papers* 14, 1911).

6 Furthermore Pecksniff may have been in part a caricature of some features of A. W. N. Pugin and his father (Saint 1983: 170, n. 1). Pugin the younger took at most one pupil, his son-in-law J. H. Powell, and his father's bad reputation seems entirely dependent on the way in which his wife ran the household rather than on his own abilities (Ferry 1861: 26–8).

7 Saint 1976: 187–91. See also the memoir by Shaw's son Robert Norman Shaw (RIBA Archives ShR/2).

8 Hosking 1841. A published version of what University College and King's College were aiming to provide can be found in Nicholson 1828.

9 Donaldson 1842: 25. It was only in the 1880s that women were admitted into all aspects of the course.

10 The *Builder* soon shifted to more conventional professional interests: see Hanson 1987.

11 *Builder*, 31 December 1842: 6. Students were to be articled as apprentices from the age of fourteen.

12 Jenkins 1961: 168. Bartholomew died in 1845.

13 Another member of this RIBA–Soanian circle was Joseph Gwilt who introduced the latest French mathematics to English architects in his *Treatise on the Equilibrium of Arches*, London, 1811.

14 Born in 1775 Papworth was the son of a plasterer and builder and after a three-year apprenticeship to a builder he was apprenticed for one year to a decorating firm. In 1805 he became a member of the Society for Encouragement of Arts, Manufactures and Commerce. In 1827 he designed 'Hygeia', a scheme for a town on the banks of the River Ohio, which may have been the target of Dickens's satire on the city of Eden in *Martin Chuzzlewit*.

15 These letters became part of his *Newleafe Discourses*.

16 Scott later argued that pupillage might ruin 'the fine art element' of architecture and proposed a 'central School of Architectural Art', enabling amongst other things a thorough study of the human figure (Scott 1864: 3–18).

17 For an equivocal contemporary view of the Beaux Arts see Burnell 1864–65.

18 Blomfield cited how the AA had abandoned its classes in sculpture because students were too busy with the examination syllabus (Shaw and Jackson 1892: 49).

19 Lethaby's position on this issue of the architect's controlling rule had also been expressed in 1889: 'How should an architect really design? I fancy it must be in the way the painter told Mr Ruskin he composed his picture – he knew what he wanted to do, and he did it. An architect wants to try something which he sees, foresees, *invents*, in a mental picture. Form, expression, colour; he has a problem to work out – a motive' (W. R. Lethaby, 'Of the "Motive" in Architectural Design', *A.A. Notes*, 4, November 1889: 24). Even in 1907

Lethaby was to bewail the failure to supply men of the 'Street, Burges or Bentley type' (Powers 1984: 69). We could add to this threesome John Sedding, to whom Lethaby was close in the mid-1880s, and Philip Webb, the subject of a posthumous book by Lethaby. Sometimes Lethaby came close to suggesting a Ruskinian dissolution of the distinctions between architect and artisan (Lethaby 1895: 334). Godfrey Rubens has dated this true Ruskinian position in Lethaby's theory to the period between 1890 and 1901 (Rubens in Backemeyer and Gronberg 1984: 49–54).

20 Powers 1982: 60–1. For the RCA see *Architectural Review*, 14, 1903: 24–5.

21 Powers provides interesting anecdotal material on this (see Powers 1984a: 46–7).

22 Naylor 1984: 43–6; see also Lethaby 1923: 405–6; 1924 Congress: 74. Lethaby's explicit rejection of ornament and historical styles also dates from this period; see his *Architecture* 1912: 243, 247. The past was to supply lessons in structural problems, building morphologies and vernacular building methods.

23 This account is based on Chaffee 1977.

24 Jenkins 1961: 166–7. Such complaints go back earlier; see *Annals of the Fine Arts*, 2, 1817: 19–25. A letter from Donaldson also appears in this volume.

25 It was proposed that the advanced 'Fine Art Teaching' would cover a number of principles. Amongst these were 'form, proportion, harmony, expression, outline and stability in composition'; ornament; colour in ornament; 'sciagraphic and orthographic rules and systems of composition in classical and gothic architecture'; the application of painting and sculpture in architecture; 'exercises to correct existing works'; and 'original composition' using new materials and omitting 'all that interferes with convenience and durability in the old or recognised styles' (Barry 1867: 307–11).

26 Cates 1887: 48. Spiers later became content with the compromises of the English situation (Cates 1887: 49–50).

27 Robert Macleod 1971: 100. On Lethaby's view of Spiers and the RA Visitors see *RIBAJ*, 23, 1916: 334.

28 For the 1884 papers see Robert Macleod 1971: 90–2; for those of 1887 see Cates 1887.

29 Reilly 1938: 205. See also Gordon Stephenson's account of his student years in the late 1920s (Stephenson 1992: 18).

30 *First International Congress* 1925: xiv. For a positive view of pupillage at this time see Birkin Haward, 'Autobiography', unpublished manuscript, RIBA Drawings Collection.

31 This view is contrary to the recuperative efforts of later modernist writers (see Kretchmer 1965).

32 See Startup 1984: 49–61. For the 1931 Act and its preliminaries see Gotch 1934.

CHAPTER THREE

The modernist academy, 1938–60

By 1931 the RIBA had acquired a very considerable if not absolute control over training and over entry into the profession. Anyone who wished to practise as a designer of buildings under the title of architect had either to undergo pupillage and take examinations set by the RIBA, probably studying part-time at an RIBA-approved course, or had to attend a full-time five-year course at a school whose own exams were recognised by the RIBA, and whose courses were vetted by Visiting Boards. Instead of the five routes into the profession that existed in the eighteenth century there were now two, pupillage and college, both regulated by a professional body with a Royal Charter. In addition, there was nothing to stop anyone from practising as a designer of buildings without qualifications, nor was there anything to stop builders and developers from erecting buildings which were not designed by architects. These two exceptions still hold; the design of buildings is still not the legal monopoly of architects, even though some 75 per cent of all new building in 1990 was architect-designed. The process by which this happened was

1863 RIBA Voluntary Examinations
1882 Compulsory RIBA Examinations for Associateship of RIBA
1895 First full-time School of Architecture, Liverpool University
1902 System of Recognition of Schools and Exemption of their students first applied to AA and Liverpool
1904 RIBA Board of Architectural Education
1923 RIBA Visiting Boards
1931 and 1938 Architects' Registration Acts

At the same time, there grew to predominance an approach to teaching and architectural style, namely the rational classicism of the French Ecole des Beaux Arts, which concentrated on the architect's metier as the producer of drawings and co-ordinator of the works, not as someone who was involved in craft or construction or the structural side of architecture. The divorce between the metier of the architect and that of the builder, of the engineer, of the surveyor or of the developer was complete.

In this chapter we will discuss two interconnected and parallel developments: first, a major change of approach to architectural style, from the Beaux-Arts to modernism; second, the funnelling of all architects through recognised schools and the virtual end of pupillage, which inevitably involved even greater centralised RIBA control. Bound up with these developments was a determined and very ambitious bid by the leaders of the architectural profession for architects to have control not only of the design of individual buildings but also of large housing schemes and other kinds of complex, and beyond even this to control the whole system of physical planning, land use and civic design – town and country planning as it came to be known. Here was the notion of a State Architecture Service, enshrined in the French Beaux Arts, taken to its limits. Some architects believed that their profession should determine public policy for the built environment as a whole, including the manufacture of building materials as well as building construction and procurement in general. Indeed there were some who advocated that architects should be responsible for all physical design, including household goods and equipment. However striking, therefore, was the change of style from classicism to modernism, it should not conceal the fact that the organisational changes were a direct continuation of those which had taken place over the previous century and a half, increasing the control of the central professional body and the reach of qualified architects over building and the built environment.

Of necessity the present chapter must take a longer and more detailed look at certain theories and policies and their implementation than has been done so far in this study. It focuses on the rise of new modernist attitudes both to methods of training and to the products of such training. It starts with an examination of the way in which modernism infiltrated the schools before the Second World War and the reasons for its appeal. The lessons learnt from the Bauhaus had a strong effect on the definition of modernist pedagogy and these will be analysed in the various forms that they took before and after the war. This first half of the chapter thus deals with the models and ideology of modern architectural education. In the second half we will describe the curricular and institutional manifestations of this education, with particular attention paid to the RIBA and to the Oxford Conference of 1958. Finally we will demonstrate how these policy issues came to be applied during the 1960s in the form of what we have termed the 'Official System'.

But what is 'modernism'? For the purposes of this account modernism is defined schematically. The promoters of the modernist architectural culture that grew from the beginning of the century to dominance by the 1950s shared a core of beliefs. These overlap and are not necessarily consis-

tent: an antagonism to ornament and style, yet a love of abstract forms; a
rhetorical adherence to industrial imagery, industrial means of production
and new materials (including the ideal of a technologically controlled
environment) and thus a relative disinterest in the executant's skill; a fascination with what were considered the peculiar conditions of modernity, particularly the flux of change; a dislike of the patterns, physical or conceptual, of
custom and tradition and instead an appeal to the natural, to the new, and
to universalism; an approach to design that believed every problem was best
solved anew using rational principles rather than empirically or by the use of
formal precedents; and finally a desire to use architecture actively to change
and redeem society, an ambition which was associated both with capitalist
and socialist tendencies. In the 1930s this collection of ideas was made artifi-
cially coherent and monolithic in the promotion of a single Modern
Movement and of the so-called International Style. Most influential were the
writings of Le Corbusier and Walter Gropius in Europe, of Philip Johnson,
Henry-Russell Hitchcock and Siegfried Giedion in the USA, and in Britain,
those of Nikolaus Pevsner and J. M. Richards and the *Architectural Review*. At
this time British modernists focused on the moral and technological interests, linking these with ideas from the burgeoning British town planning
movement to form a vision of replanning enabled by all-encompassing
administrative powers. After the war this form of modernism swept aside the
by-laws and acts that preserved urban continuity, giving the architect, who
often worked anonymously in state bureaucracy, virtually unprecedented
scope.

The Bauhaus in Germany, 1919–33

For most modernists it was a German school, the Bauhaus, that most stimulated their ideas for reform. In fact for the first time a movement was identified not with a corpus of buildings and theories but with a school. We need to
explain the peculiar fascination that this school had for British architects.
When it was set up under the direction of Walter Gropius at Weimar in 1919,
the Bauhaus was the culminating result of long efforts to reform design education in Germany.[1] It combined the Academy of Art and the School of Arts and
Crafts, claimed the medieval workshop as its ideal and promised that there
would be a guild spirit linking artists and craftsmen devoted to expressing a
shared spirit and living as a community. In 1919 Gropius proclaimed 'the ulti-
mate aim of all visual arts is the complete building', yet oddly there was no
architectural course during the Bauhaus's earliest and most important years; it
was a school of art and design, not a school of architecture.[2] The only architectural experience that students gathered for many years was by working for
Gropius's private office.

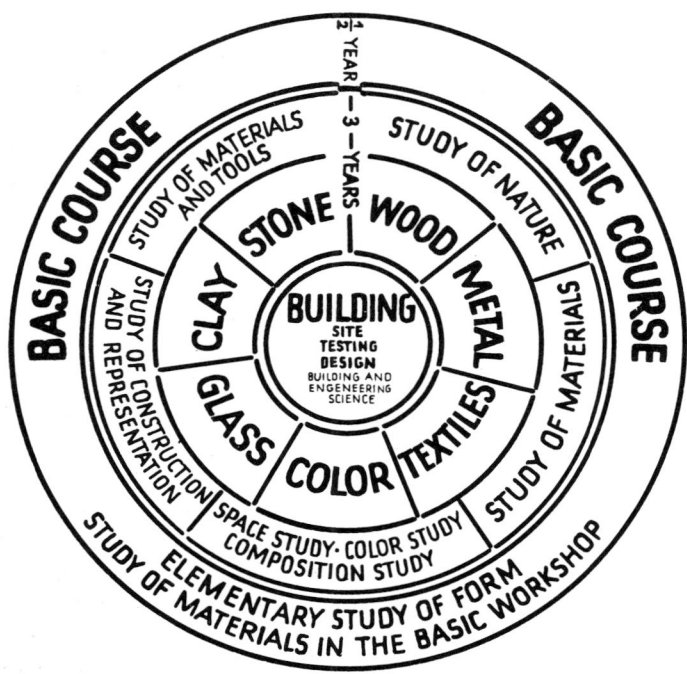

29 Johannes Itten: diagram of the Bauhaus curriculum (1923)

In its earliest years (1919–22) the Bauhaus was dominated by the figure of Johannes Itten, an art school teacher who had been strongly influenced by mysticism and the educational theories of Franz Cizek, Frederick Froebel, J. H. Pestalozzi and John Dewey. These theories of progressive education also entered architecture in other ways, but Itten was to provide one of the major conduits. Frank Lloyd Wright, for instance, experienced Froebelian kindergarten methods, and Le Corbusier may have been influenced by Pestalozzi's geometrical drawing exercises (Wilson 1969: 99–104). Interestingly, Froebel himself had experienced both apprenticeship, to a forester-cum-land surveyor, and an uncompleted university education. He also had ambitions to be an architect (Wilson 1969: 99–100). Much of this progressive education that Itten drew upon, whether 'learning by doing', representing primary sensations, the value of play activities, or the principles of form derived ultimately from Rousseau's notions of nature as a pure state of divine endowment and of the educational effects of environment and guided self-discovery. Most of such theory was focused on studies of child learning and its findings were intended to be applied only to children's education.

Of the very greatest importance for subsequent architectural education was the Bauhaus's *Vorkurs* for first-year students, devised by Itten in 1920 (**29**). This aimed to stimulate individual creativity through a succession of exercises teaching abstract relationships of forms, materials and colours, problem-solving and expressive freedom, and using a progressive development from simple to complex. The *Vorkurs* started with free associative drawing and moved on to an exploration of tones and planes. Then materials were examined through collages and careful studies of natural forms. More complex studies followed, including abstract analyses of old masters in terms of mathematical proportions, rhythms and colour theory.

Itten regarded the *Vorkurs* as a spiritual rebirth. In other words, the *Vorkurs* cleansed students of their formal preconceptions, treating them as corrupted bodies laden with a ragbag of cultural detritus; as Itten explained, 'Every new student arrives encumbered with a mass of accumulated information which he must abandon before he can achieve perception and knowledge that are really his own' (quoted in Banham 1960: 278). Itten envisaged his students as returning to a child-like state, from which he would develop their innate abilities. This point is an important one because when the *Vorkurs* method came to be applied to the training of architects it marked a radical shift away from the dominant, if implicit, ideas underlying both academic training and pupillage, that education functioned accretively and that objective knowledge and skills were built on the basis of previous learning – that there was no need to reinvent the wheel. In contrast, for Itten, every problem had to be thought out from scratch. Hence the fact that neither history of art nor history of architecture were taught in any substantive way at the Bauhaus.

After the *Vorkurs* Bauhaus students learnt crafts. They studied in traditional workshops and were known as 'apprentices' and 'journeymen'. This changed however when Gropius, under the influence of Theo Van Doesburg and his De Stijl theories, altered the programme in 1922 and Itten left in 1923. From this time dates a new elementarist formal language at the Bauhaus, as well as Gropius's interest in preparing students for industrial design. According to elementarist theory it was intended that the forms of designs would be derived not from the subjective resources that Itten aimed to plumb, but from the methods of machine production, the constraints of materials and the needs of the programme. Such forms would thereby be imbued with the spiritual expression of modernity. Standardisation could thus be, for Gropius, a quasi-spiritual discipline.

After 1923 the Bauhaus workshops were used less for crafts training than for the conception and execution of prototypes for mass production. Laszlo Moholy-Nagy and Joseph Albers, who succeeded Itten, moved the *Vorkurs* in a constructivist direction with abstracted experiments in balance, tension, compression and transparency. Collages and the old master exercises were dropped. Thus under Moholy-Nagy and Albers the *Vorkurs* became less the ritualistic way of life envisaged by Itten, and more of a play-therapy (Rykwert 1982: 48). One architectural student described the course in 1928:

> What Albers did was to seat us at long tables in the workshop wing of the Bauhaus and confront us with some unlikely materials such as wire mesh, paper, corrugated cardboard, sheet metal, matchboxes, newspapers, or what not. We were supposed to do something with these – just *basteln*, or play around with them, to see if we could make something out of them or discover something about them (Dearstyne 1986: 90–1).

The problem-solving remained, but it was now purged of its mysticism. However, in both its manifestations, despite the claim to liberate individual creativity, the *Vorkurs* dominated the aesthetic approach that students brought to their later work. Under Itten this was a mixture of expressionism and Arts and Crafts; under Moholy-Nagy it became cooler, run through with the pure universal geometry of elementarism and constructivism.

It was only in 1927 that an architecture department was formed at the Bauhaus by the Communist Hannes Meyer, and its success was regarded with some equivocation by Bauhaus teachers.[3] In 1928 Gropius resigned and Meyer took over, remaining as director until 1930 when Mies van der Rohe replaced him. Meyer steered the Bauhaus firmly towards the problems of mass housing and standardisation and concerns with planning, light, heat and acoustics. The architecture course was expanded so that it dominated the school, guided by a Spartan and rationalist view of design as technologically determined and in the service of a certain social programme, in this case Communism. Supporting this were lectures on sociology, economics and psychology. Then, under Mies's direction, and with the harsh political climate of the early 1930s, the social aspects were generally withdrawn in favour of formalism (30).

The greatest achievement of the Bauhaus is often said to be its propaganda. Even before it was finally closed down by the Nazis in 1933, it had spread a potent image or myth of itself through the publication of fourteen *Bauhausbücher* between 1929 and 1930. This propaganda glossed over the Bauhaus's complex history, its problems and its contradictory theories. Some of these should be pointed out. The link with industry, for example, was only tenuously achieved after 1925, and both the early guild imagery and the later functionalism consorted uneasily with the *Vorkurs*'s aim to produce creative artists. Similarly, the dissolution of distinctions between the arts and the crafts was made difficult, especially in the early years, by the inflexibility of the teachers. A continuing problem was that the dual origin of the Bauhaus in the Academy and the School of Arts and Crafts remained in the division between *Formlehre* (the teaching of form) and *Werklehre* (the learning of crafts), and

30 Bauhaus architecture class under Mies van der Rohe: redesign of department store, Dessau (1932)

this was never resolved. Another issue concerns the role of architecture at the Bauhaus. As both Moholy-Nagy and Gropius later explained it, the reason architecture was not taught at the Bauhaus until 1927 was that it was felt that creative, manual and visual skills must be learnt first. Yet the real reason for this absence, as Andrew Saint has shown, were chance political and economic cirumstances involved in the original setting up of the school (Saint 1983: 119–27). Finally, the complex permutations of Itten's original *Vorkurs* inevitably became subject to simplification in the pursuit of various later dogmas.

The Bauhaus idea in pre-war Britain

Standardisation and rationalisation, using glass, concrete and steel in simple uninflected forms, became the dominant idea and visual images of the Bauhaus when Gropius and others came to write about it in later years. Itten and the expressionist and mystical elements of the Bauhaus were little known about until quite recently.[4] Gropius's *The New Architecture and the Bauhaus* (first published in England in 1935) and his *Bauhaus, 1919–1928* (1938) jointly written with Herbert Bayer, were two of the most influential books in moulding this image of the Bauhaus. In *The New Architecture and the Bauhaus* Gropius made no attempt to unravel the Bauhaus's complex development or its contradictory theories. The Bauhaus was carefully distanced from the Arts and Crafts tradition by describing the course as it stood after 1922: the workshops were presented as places where type-forms were designed for massproduction; research and teamwork were stressed; the curriculum was presented as balanced between 'practical instruction' and 'formal instruction'; and the *Vorkurs* was seen as a liberation of individuality aimed at developing 'elementary self-expression' (Gropius 1935: 51–97). Style was stigmatised as applied fashion and rejected in favour of the notion that a supposedly universal language of forms could emerge from an objective understanding of modern society and modern technology.

The Bauhaus was widely known about in Britain before the war. The Building Research Station was in contact with it in the 1920s (W. Allen, pers. comm.) and Gropius and other continental modernists came over in the mid-1930s, Gropius bringing an exhibition of some 170 drawings and photographs of his work to the RIBA in 1934 and then later briefly setting up in practice with Maxwell Fry. As we will see, the style of rendering and the arrangement of dwellings in the housing schemes exhibited in 1934 clearly had an impact on AA students, but Gropius gave little indication, either in the exhibition or in a lecture he gave to the Design and Industries Association in May 1934, of how students were actually taught at the Bauhaus. The exhibition was opened by Raymond Unwin who linked Gropius's theories with those of Philip Webb and

[handwritten margin note: escape from aesthetic choice]

[96]

William Lethaby, on the basis that all three emphasised structure rather than style and believed in the practical understanding of building through contact with materials and site work.[5]

By this time, of course, the Bauhaus had ceased to exist except as an idea, and it was largely discovered in Britain through books. As well as Gropius's *New Architecture and the Bauhaus*, there were accounts of the Bauhaus in Herbert Read's *Art and Industry* (1934), an essay by Gropius on the Bauhaus curriculum in *The Year Book on Education* (1936), an extract from this in *Circle* (1937), the collection edited by Leslie Martin, Ben Nicholson and Naum Gabo, and several accounts by Nikolaus Pevsner (Pevsner 1940: 276–81; 1936b; 1936a). These works, in conjunction with Moholy-Nagy's *The New Vision* (published in England in 1934), presented the Bauhaus as a synthesis of certain ideas: the freeing of individual creativity, the use of constructivist and elementarist forms, the adaption of functionalist ideology and the need to make a range of activities, from industrial design to planning, the concern of education.

It is hard, however, to see that the Bauhaus had much of an impact upon British architectural schools before the war, and certainly not in terms of any systematic educational theory. By the mid-1930s young student architects such as Percy Johnson-Marshall at Liverpool, Arthur Ling at the Bartlett and Anthony Cox and Leo de Syllas at the AA were certainly enthused by its idea of a comprehensive view of the built environment and by some perhaps vague ideas of what it stood for in terms of approaches to materials and clients (P. Johnson-Marshall, pers. comm.). At the AA some of the younger pre-war teachers have claimed that they were 'avidly aware of [it] and stole ideas from it' (D. Jones, pers. comm.). As we shall see later the AA unit system, with its aim of group working, was sometimes loosely compared to the Bauhaus, but it seems more likely to have been inspired by the theory of Patrick Geddes, the pioneering sociologist and town planner. AA student knowledge of the Bauhaus is well represented by the reviews of Bayer and Gropius's *Bauhaus, 1919–1928* that appeared in *Focus*, the magazine of the AA students, in 1939. The most interesting of these, by Robert Townsend, actually attacked the Bauhaus for its concern with aesthetics over social problems, for its lack of a substantial link with industrial concerns and for its use of kindergarten play therapy (*Focus*, 4, summer 1939: 32–3). The lessons that could be drawn from the Bauhaus for architectural education, according to Townsend, were five-fold: that it broke with academic traditions; that it analysed everything into its components; that students played a role in making decisions; that education was conceived as a developing process; and, finally, that Gropius amalgamated the School of Arts and Crafts and the Weimar Academy of Art (*Focus*, 4, summer 1939: 34). As expressed in these general terms, there was nothing specific in these lessons to the Bauhaus, for all of them had been aspects of the AA's emerging modernism and indeed of its earlier Arts and Crafts approach. Townsend in fact was using a highly selective interpretation of the Bauhaus to throw into relief the particular conditions of the AA's modernist revolution.

One of the leading teachers at Liverpool at the time of Gropius's visit in 1934 was the architect and town planner William Holford. In 1938 Holford used the notion of a similar basic training for all the building professions, with workshops for handicrafts, to link the Bauhaus with the position of the Memorialists of 1892. This connection with the Arts and Crafts Movement was often to be used by British supporters of the Bauhaus; Unwin, for example, had used a similar comparison in 1934 (*RIBAJ*, 19 December 1938: 171). But Holford also argued that the Bauhaus and its 'New Architecture' made traditional practices seem expendable; for Holford there were 'no permanent architectural values save those founded on the elementary requirements of living, the laws of gravity, and of the human eye' (*RIBAJ*, 19 December 1938: 169). If there were no such values, there could also be no reversion to historical styles. Style itself was a fallacy; it was to be replaced by a rational analysis of needs wedded to the forms of industrial production. But Holford did not carry out these ideas at Liverpool and, as we shall see, he was unable to make an impact on an important RIBA committee on which he intermittently sat during the war.

In the 1930s, then, there was a sense of the ideas generated by the Bauhaus but there was little appreciation of how, if at all, they might constitute a complete form of architectural education. Indeed the architecture department at the Bauhaus itself had only lasted for six years, barely time enough to produce one class of students. Although there was an awareness of some of the Bauhaus's approaches, there was no British architectural school which had recreated itself in the image of the Bauhaus.

It is useful to compare the *Vorkurs* with what was expected of students taking the RIBA Intermediate examination in 1938, for this examination would have guided the way most architectural schools ran their first-year courses. The RIBA syllabus for the first year was dominated by drawing. This included studies of ancient, medieval and Renaissance buildings (31); drawings of the Orders; constructional studies and architectural geometry; freehand drawing of details; and the sketching and measuring of portions of buildings. There was also some work on mathematics and elementary science. In the following three years these exercises would be extended while history (up to the Renaissance), construction, structures and principles of design would be added.[6] To summarise, the concerns of the *Vorkurs* were with the pre-cultural, with self-discovery, with personal expression and with technological or material boundaries. By contrast, a Beaux-Arts first year implied a belief that education functioned accretively on the basis of a cultural inheritance and rational

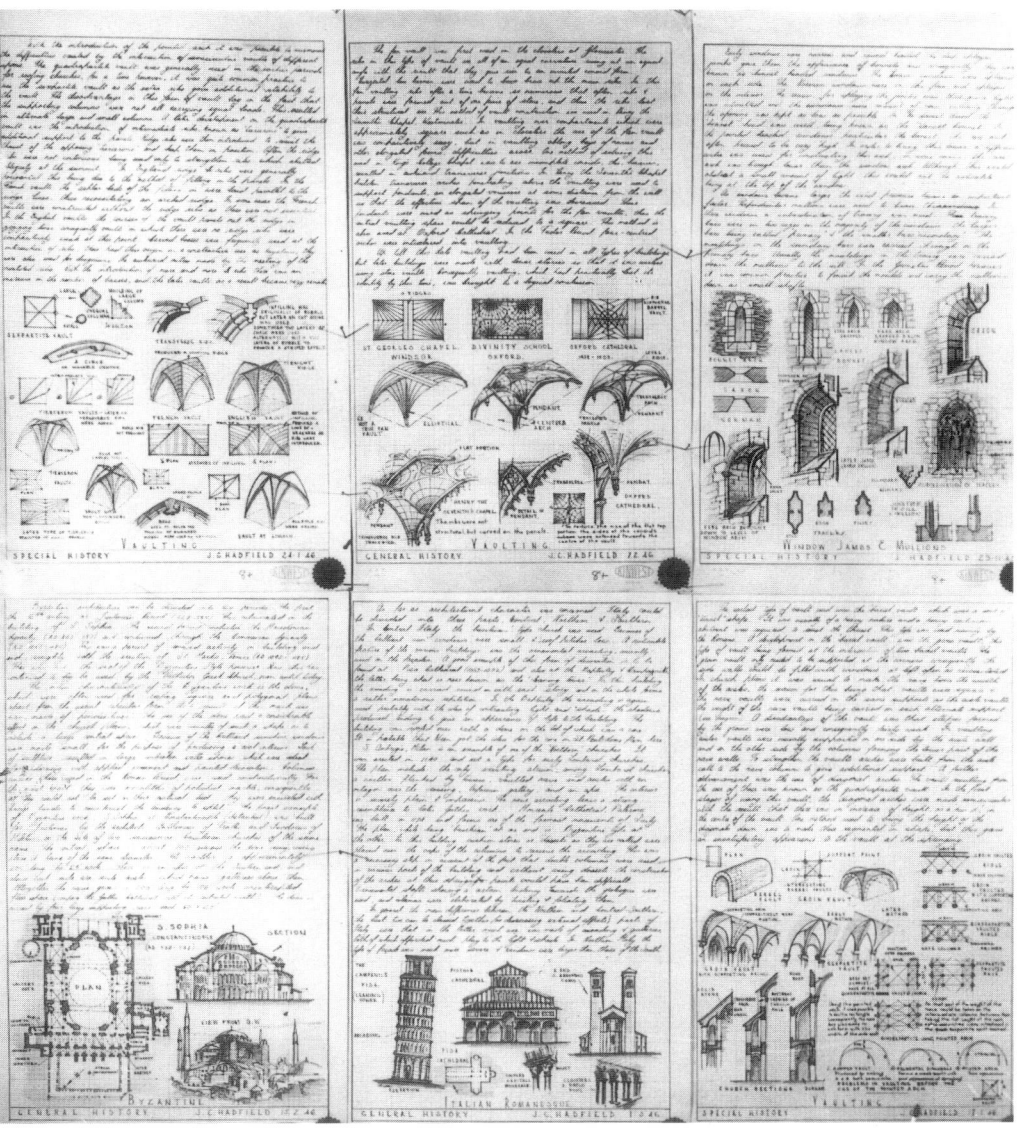

31 School of Architecture, Manchester College of Art: first-year history sheets (1946)

processes, and that to these would be added a body of knowledge and an ability in drawing skills (32).

Clearly if the young modernists were to bring about the architectural culture that they desired, not only would they have to change their own schools, they would also have to revolutionise the policies of their own professional body.

[99]

A GREEK COMPOSITION

32 F. R. S. Yorke: Greek composition, first-year work at Birmingham School of
Architecture (1925)

Modernism at the Architectural Association and elsewhere in the
1920s and 1930s

> We were born in the war. Much that follows in this journal can be orientated to that
> one fact. We were born into a civilisation whose leaders, whose ideals, whose culture
> had failed. They are still in power to-day. But we, the generation who follow, cannot
> accept their domination. They lead us always deeper into reactions that we are con-
> vinced can only end in disaster.

It was with these words that a group of AA students launched their new
journal, *Focus*, in 1938. The same sense of aesthetic and political conflict
between generations also racked the organisation of the AA at this time. It was
an important moment in the history of British architectural education because
the heightened conflict enabled the young modernists to find and express an
educational identity both by linking a group of ideas around their project and
by locating and characterising the ideas from which they were reacting.

As we saw in Chapter Two, the AA had adopted many Beaux-Arts methods
before and after the First World War. But in the 1920s the school was open to a
heady mix of influences. While Howard Robertson preached Julien Gaudet's
Beaux-Arts theories of composition, and often used modernist examples to

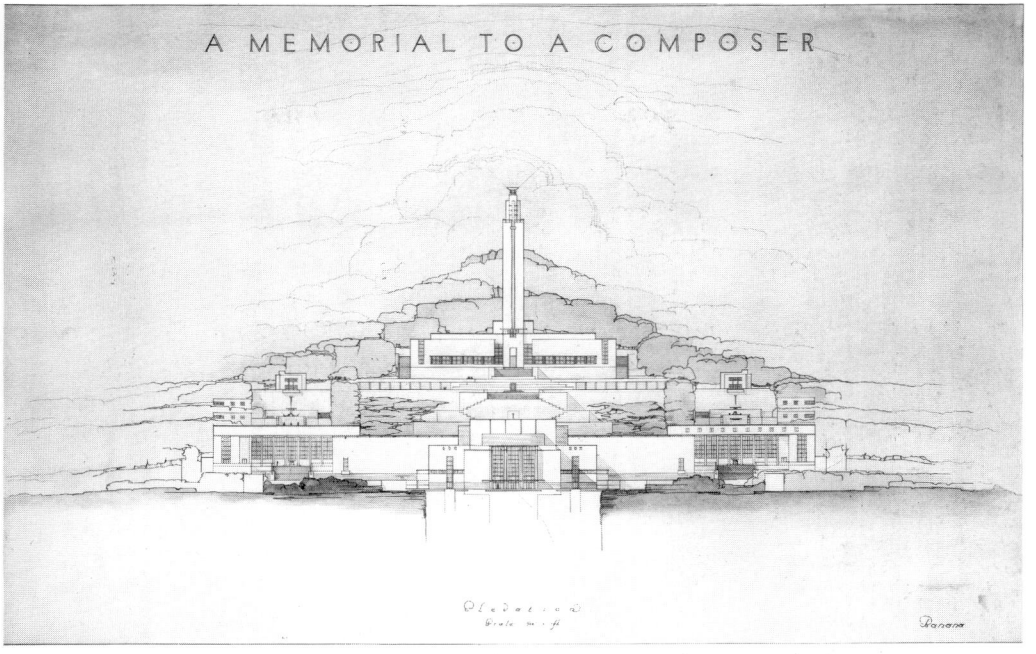

33 Elizabeth Scott: 'A Memorial to a Composer', Rome Prize entry by an AA student (1929)

expound them, F. R. Yerbury introduced contemporary European architecture both at the AA and through his photographs and articles in the pages of the *Architect and Building News*. Meanwhile the students independently digested the theories of Le Corbusier almost as soon as they were published in France (Gowan 1975: 71). Students began to inject modernist references into their work, especially in sketch designs; typical of this would be 'an axial plan and elevations with suggestions of the Einstein Tower in one corner'.[8] In the 1930s the Beaux-Arts formulas for classical monumentality were increasingly dressed in the fashions of contemporary European architecture (33). Modernism, as a style, was accepted by most students and many staff as early as 1932, according to one report, although the curriculum still included many Beaux-Arts programmes (Patrick 1958: 151–2).

The AA's increasing modernist orientation in the mid-1930s was officially recognised by the appointment of E. A. A. Rowse to succeed Robertson as principal in 1935. Rowse was a town planner with an interest in Third World matters and a desire to bring operational research into the classroom. In his first year Rowse set up the School of Planning and Research for Regional Development within the AA. In the spring term of 1936 he reorganised the AA from its five progressive 'years' to a system of fifteen 'units' each of about seventeen students run by one teacher. These semi-autonomous units were intended to encourage teamwork, rather than the supposed individualism and competitiveness of the Beaux-Arts, by conducting integrated research on a studio project.[9] At the beginning the broad aim of this unit system was to bring the sociological methods of the town planning movement into architecture. Rowse had picked up these methods from his mentor, the visionary sociologist Patrick Geddes (1854–1932), and through Geddes their genealogy dated back to the nineteenth-century social science of Auguste Comte and the pioneering social surveys of Frederick Le Play (Meller 1990). Rowse was also interested in the scientific management of Frederick Taylor and wanted to use studies of behavioural patterns as the generator of design. Furthermore, he and others also favoured more analytical investigation at the beginning of design projects and wanted to phase out the quick *esquisse* (*Focus*, 3, spring 1939: 85). Rowse brought in a number of young teachers all of whom claimed left-wing views, and by 1937 they had forced the school to give up the teaching of the Orders. H. S. Goodhart-Rendel's comment on this was, simply, 'I hope you know what you're doing.' By 1940, however, he agreed: '[the Orders] have now outstayed their usefulness . . . [they are] no longer an aid to expression but a hindrance' (D. Jones, pers. comm.; *Builder*, 3 May 1940: 586).

It is worth saying something more about the influence of Geddes here, since it was so crucial for Rowse and other modernists and town planners in the first half of the century. The title of his 1904 essay 'Civics as Applied Sociology' sums up his approach, and William Holford regarded him as 'the great educator and interpreter of the function of environmental planning in modern life' (see his Foreword to Mairet 1957: xi). Geddes devised a multidisciplinary or 'biotech-nic' approach to planning involving biologists, psychologists, sociologists and economists, amongst others. These teams would be brought together by planners with Olympian powers of observation and detachment. Yet Geddes's often sensitive patching and improving attitude to planning and his respect for cultural influences were usually forgotten in attempts to make use of his more formulaic idea of urban society as the organic merging of 'Place, Work, Folk'. The organism of the city was placed in the habitat of its region, and both needed to be studied in what Geddes called a Regional Survey, compiling information and analysis of every possible aspect before embarking upon design; a method that appeared to give planning a scientific basis. On another level, Geddes was also very antagonistic to 'text-book-perpetrators' and 'examination and machine bureaucrats' because he believed they stifled creativity (Boardman 1944: 266).

Returning now to the AA, in the same year as Rowse's appointment, H. S. Goodhart-Rendel had been made Director of Education, a position superior to that of Rowse. Goodhart-Rendel was a lordly figure with a strong and unfashionable love of Victorian architecture. He was a keen musician, the owner of a country house, an ex-Guards officer and author of the *Grenadier Guards Squad Drill Primer*. He thus epitomised many of the values to which the younger generation at the AA were opposed.

The differences that caused the ensuing confrontation between Rowse and Goodhart-Rendel are clear but they partly depended upon a fallacious if understandable identification of style and politics that was only made stronger by the apparent social distance between the opponents. This was a situation in which flat roofs were seen by both sides as a symbol of social revolution; the red-painted roads on a student model were taken to have political significance; and Goodhart-Rendal antagonised many of his staff by sitting at staff meetings in top hat and tails with a Rolls-Royce waiting outside to take him to the opera (D. Jones, pers. comm.). Just as the students rejected a war that Goodhart-Rendel had fought in, so they saw the architecture that they supported being attacked by militarists in Nazi Germany; in 1939 *Focus* published a view of the Weissenhof Seidlung at Stuttgart on which the Nazis had montaged Arabs and camels, labelling it 'Arab village'. But the modernists' position depended on a deceptive parallelism. Much as Goodhart-Rendel's own architecture at this time was a negotiation between tradition and modernity through notions of an abstract aesthetics derived from Reginald Blomfield and Geoffrey Scott, so it would be mistaken simply to characterise Goodhart-Rendel's position on education as a reactionary form of Beaux-Arts. In fact he supported the new unit system and backed Rowse's interest in planning (Powers 1982: 292). Later he came to agree with the rejection of the Orders and to worry deeply over what new rules or formal conventions could replace them, to stress the dependence of architecture on a knowledge of building construction, and to castigate the British version of the Beaux-Arts for mistaking 'means for ends' and for leading the British architect 'to hug his chains' (Goodhart-Rendel 1940). However, he did see an individual training in design as the central function of an architectural school and he wanted to maintain such Beaux-Arts practices as the *esquisse*. Where Rowse's support came from most of the students and many of the staff, Goodhart-Rendel's came from the AA Council and the RIBA Board of Education.

The most active students at the AA sided with Rowse, and in June 1937 they published a report itemising their suggestions for changes to the course. This report, which, due to the colour of its binding, became known as 'The Yellow Book', is one of the first manifestos of modernist architectural education produced in this country and many of its points became firm policy when this generation of students attained institutional positions after the war (it was reprinted in *Focus*, 3, spring 1939: 87–96).

The force of the Yellow Book was based on the conviction that 'students do not feel that they are part of a social, technical and cultural process with almost limitless possibilities for architectural invention'. One of the main blocks to this

was the 'elaborate system of consciously imposed competition', which compelled students to work for it as a thing in itself. Entry requirements to the profession, it argued, should depend less on artistic ability and more on scientific
knowledge. The report supported the unit system but wanted certain adjustments to its content; the effect of structure on design, for example, had to be
demonstrated through a range of materials. In the studio, design, construction
and other subjects were separated out into 'watertight compartments', thus
enabling design still to be taught as 'empty formulae of proportion and duality'
while construction was 'a spiritless copying from textbooks'. Sketching exercises needed to be related to studio work and decoration must be removed
from a 'period bias'. In teaching history the report was totally opposed to a
chronological survey starting with ancient Egypt that tried to arm the students
with an awareness of particular styles or 'paragons of achievement'. Instead the
subject should be taught as a 'history of social movements', with architecture
'incidental to the pattern of the age'. It was this interest in a wider field of influences on and references for architecture that was one of the modernists' most
fundamental disagreements with Goodhart-Rendel. The reason for this was a
form of social determinism: 'it is the particular social organisation of the time,
and the relations of man to man that spring from it, that determines what specific type of building needs will be developed during that period'. Since 'it is
our present position that is of most interest to us', history courses must start
with the nineteenth century and only in the second and third years go back to
ancient Egyptian times.

In 1937 one of the most famous of early modernist student projects was
designed – 'Tomorrow Town' (34, 35). The project exemplifies the aspirations
of the AA's modernists at this time. It was a group project by Unit 14 (taught
partly by Anthony Cox and including Richard Llewelyn Davies, later to become
principal at the Bartlett) that dealt with the social problem of rehousing
through a mixed scheme of three-storey, flat-roofed terraces and slab blocks in
a parkland setting (Pattrick 1958: 153). It thus bore strong resemblances to
Gropius's Siemenstadt development in the suburbs of Berlin or his riverside
housing scheme, both of which had been exhibited in England three years
before. It was rendered in precise outlines, devoid of rendering and washes. Six
principles had guided its development: the provision of an optimum diet; the
separation of industry; a tranquil and healthy domestic life; a diversity, yet
community of interests; and lastly an economy in cost, based on standardisation (Rowse 1939: 169). In its social content and aesthetic form it seemed to epitomise the radical utopian vision of the AA's young modernists.

With the Yellow Book and projects like Tomorrow Town the AA modernist
slate was established. It covered the kind of qualifications necessary to enter
training, the educational format itself and of course the content of that education. The Yellow Book had optimistically set out to enlarge upon the changes

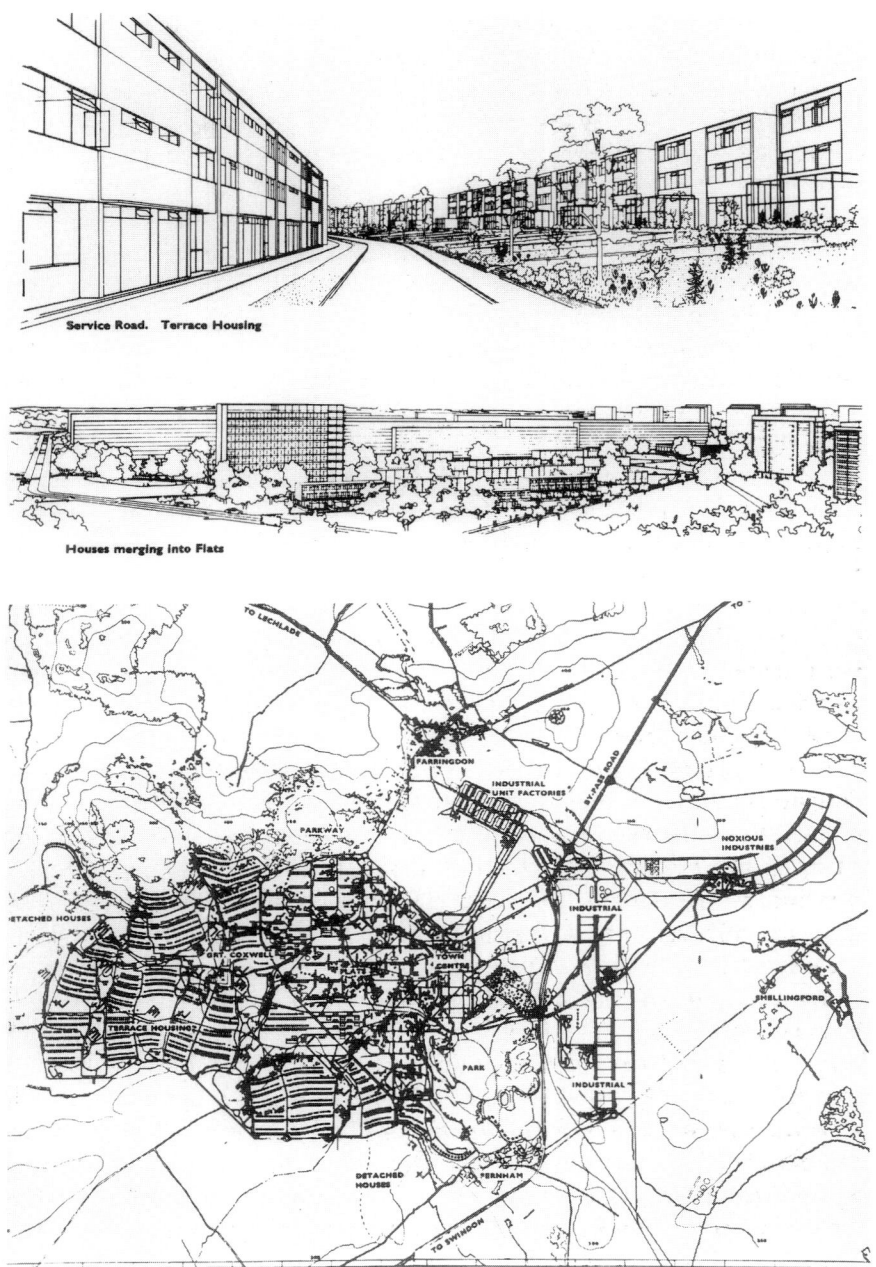

Service Road. Terrace Housing

Houses merging into Flats

34,35 AA Unit 14 pre-thesis project: 'Tomorrow Town' (1937–38)

that Rowse had already set in train at the AA. But those changes soon looked like being derailed.

The differences between Goodhart-Rendel and Rowse came to a head in 1938. Early in that year Goodhart-Rendel delivered his own educational manifesto, 'The Training of the Architect', marking a renewal of some Beaux-Arts policies (republished in Gowan 1973). Soon afterwards Rowse was dismissed and replaced by the French classicist Fernand Billerey who was notably antagonistic to the unit system. The staff wanted Maxwell Fry, a young Liverpool-trained architect who had made a mark with several modernist houses (D. Jones, pers. comm.). It was shortly after this that the first issue of *Focus* appeared, with its editorial call-to-arms quoted at the beginning of this section. The AA students and younger staff members like Robert Furneaux Jordan, Douglas Jones, Richard Sheppard and Max Lock, all brought in by Rowse, strenuously opposed the new regime and in the summer of 1938 Goodhart-Rendel was forced to resign. A conciliating modernist, Geoffrey Jellicoe, replaced him and the posts of Principal and Director were combined. Early in 1939 Jellicoe appointed an advisory committee strongly loaded with modernists, to make recommendations on educational policy.[10] The AA's course had been set.

This AA crisis in 1938 marks the leading edge of modernist change in British architectural education. It was partly about students' right to have a say in their education (ironically, at an institution that had originally been set up by students), because the Board of Architectural Education had weighed in on Goodhart-Rendel's side by criticising the power of student opinion at the AA.[11] Mainly, however, it was about teaching methods and content. The modernists saw that the unit system and group working were under threat, and that their desire for a combination of 'creative design', research, and a 'sociological outlook' was baulked, if only, as it proved, momentarily (*Focus*, 3, spring 1939: 100). Aspirations towards mass-production and territorial planning were opposed by defenders of craft and civic design. In Britain's most public – if independent – architectural school, the years leading up to the Second World War had seen 'the questions of science, sociology, and politics [raised] like Hydra's heads to scatter and confound their elders' (*Focus*, 4, summer 1939: 10)

The AA's crisis in 1938 dramatised changes that were also happening more quietly in several other architectural schools. This could occur simply at the level of students using contemporary modernist architecture as inspiration for their designs. This happened, for example, at Leicester School of Architecture where Dudok villas were popular models in the 1930s (R. Cave, pers. comm.). It could also take place at a more deliberate theoretical level, directed by the faculty. This was the case at Hull where the twenty-six-year-old Leslie Martin was appointed head in 1934. The course, as Martin has described it, was based around solving contemporary problems rather than the pre-set notions of

36 William Holford: 'New Cities of Light', sketch design (1935) (produced while he was an instructor at the Liverpool School)

classicism (Sir L. Martin, pers. comm.). Breuer, Moholy-Nagy, Maxwell Fry, Morton Shand, Chermayeff and other leading modernists all visited Hull. However, apart from the AA, the most important school for modernism at this time was Liverpool University.

Liverpool's architecture school had set up strong links with the town planning movement when a chair in that subject was established there in 1909, first filled by S. H. Adshead and then from 1914 by Patrick Abercrombie who made it into a kind of national 'information bureau' (Dix 1981: 104). Liverpool students had long been persuaded by Reilly to go in for work with local government. The inspiration for such interests was clearly the bureaucratic power built into the French and American Beaux-Arts systems and Reilly, as we have seen, had remodelled Liverpool's syllabus on Beaux-Arts lines. Reilly himself always remained an adventurous eclectic open to new developments, and by the early 1930s he had come openly to espouse modernism. Students continued to learn about mathematical proportions, but in 1936 teaching of the Orders was abandoned – a year earlier than at the AA. More futuristic exercises, such as six-hour *esquisses* on 'The Shape of Things to Come', began to be set at this time (**36**). Abercrombie was a disciple of Geddes and, until his transfer to become head of the department of town planning at University College in 1935, he taught town planning less as an aesthetic or technical than as a socially-considered activity, guided by the Geddesian triad of 'Place, Work, Folk'. Such approaches were aided by Reilly's introduction of sociologists like Ruth Glass. The year 1934 saw important visits to the school by Mendelsohn, Chermayeff and Gropius, who lectured and took part in project criticisms, and indeed Gropius seems to have had no qualms about identifying himself closely with the school.[12] These currents were also fed by ex-students. Gordon Stephenson, for instance, had worked with Le Corbusier between 1930 and 1932, when the Soviets' Palace design and the plans for Algiers were on the master's drawing-board. On his return Stephenson was given a teaching job at Liverpool and soon Corbusier pastiches began to appear in his students' work (37; Stephenson 1992: 29–44).

A glance through Liverpool's Prospectus for 1935–36 shows that some but by no means the majority of the students had adopted modernist styles by this time, although they produced them within the old Beaux-Arts programmes, using Beaux-Arts rendering techniques. When Gropius reviewed the students' work for that year he drew attention to its cell-like groups and its research work on programmes for 'working-class flats, municipal buildings, concert halls, airports, factories' (Gropius 1936: 7). Many of Liverpool's younger faculty members and students during the 1930s became leading public service planners and architects after the war, including William Holford, Gordon Stephenson, Peter Shepheard and the brothers Stirrat and Percy Johnson-Marshall (38).

With Liverpool, as at the AA, there is an important distinction to be made between work produced in a modernist mode and distinctively modernist educational techniques. By and large the second of these were absent in British schools. The question was, of what did these techniques consist, and where could they be seen? It was a question that came to be more urgently posed in the post-war years.

Modernist schools in the 1940s and 1950s

After the start of the Second World War modernism continued to be taken up by many schools while formal vestiges of the Beaux-Arts were neglected, edged out in favour of what appeared to be more pressing curricular requirements, or actually abolished. In Nikolaus Pevsner's words, Britain was in a transitory state 'pending a restatement of the problem in contemporary terms' (Pevsner 1950: 367). In most schools, although such a restatement may not have been made, there were at least strong modernist tendencies by the 1940s and the early 1950s.

For example, the departments at both Leicester College of Art and Cambridge University were full of students working on modernist studio projects.[13] Under the headship of Douglas Jones from 1940 Manchester had a

MERSEYSIDE MUNICIPAL OFFICES
AND AUDITORIUM

AXONOMETRIC VIEW

37 A. L. Williams: municipal offices and conference hall for Merseyside; Liverpool School fifth-year work (1936)

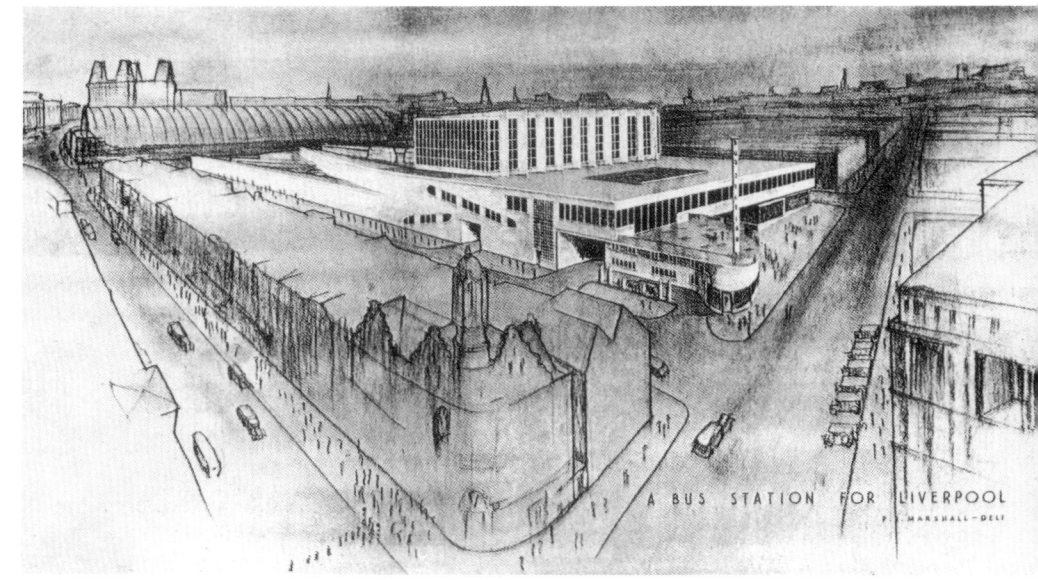

38 Percy Johnson-Marshall: bus and coach terminal station for Liverpool – fifth-year project, Liverpool School (1936)

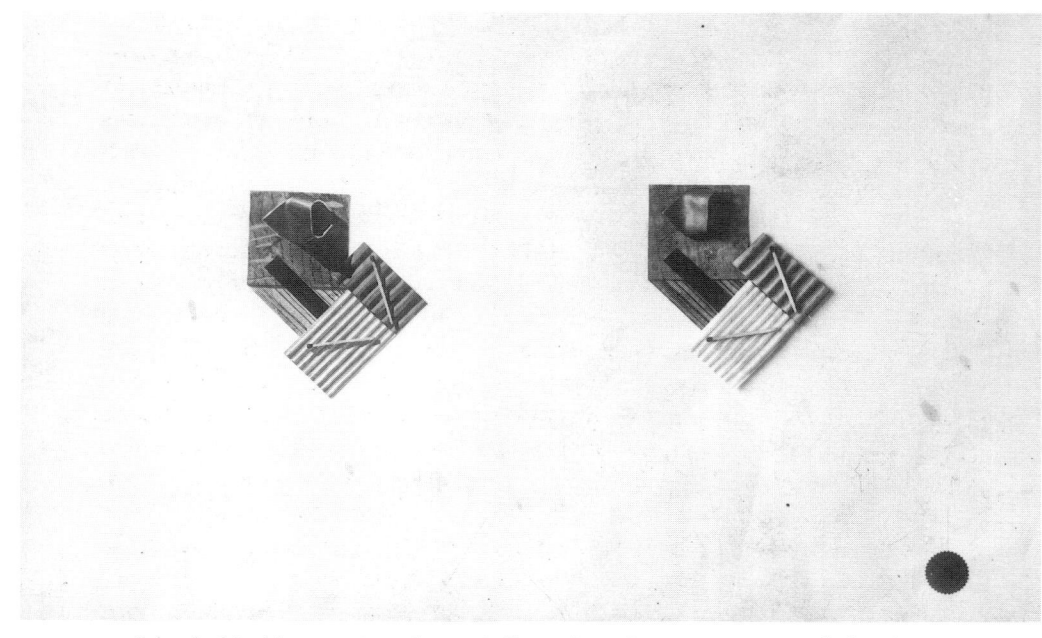

39 School of Architecture, Manchester College of Art: first-year texture study (1941)

modernist painter, Olive Sullivan, using *Vorkurs*-derived methods with architectural students, especially for exploring colour. For first-year students she cribbed such projects as the making of a mixed-media assemblage which was then painted as illusionistically as possible (**39**; D. Jones, pers. comm.). In the late 1940s the AA also instituted a form of *Vorkurs* for first year students (Banham 1968: 390).

Elsewhere, the architectural school at Kingston was 'directed like a Bauhaus version of a puritan grammar school' (Gowan 1975: 13). The RIBA, however, refused to extend exemption to Kingston. This may have been part of a regional distribution policy (Startup 1984: 71), but it clearly fitted the RIBA's immediate post-war policy: it saw that Kingston was too far gone for compromise. C. H. Reilly agreed that the issue was to do with the content of the curriculum there. In Reilly's view the course at Kingston was

> Of a rather Bauhaus kind . . . getting remarkable results if not quite on the lines of those wonderful R.I.B.A. testimonies of studies . . . There was a definite break with Beaux Arts traditions and a return to fundamentals in the relation of design to construction, often illustrated by models, which was very refreshing and seemed to me more than comparable to the break I engineered at Liverpool forty-three years ago from the Victorian Revival stuff then being taught (C. H. Reilly in *A & B N*, 25 July 1947: 67).

Birmingham was another school leading the way to new methods, yet in its case trying to combine them with hands-on crafts and construction classes. It had been a conventional school of the British Beaux-Arts type under the direction of George Drysdale, who had been trained at the Ecole des Beaux Arts. When Douglas Jones moved to become head of the school at Birmingham in 1947 it became notably influential, especially for its 'live' projects, and Jones's impact was for a time compared with that of C. H. Reilly at Liverpool (*A & B N*, 22 February 1961: 258). Jones had first tried live projects at the AA before the war. He started them at Birmingham in 1950 as a way of combining design and building exercises with hands-on experience of construction. These projects always used small, relatively simple buildings in order that the project might be seen through to completion – from preparing a brief to supervising construction – by students taking on new jobs in their third year and, hopefully but not always, finishing them by the end of their fifth year. Often criticised by other modernists for limiting student creativity, the live projects typically built laboratories, housing, clubhouses or village halls, using pitched roofs and mixed facing materials. Jones could defend them against critical Board of Education members like Donald MacMorran and Anthony Chitty through his friendship with the influential Donald Gibson and C. H. Aslin (D. Jones, pers. comm.).

First-year students at Birmingham in the late 1940s made abstract models in the manner of the constructivist art of Tatlin or Moholy-Nagy, but they also learnt the rudiments of building crafts (brickwork, carpentry, plumbing, plastering) and worked on 'conglomerates' – construction exercises using full-size components, whose use was spread to other years by the 1960s (40). In a *Vorkurs* manner design was postponed until after students had learnt to appreciate 'the abstract qualities of architecture, of proportions, rhythm, colour and texture' (*A & B N*, 193, 28 May 1948: 474; *AJ*, 130, 15 October 1959: 353–5).

40 Birmingham School of Architecture: 'Upper school conglomerate' (1961)

Birmingham may have been unusual in delaying design for even the more 'progressive' schools started students on simple design work (*AR*, 107, June 1950: 371). In this respect at least, Birmingham was closer to the American model; at Massachusetts Institute of Technology design began after one year and at Mies van der Rohe's Illinois Institute of Technology it did not begin until after three years (*AR*, 107, June 1950: 371). Yet Birmingham remained traditional in its insistence on acquiring drawing skills through measured drawings of buildings and details and sketch designs (of non-architectural subjects), and it resuscitated a Lethabitic element in its insistence upon hands-on experience (*AJ*, 157, 25 April 1973: 956; *A & B N*, 219, 22 February 1961: 257–63). The point was to have the student ask, at every stage of design, how is this to be constructed?

What could be termed a more conventional modernist line was followed at Edinburgh. Following his work for the LCC Robert Matthew became head at Edinburgh in 1953. He thus pursued a route that was to become common amongst his contemporaries; from planner or public service architect to 'tarmac professor' (the term given to academics with international practices). In his inaugural address Matthew made it clear that his policy would primarily be to train architects for work in public authorities. The student at Edinburgh was to be taught to master industrial production and to bring a progressivist ethos to design. Policies that involved patching up the cities were inappropriate for the new modes of life, because the new forms 'must bear little relation to those of past ages, as little as our own culture bears to those of history' (*AJ*, 118, 26 November 1953: 658–61).

Robert Gardner-Medwin left the LCC at the same time as Robert Matthew in order to take up the chair at Liverpool. There he not only advocated the development teams that had been used at the LCC, but also a widening of the curriculum and the introduction of building science. A faculty of environmental studies was established, and to the usual architectural disciplines were added the pure and social sciences including psychology and public health (*AJ*, 117, 2 April 1953: 427).

By the early 1950s, then, many architectural schools considered that they had a form of modernist education in operation. Few of them, however, had revised their curriculum – or 'restated the problem' – in a thoroughgoing way. Furthermore there were other schools where Beaux-Arts practices still survived, the odd one (such as Brixton) where Arts and Crafts ideals were overlaid with the new fashions, and of course a large number of part-time schools. About 46 per cent of architects in the early 1950s qualified by taking the RIBA external examinations. The situation was one of great flexibility. The RIBA may still have deliberately withheld recognition to part-time schools with greater aspirations.[14] If so the result was to retain the opportunity for many architects to enter the profession through a combination of pupillage and part-time education. The situation was thus one of some variety in the early and mid-

1950s. The point here is that although, unlike the situation in the eighteenth century, entry into architecture was regulated by a certain notion of professional competence, there was still some looseness in the structures that could enable one to reach this level.

Models for modernist education after the war

We need now to examine the models that were available to enable architectural schools to restate the problem in the post-war years. They can be divided into four main ideas: the example of the Bauhaus; the working methods developed for the Hertfordshire schools; the ideal of faculties encompassing all the building professions; and finally, a new system of town planning, for which a new form of architect had to be produced.

The Bauhaus model in the post-war years

After the war a revised version of the Bauhaus method seemed to offer some architects and teachers a proper modernist mode of training. Whereas before the war British modernists had only seen rather vague principles embodied by the Bauhaus, in the post-war years they began to perceive it as having offered a systematic form of training. This was the result of several factors. For a start, more was now known about the Bauhaus and particularly the philosophy of its *Vorkurs*. Moreover, in the USA schools had in the meantime been set up in the image of the Bauhaus (though often differing significantly from it) led by ex-Bauhauslers and operating a lively propaganda machine. Through the Congrès Internationaux d'Architecture Moderne (CIAM), modernists had organised an international circus of talents with well-publicised conferences that often dealt with the subject of architectural education. The final factor was that British architects by now had experience in organising or working within research and development teams that espoused Bauhaus values.

The crucial element in the influence of the Bauhaus after the war was that many of its teachers had settled in the USA and established or reformed schools there on Bauhaus lines. After Liverpool had flirted with employing him, Gropius had moved to the States and became chair of the Harvard Graduate School of Design in 1937; Mies and Hilberseimer went to the Illinois Institute of Technology; Moholy-Nagy was made Director of the School of Design, Chicago (later to be merged with IIT). By 1954 Bauhaus-derived courses were regarded as the norm by the American Institute of Architects (Bannister 1954, vol. 1: 106–7).

In the post-war years Gropius became even more of an inveterate proselytiser for his vision of architectural education. He gave papers on the subject at the CIAM conferences held in Britain in 1947 and 1951, as well as a talk on BBC radio in the latter year, and his collection of essays *The Scope of Total*

Architecture (1943) – many of which were on architectural education – quickly went through several editions. The image was now refined. The *Vorkurs* was presented as having aimed at uncovering the 'biological centre' of the student, who could then apply a 'special language of shape' based on a 'scientific knowledge of objectively valid optical facts' (Gropius 1943: 24; Giedion 1951: 44). Thus architectural grammar would not be inherited from the past but handed over by the datum of science and then applied according to subjective resources. As Gropius put it, 'I must empty my soul that God may enter' (Gropius 1943: 32). Manual, industrial and building competences would follow this initial stage, based on a 'direct participation in the techniques and processes of making things' (Giedion 1951: 43).

It is particularly interesting that the student-as-blank-sheet aimed at by the *Vorkurs* was often linked in these post-war years to the notion of the city as a *tabula rasa* and the ideal of architect-led collaborative teamwork producing anonymous architecture (Giedion 1951: 46). The latter was an idea that had great appeal to British modernists working in large public offices. But we can also see the deep resources of the Bauhaus legacy, for those individualistic and creative aspects of its course could be recovered again when the image of the anonymous public architect had lost its gloss.

The notion of a natural (aesthetic) rightness like the 'unprejudiced receptivity of . . . childhood', in other words those aspects of the educational theories of Froebel or Dewey that Itten had used, was now directly related to the solving of social problems. Furthermore, theories that had been devised in order to understand child development were now applied to the training of young adults. The *Vorkurs* thus became a model for the design process as a whole; the issue had to be considered completely afresh, rejecting older solutions as one rejected the ideas of unreliable adults, and applying the openness of innocence in conjunction with the infallibility of science. Moreover the establishment of various Bauhauses in the USA, particularly at Harvard, seemed to show that they could work within academia, and could take over what had been the preserve of the Beaux-Arts. Gropius himself, however, expressed reservations about this academic framework that seem rarely to have been held by his counterparts in Britain.[15] Furthermore, while the British modernists were beginning to join or infiltrate their professional body, the RIBA, Gropius was expressing a position opposed to professional autonomy: 'I am going round telling every student that he should not follow the so-called ethical outline of the leading professional organizations . . . I can see hope for the profession only if he joins hands with the engineer and contractor, that is to say that he goes back into the building production' (*A & B N*, 201, 3 January 1952: 6).

With all this expansion of architectural ambition, this rush to keep pace with 'the convulsions of our mechanical age' (Giedion 1951: 44), something had to be lost. Two losses at least were admitted. First, history as a continuous body of knowledge about architectural practices was replaced by the search for principles which were believed to underlie each period. Second, traditional drawing skills were to be subordinated to imagination and the experiment and enquiry of science or even forsaken altogether (Giedion 1951: 44; CIAM 1951). The eclipse of building and ornamental skills by a concern with industrial mass-production and an abstract formal language was a third but unadmitted loss.

The Hertfordshire school building programme

Some models already existed in modernist British architecture which were related to the Bauhaus ideal in education. Most notable was the experience of the Hertfordshire schools architects which now attained an exemplary status. Under C. H. Aslin, but effectively run by Stirrat Johnson-Marshall, the architectural department of Hertfordshire County Council pioneered the mass prefabrication of schools from 1947, and within four years the department had completed forty of them. Here, more than anywhere in Britain, was an example of how to design according to needs discovered through consultation, and of how to set up a research programme, in collaboration with the Building Research Station, that could create a flexible system of mass-produced components, and research building science, colour and ergonomics, treating these as subjects to be objectively resolved. The discipline imposed within the production team and their functioning as a 'Composite Mind', to use a term invented by Patrick Geddes (Johnson-Marshall n.d.), with a working partnership between designers, manufacturers and craftsmen, could be seen as the practical application of the Bauhaus ideal and of the teamwork that AA modernists desired. Here that voguish term 'research', bandied about by MARS Group modernists, came to mean something more recognisable to such socialist scientists as J. S. Bernal and J. B. S. Haldane (Saint 1987).

At Hertfordshire the role of the architect was effectively redefined. Often aloof from design, drawing and the skills of detailing, the architect became an anonymous but powerful manager, researcher and administrator, working within a form of Socialist Fordian ideology. To make prefabrication and research serve flexible design seemed to be one of the essential conditions of a modern democracy, and these were the key tenets of what came to be called the 'New Humanism'.

There was another way in which the post-war Hertfordshire schools may have offered not just exemplary practices but also educational theory for architecture. As we have seen, the Bauhaus was more widely known about in the post-war years. In addition, British modernism began to take in more of the 'progressive' educational theory upon which some aspects of the Bauhaus system had been based. This kind of education, it was believed, would create the new citizens able both to design and to appreciate the new architecture. The schools' architects

41 Henry Swain, Nottinghamshire Deputy County Architect, giving Cambridge students a crit (1962)

rapidly came to transmit their experience to architectural education. Both Henry Swain (head of the Nottinghamshire schools programme) and Stirrat Johnson-Marshall, for example, were members of RIBA Visiting Boards in the immediate post-war years. Architects such as Stirrat Johnson-Marshall, David Medd and Bruce Martin and other schools architects from Hertfordshire, Nottinghamshire and the Department of Education and Science were much in demand to teach and lecture in architecture departments (41). As well as the research and development lessons of school building they may have brought with them some of the values of the post-war educationists, in particular the belief that progressive art education could be a model for all education.

The two most prominent educationists to be involved with the post-war school building programme were John Newsom, Chief Education Officer for Hertfordshire, and Henry Morris, who before the war as Chief Education Officer for Cambridgeshire had been instrumental in commissioning Gropius to design the Impington Village School. After the war Morris advised on the cultural development of the new towns. In both roles he acted on the belief that art and architecture, with education, could be agents of social development (Rée 1985; Baynes 1973: 369–70). He believed in a powerful architectural profession to counter speculative building and wanted a 'laboratory city' that could offer the chance 'to carry out research into every aspect of modern living' (*Focus*, 4, summer 1939: 99–100). In 1948 Morris planned an institution which would have been the nearest England had come until then to a Bauhaus. Morris's Cambridgeshire Regional College of Technology and Design was meant, like the Bauhaus, to combine the functions of an old Technical College and a School of Art. It was intended to bring together the concerns of design, craftsmanship and industry, and for its three-year courses in architecture fully to participate in this. However, the scheme was eventually abandoned because of a cut in funding (Rée 1985: 106–7).

Both Morris and Newsom believed that the child learnt through the environment in which he or she was educated, as well as by the methods used in that environment. Light, colour and spaciousness were essential components of this environment, and also key areas of study at the Building Research Centre. They were also, of course, important aspects of modernist aesthetics in general and, as we shall see, of the revamped idea of building science. Furthermore, in the wake of the 1944 Education Act, which Morris had some influence upon (Rée 1985: 91), the reforms advocated by the educationists were also seen as essential elements in the reform of society, much as the modernists saw their 'New Architecture'. The sympathy between educationists like Morris and Newsom and modernist architects indicates how the educational theory behind the Bauhaus might have been perceived even more vividly by those with eyes on reforming architectural education.

Faculties of environmental design

An important and fascinating result of the Liverpool ethos, of lessons learnt during the war, of the Bauhaus ideal, and even of some Lethabitic notions, can be found in the career of Percy Johnson-Marshall and in his development of the idea of large faculties of environmental design. From 1931 to 1936 Johnson-Marshall had studied at Liverpool with his brother Stirrat. There they were taught by Charles Reilly, Lionel Budden and Patrick Abercrombie. Both of the Johnson-Marshalls were present when Gropius brought his exhibition of Bauhaus work to Liverpool in 1934. As reported by Percy,

> This changed our direction of thought and design – how to come to terms with technology? . . . We were also becoming strongly influenced by social issues, and wished to take part in the 'scope of total architecture'. We both decided to go into some form of public service (Johnson-Marshall n.d.).

After training Percy Johnson-Marshall joined the MARS Group and helped with the MARS plan for London. He worked with Donald Gibson on plans for

Coventry until 1941 and then joined the Royal Engineers and was sent out to Burma and India, where he had been brought up as the son of a British civil servant. When he returned to England after the war he took the planning course that Rowse and Jacqueline Tyrwhitt had set up and then joined Holford and Stephenson's Planning Technique Office at the Ministry of Town and Country Planning in 1946.

Return home was not just a return to the notion of the architect-planner. Johnson-Marshall's experiences in India and Burma had a significant impact on his organisational skills and his notion of architectural education and he was to campaign for this new thinking both within the RIBA and outside it during the late 1940s and the 1950s. As a Royal Engineer he had been unusually active in creating new initiatives, especially through the Service Arts and Technicians' Organization (SATO) which he helped to establish and of which he became the head in 1942. He and William Tatton Brown, an architect with fine modernist credentials, having worked with André Lurçat and with Lubetkin in the Tecton office, used this organisation as a way to carry out educational programmes, to discuss the reconstruction of London and to make planning schemes (42).[16] Johnson-Marshall was particularly interested in setting up Bauhaus-like educational projects such as his proposed syllabus for a School of Indian Architecture and Regional Planning at Calcutta University and his proposed Faculties of Planning, Design and Technics for Indian Universities (*AJ*, 103, 2 May 1946: 340). Another inspiration may have been the university that Geddes had planned for central India just after the previous war (Meller 1981).

The proposed faculties were to be established in Calcutta, Delhi and Madras, and to replace the only existing school, at Bombay (which had exemption from RIBA Intermediate exams). The assumption behind these faculties was that unity of design depended upon the common background of artists and technicians, and that this background could only be obtained in faculties 'where all branches of design and planning are taught, in close proximity to manual work and scientific materials research' (Johnson-Marshall 1944). Both a theoretical and a 'hard', operational notion of research, on the model of the Tennessee Valley Authority research on geology and planning, was to be at the heart of this educational enterprise.[17]

Less systematic, but none the less interesting as experiments in aspects of education, were the polytechnics set up by SATO in 1945 and 1946 at Pegu and Rangoon in Burma (Johnson-Marshall 1946). These were institutions loosely established on an *ad hoc* basis in order to train troops in local building techniques and in some of the building skills that might be useful in reconstruction work at home. The polytechnics seem to have been close in intent to the Brixton School of Building. In Johnson-Marshall's words they were an 'attempt to break down the artificial barriers of the building industry by uniting the

42 Percy Johnson Marshall explaining a project to the Governor of Burma, Sir Reginald
Dorman-Smith (1945)

artist and technician in a common purpose-training for Reconstruction' (*AJ*,
103, 2 May 1946: 340). Short courses were set up with Rowse as one of the teachers. Echoing Brixton's teaching, bricklaying was learnt by constructing model
houses within the polytechnics' large workshops (43), and students were
encouraged to learn the use of indigenous materials such as bamboo to rebuild
village dwellings (W. Tatton Brown, pers. comm.). Indeed, adopting and
improving the local vernacular seems to have been one of the aims in both the
polytechnics and the proposed faculties.

The war and the colonial setting had, in effect, enabled Percy Johnson-Marshall to hatch educational reforms and to conduct a series of experimental projects on education and planning. But from the first these projects had been intended to have wider lessons. It was hoped that similar Technical Training Centres would be set up in all countries, with an International Commission upholding technical education standards (Johnson-Marshall 1944). More practically, while he was in the Far East he had managed to gather information about existing British architectural schools and had sent his SATO educational proposals to the Board of Architectural Education. When he returned to England he continued to press these proposals on the Board (RIBA Archives 7.1.4., 1946). He was determined to change what he regarded as a narrow and out-dated aesthetic approach to architectural education. By contrast,

43 British and Indian soldiers learn bricklaying at the SATO Burma Polytechnic by building a model Indian house designed by SATO architects (1946)

modernism represented for Johnson-Marshall, as it had for Rowse and others at the AA, a broader encompassing of environmental and social interests. Sponsored by the MARS Group to lecture at the RIBA in 1946, he advocated much closer unity between architects and technicians, argued that technical education should be thoroughly reorganised, and urged ex-SATO members to join trade unions and agitate for progressive institutions (Johnson-Marshall 1946: 342). In a lecture at Brighton in 1947 he criticised the 1946 Report on Architectural Education for coming thirty years too late and suggested instead that the defects of the architectural schools should be corrected using the lessons of the Bauhaus. These lessons, he argued, could be distilled through his own proposal for new faculties in India. In these the idea was to have a Faculty of Planning, Design and Technics based around a Building and Planning Research Centre:

> It was presumed that all students of the Planning, Building and Works groups would have a common basic Art and Science Course. Most of the Engineering students would then go on to the existing Faculties of Engineering, and the rest would go to the new Faculty, including Architects, Landscape Architects, Town Planners, Structural Engineers, Heating, Lighting and Ventilating Engineers, Industrial Designers, Painters and Sculptors. After an initial common training they would all proceed to specialized departments.

This proposal, Johnson-Marshall suggested, was 'eminently suitable for adoption in this country' (Johnson-Marshall 1947). Accordingly he continually pressed the Board of Architectural Education to consider his Indian schemes, in other RIBA forums he argued for a widening in the compass of the schools, and we may be sure that this campaigning redoubled when he joined the Board in 1953 (*RIBAJ*, 56, February 1949: 166; 57, May 1950: 267).

Percy Johnson-Marshall saw his proposals as a drawing together of lessons learnt from Gropius, Lethaby and his own planning experience. By 1957, in an article entitled 'From Schools of Architecture to a New University Faculty', he re-emphasised that the place for these new faculties could only be in the universities and that they would be for building professionals rather than, as at Brixton, for building artisans. Although he claimed Lethaby as a mentor in the area of shared training his professional vision of these faculties marks a fundamental difference from Lethaby. The vision was only slightly nearer to Gropius. Only when Bauhaus ideas were carried 'to the stage of integration with the university system' – a lesson that Johnson-Marshall had learnt when devising his Indian faculties – could the demand for specialised and co-ordinated teams of experts working in an industrialised building operation be satisfied. The essential ingredients of the faculties would be a common preliminary course and a main course of branching specialisms. Both of these would be hubbed around a research centre where experiments in teamwork would be a key area of study, and this centre would have links to a regional Building Research Centre.[19] Johnson-Marshall would have continued to advocate these large faculties when he attended the Oxford Conference in 1958, which we shall discuss later in this chapter. On one level, faculties of environmental studies were simply intended to create conditions so that professions that would work together could study together, and practically they enabled equipment and specialist staff to be pooled. But on another level they were seen as providing the framework for learning about professional architectural practice in the modern world, and thus were essential to the notion of architectural education shared by most modernists.

The new system of town planning after 1947

The fourth development that affected architectural education came from post-war town planning. Of overwhelming importance to the way in which archi-tects, builders and developers have operated in the post-war years has been the new system of building controls introduced by the 1947 Town and Country Planning Act. This act was generally acknowledged at the time as Britain's special and for a long time unique contribution to modern architecture, enabling the planner to treat the existing city as a *tabula rasa* – though the basic ideas derived from Le Corbusier's book *Urbanisme* of 1925. The framework of the act was devised by a team led by Sir William Holford at the Ministry of Town and Country Planning between 1943 and 1945. Holford was a product of Liverpool under C. H. Reilly in the late 1920s and early 1930s, and had been appointed Professor of Town Planning at Liverpool in 1935, at the age of twenty-eight.

Before the new act building controls had been exercised through the Public Health Acts, the Model Clauses of the Local Government Board and the London Building Acts. A landowner possessed the right to build on his own property as well as to rebuild existing buildings; local authorities could not prevent him from doing so, but they did have the power to make by-laws under the Public Health Acts. These by-laws laid down enforceable rules about how a landowner must build; about adhering to the building line in a street, and about the width of new streets. The London Building Acts also set limits for the heights of new buildings. Accordingly, the Local Government Board issued Model By-Laws which prescribed minimum widths for streets depending upon their length and function. For example, any street longer than 100 feet had to be a carriage road and had to be at least thirty-six feet wide. These laws were readily intelligible and easily enforceable through a corps of District Surveyors. At the same time, like all simple regulations, they undoubtedly resulted in a somewhat regimented and unimaginative layout of buildings.

Both the philosophy and the provisions of the 1947 Town and Country Planning Act were totally different. By-law regulations were replaced by a

Development Plan, which every local planning authority was obliged to produce within three years, showing 'the manner in which they propose that land in that area should be used'.[20] These were to be shown on maps designating roads, open spaces and new buildings both public and private. No development could any longer be carried out without permission from the planning authority, and the authority had powers to give or refuse consent 'as they think fit', so long as they '*have regard to* the provisions of the development plan'. All owners' development rights were nationalised in exchange for £300 million, which solved the problem of compensation for the loss of property rights. In addition, the planning authority had powers to designate land for Comprehensive Development. The definition of a Comprehensive Development Area was one which 'should be developed or redeveloped as a whole' in order to deal with war damage, to remedy 'bad layout or obsolete development', or to provide for relocating population, industry or open space.

Central to the workings of the new planning system was the almost complete discretionary power over development given to the planners, subject only to the right of appeal to the minister. Post-war planning authorities were not even bound to adhere to their own Development Plans as the basis for granting permission. They only had to 'have regard' to the plan, and could disregard its provisions if they thought fit. The modernist architects and planners who framed the legislation deliberately wanted this to be vague, and not tied down to specific rules and codes. They wanted this because planning was, they argued, 'a continuous, not a static process', not an 'act of design'. This simple formulation is very significant. That significance lies in the total rejection of the notion of civic design, which had been central to town planning as it had been practised in Britain since the seventeenth century. (As we shall see in Chapter Four, one of the people who worked on the act, William Allen, who also played a key role in devising the new system of education, took the view that even the practice of architecture itself should not be an 'act of design' but the formation of rational policy.)

In short, this new flexible system of control at the discretion of the local planners (who were expected to have been trained as architects) freed modern architects from the tightly drawn rules of the old by-laws which, because they envisaged building within the context of the 'corridor street', had very much restricted architects' capacity to realise the new kind of buildings they wished to design. Especially with the power to redevelop a whole area through Comprehensive Development Orders, the architect was able to dispose buildings of all kinds, of different shapes and sizes and materials, on a large site without the constraint of existing streets, neighbouring buildings and restrictions on height. The bearing of this upon education is obvious. The architect of the future had no need to learn to design within the traditional codes of the British city, and therefore much of that traditional knowledge seemed to have become obsolete. The new architect needed to learn to think imaginatively about the openings which the new freedoms offered. Hence 'education for change'.

Changes in the educational policy of the RIBA, 1945–60

These models helped to mould the new form of training, but to bring this about the RIBA also needed to be reformed. This internal history is not just of institutional interest, however, for in bringing about these reforms the modernists also created a powerful central force – in effect a Ministry of Architecture.

1. The shift of power from the Beaux-Arts to modernism

The history of the debates about architectural education within the RIBA in the 1940s and 1950s is complex. In the Board of Architectural Education the period saw a continual jockeying for position and for support, interrupted by moments of apparent stillness and brief spurts of reaction. Generally however the modernists and modernisers gradually succeeded in gaining positions, and then in the mid-1950s suddenly acquired complete power. In the 1930s and early 1940s there had been the odd modernist, like Leslie Martin or Frederick Gibberd, within the Board of Education. Immediately after the war their numbers slightly increased, so that in 1947, for example, Beaux-Arts practitioners and neo-Georgians like Hector Corfiato, A. E. Richardson, Lionel Budden, Stephen Welsh, Edward Maufe and Darcy Braddell held the majority over a small group of modernists like Richard Sheppard, John Summerson and Ralph Tubbs (RIBA Archives 7.1.1, 1947). But pressure was mounting outside the Board from the MARS Group and the modernist-oriented Association of Building Technicians, impatient of the still strong weight of tradition (P. Johnson-Marshall, pers. comm.).

Whatever the preferences of its individual members the Board as a whole began to recognise the need to update the education it controlled. In 1948 the historical ingredient in the Intermediate syllabus was extended to 'stress the continuous and evolutionary character of the subject and to link the past with the present'.[21] In the following year books by Gropius, Le Corbusier, Wright, Giedion, J. M. Richards and Pevsner were added to the reading list for the history quota of the Intermediate syllabus (RIBA Archives 7.1.1., 1949). It is interesting to note that no such names were mentioned in the general reading list, where writers like Reginald Blomfield, Geoffrey Scott (who could be taken, if mistakenly, as a formalist by modernists) and Clough Williams-Ellis still held sway.

The problem for modernists was whether there was a suitable modernist way to teach history if indeed history needed to be taught after the Bauhaus revolution; as Pevsner had noted in 1950, in the progressive schools it was seen as an 'unavoidable nuisance or acceptable entertainment wholly detached from the tasks of today' (Pevsner 1950: 371). The lead was eventually taken by the Board of Architectural Education, which by 1957 had redefined the approach to the subject in its examination: 'History of Architecture is part of the study of civilisation itself . . . it must be based on the study of the ways and means by which the architectural needs of people at different times and in different places were satisfied'.[22] In a curious way, by treating architectural history in terms of its relationship to the life of societies – as the 'chromosomes of social activity' (Banham 1962–63: 46) – the subject was even more firmly segregated from the life of architects.

It was in this period also that building science began to be canvassed as a modification of the syllabus, extending the area then known as 'services' into a major subject (RIBA Archives 7.1.1., 1948). Building science was one of the pennants under which the modernists marched. It could be a catch-all for any study of the technology and technical principles involved in building; it might sometimes mean the consideration of heat, light and sound, and sometimes the basic principles (equilibrium, gravity, tension etc.) governing structures. Whatever it included it always stood for scientific principles, a quantitative study of the technical aspects of buildings and a greatly enlarged place for that study within the curriculum and within the process of design. The history of this subject is relevant. It was first canvassed as part of architectural education in the late 1920s and 1930s by J. L. Manson, a Board of Education inspector. Manson was on the advisory committee for Robert Fitzmaurice's book *The Principles of Modern Building* (1938). This work became a best-selling 'Bible', presenting 'the application of scientific methods of analysis to . . . functional requirements and the principles that determine success in meeting them' (Lea 1971: 179). In 1946 the Building Research Station set up a new division specifically dealing with the building aspects of heat, light and sound, treating them as the province of science where previously they had been determined empirically and by custom. In the following years the BRS pressed to have building science accepted as a degree subject as well as to have it integrated into architectural education (Lea 1971: 168). The BRS also developed the linked science of ergonomics, published booklets on building science, and ran what was in effect an informal kind of postgraduate school immediately after the war that proved to be influential in disseminating its work (Saint 1987: 25; W. Allen, pers. comm.). In the mid-1950s Liverpool became the first university to have a Department of Building Science. Sheffield and Manchester College of Technology soon followed. Today, where there is no separate department, building science is taught by members of architectural schools. Just as Fitzmaurice's book ignored methods of building construction, so building science has tended to shunt that subject out of architectural education (*RIBAJ*, August 1979: 356–7).

Meanwhile other aspects of the examination system had hardly changed. The subjects given in 1948 for Testimonies of Study in historical design were exemplified by an orangery in a seventeenth-century English garden (RIBA Archives 7.1.2., 1948), while those given as design problems in 1949 included a bird observatory, a kindergarten schoolroom, a royal retiring room and a studio (RIBA Archives 7.1.1., 1949). In 1948 the examination committee disagreed over whether a Testimony of Study in 'Construction Applied to Elementary Design' would be best served by a subject of a house 'in one of the local styles traditional in this country'. Those against this exercise argued that it would produce 'dull and elaborate drawings of semi-obsolete methods' (RIBA Archives 7.1.2., 1948). An interesting incident occurred in 1949 when the Board of Architectural Education proposed to abolish the *en loge* competition for the Tite and Soane Prizes. After letters of complaint had been written by John Brandon Jones, Louis de Soissons, Sir Giles Gilbert Scott and others, the Board backed down on its decision later in the year (RIBA Archives 7.1.4., 1949).

These examples reveal that RIBA educationists were divided and probably a little confused about the manner in which education should be reformed. Besides, it seemed as if examination syllabuses set up by the RIBA could only change in a piecemeal manner. The schools themselves became less ruled by these syllabuses. Indeed the strategy of modernists on the Visiting Boards in the early 1950s seems to have been to advise schools not to base their courses too closely on the examination syllabus (see Bristol's Visiting Board Report in RIBA Archives 7.1.2., 1953). Modernist reformers began to see that the system itself would have to be changed and to do this they would have to direct RIBA policy.

2. The 1946 report

The first of the post-war reports on architectural education appeared in 1946. Serious debate about architectural education had not stopped with the declaration of war in 1939. Although the wartime schools momentarily stopped being arenas for conflict and change, there was some augmentation of the small ideological changes that had occurred in the RIBA before the war through the infiltration of some committees by young modernists.

The RIBA set up a Special Committee on Architectural Education in 1939 and this met thirty-five times throughout the war years. It may have been intended as a response to events at the AA, but officially it met to take stock of changes made since the 1924 conference. Amongst its members were Martin Briggs and Lionel Budden, who had both spoken at the 1924 conference. The RIBA President and Vice-President, W. H. Ansell and Darcy Braddell, were in attendance and the two leading schools were represented; Liverpool by Budden and W. G. Holford (who missed many of the meetings due to his involvement in framing the new town planning policies of the Ministry of Works and Planning – it is possible that if he had been able to attend more the final report would have been a considerably more radical statement), and the AA by Geoffrey Jellicoe. Two interim reports were issued in 1942. The first recommended that students entering training should have passed one recognised examination, replacing the existing system based on letters of recommendation and the submission of drawings. The second interim report suggested that an advisory booklet on office procedure should be issued and argued that the requirement of office experience should be extended from one to two years before Associateship could be gained. Cautious steps were thereby made to encourage a different kind of student to enter architectural education and to reform the relationship of education to office work.

The bulk of the main report issued in 1946 concerned the syllabus itself. Its suggestions were a fudge, with a smattering of safe concessions to new pressures. On the principles and aims of architectural education and the function of the architect, the report came down in favour of an image of the architect as a humanist distinct from the engineer and imbued with the literature, arts and architecture of the past, one who would 'approach his work as an artist aware of science rather than as a scientist aware of art' (RIBA 1946: 7). Although architectural education was to be directed firmly away from an obsession with recent technology, neither was it to be aimed at traditional forms and styles. Instead, in a grand and vague flourish, planning, construction and design were to be melded into one activity and guided by aesthetic principles rather than any specific teaching method.[23] Elsewhere in the curriculum the emphasis was to be on techniques of presentation (including measured drawing, lettering, sketching and sciagraphy), the theory and history of architecture, construction, and town and country planning. What the Beaux-Arts educationists and the modernists could agree upon was a statement of intent that training would be full-time, five years long and firmly based in the schools, since pupillage, which still persisted in the regions, 'will and should fade away'. Ironically, Budden thought that the inclusion of schools of architecture in universities would actually protect them from the 'hazards of revolutionary experiment' (Budden 1945: 250).

The 1946 report was opposed to the domination either of the Beaux-Arts tradition or of modernism. Of the former it noted that, if its prestige had dimmed, many of its accoutrements still survived in the form of ateliers in London, the stressing of 'logical and organic coherence in planning', the problem method and the use of juries to assess student work (RIBA 1946: 22). On classicism it advised that 'though the orders may still be studied, it is in their historical context and as examples of perfect proportion, articulation and detail, rather than with the idea of perpetuating them as architectural forms' (RIBA 1946: 22). In accordance with post-war needs more attention was to be paid to housing. On modernism it commented piously that 'standards of rationality rather than of conscious modernity are prevailing' (RIBA 1946: 28), yet it was opposed to social or economic research in the schools. In the RIBA exams historical coverage was to be extended to the present day, and generally history was to be taught with an eye both to its value as a 'record of means and processes by which the needs of society at different times in different places were satisfied' and to the 'permanent principles of architecture' (RIBA 1946: 32–3).

Thus the 1946 report tried to find a middle way by retaining the acceptable aspects of Beaux-Arts training and adding to them a recognition of modernity, while staking a claim on the neutral ground of good sense, sound practice and an education based primarily on aesthetic considerations. It was not a course designed to appease modernists who criticised the report for being narrowly professional in its concerns, for coming thirty years too late, and for not making the building sciences the primary and foremost study out of which architectural beauty would arise (RIBA Archives 7.1.4., 1946; *AJ*, 105, 8 May 1947: 388; P. Johnson-Marshall, pers. comm.). But this middle way did try to absorb the differences between figures like Budden, who in 1945 seemed to be proclaiming a counter-revolution against the influence of Gropius and other modernists (*RIBAJ*, August 1945: 308), and Holford who seemed to want to fit the Bauhaus into an English Arts and Crafts tradition (*RIBAJ*, December 1948: 165–74). The compromise between these factions remained official RIBA policy into the 1950s,[24] and it was well represented by the introduction in 1951 of a requirement for one year of practical training during all courses.

3. The 1952 Ad Hoc Report

Beaux-Arts figures such as Hector Corfiato, Lionel Budden, Darcy Braddell, Stephen Welsh and Albert Richardson remained on the Board of Architectural Education into the early 1950s. However, their power had considerably diminished there and now mostly resided within their own schools. A good example of this, and of the renewed centralist tendencies, is the 1952 Report of the Ad Hoc Committee on Architectural Education which attempted to increase formal control over the schools' examinations through lists of suggested external examiners. This had been resisted in the 1920s by individual Beaux-Arts heads (Reilly 1938: 214). The 1952 report was supported by the odd traditionalist member of the Board such as Donald MacMorran but resisted by such heads of schools as Budden, Corfiato, Welsh and W. A. Eden (RIBA Archives 7.1.1., 1951). It is significant then that leading advocates of the Beaux-Arts system in Britain all resisted central control. A more general example of their diminished power is the way that the Board, in a kind of anti-Beaux-Arts alliance of modernists and pragmatists, began to address the criticisms made of the Beaux-Arts methods by stressing the relation of the curriculum to practice and advocating more site, workshop and factory visits, and a clearer grasp of architects' responsibilities within the design team (RIBA Archives 7.1.1., 1952).[25]

4. The 1955 MacMorran Report

When a new committee to examine architectural education was formed in 1952 under the chairmanship of Donald MacMorran, many thought that its report would spearhead an attack on the architectural schools (*AJ*, 121, 10 February 1955: 187). It was intended that the report would investigate the training methods actually in use, especially those based on part-time attendance. An Interim Report submitted in 1953, however, sought only to modify what was already in place, recommending, for example, that while more attention should be given to twentieth-century architecture in the Testimonies of Study, there should also be more emphasis on domestic subjects in design work, as well as more sketching. The examination system, the report argued, 'remains the instrument with which the Royal Institute can, itself, shape the course of architectural education', and pupillage 'will, and should, continue to be a means of entry into the profession' (RIBA Archives 7.1.1., 1953). In other words older methods would be encouraged to heal the breach with practice. Not surprisingly, the Interim Report was opposed by such modernist members of the Board as Percy Johnson-Marshall, Robert Matthew, Robert Gardner-Medwin (all three of whom were public sector architects who gained influential posts in architectural schools), and other commentators who pointed out its 'reactionary folly' (*AJ*, 121, 10 February 1955: 187), and called for the phasing out of pupillage and part-time education (RIBA Archives 7.1.2., 1954). MacMorran was seen as somebody who wanted to put a break on experimentation in favour of traditional notions of technical competence – a 'noisy counter-revolutionary' (D. Jones and R. Cave, pers. comm.).

MacMorran's Final Report, published in 1955, proposed other ways of dealing with the perceived distance between education and practice. Its most important recommendations were to end the requirement that drawings should be submitted for entry into training, to extend practical training from one to two years (a suggestion already made in the Special Committee's Interim Report of 1942), and to make the standard of examinations in the schools similar to those of the RIBA (*RIBAJ*, February 1955). If in the eyes of modernists 'nothing more innocuous could be expected' (*AJ*, 121, 10 February 1955: 187), it was now clear that if pupillage was to be phased out then the system within the architectural schools would have to be more carefully geared to office practice. Furthermore, a period of one or two years of practical training following the Intermediate level was thought sufficient to supply experience of office training and thus do away with any need for pupillage.

One of the most interesting of the recommendations was the seemingly insignificant replacement of the RIBA design examinations with an examination based on Testimonies of Study. What was actually happening here was the abolition of one of the last vestiges of the Beaux-Arts tradition, the *en loge* design exercise in which the student was asked 'to analyse a paper problem, produce a series of outline solutions, choose the most promising, and develop it on more or less conventional lines within a limited time' (RIBA Archives 7.1.1., 1954). According to MacMorran's report 'this particular skill is now held in less esteem, and it is felt that the process of design, to be of value, should be based on more detailed researches into the nature of the problem, the means of construction, and other factors capable of influencing the solution' (RIBA Archives 7.1.1., 1954). This move did not go unresisted. Rowland Pierce, a member of MacMorran's committee, was notably vocal in defence of the old system when the recommendation was discussed by the Board of Architectural Education. Pierce pointed out that the *en loge* system was still used by the British School at Rome. Nevertheless when voting took place only five members of the Board wanted to retain the design examination, while nineteen were against it (RIBA Archives 7.1.1., 1954).

5. The modernist takeover of the RIBA, 1954–56

British modernists were not happy with the state of architectural training in the post-war years. They wanted to reform all architectural institutions and to create a uniform system aimed at serving a largely nationalised architectural production. They saw that the way to do this was to take over the RIBA and to give it a much larger role in overseeing what took place in architectural education. By 1955 a new breed of younger, public authority modernists had come to dominate the Board of Architectural Education and the RIBA Council. By 1958 a rigged conference at Oxford had set out the necessary framework and by the early 1960s the RIBA had been made into a kind of crypto-government department to carry this into effect. It is necessary now to understand the way in which this domination had come about.

The number of salaried architects had been growing rapidly both in proportion and in total for two decades. In the late 1930s the RIBA's ideal of the 'independent, artist-constructor-businessman acting in a fiduciary relationship to his client' began to be challenged, particularly by the Association of Architects, Surveyors and Technical Assistants (AASTA, renamed the Association of Building Technicians in 1942) and by a new ideal of permanent salaried employment in large local or central government departments (Summerson 1942: 235). In 1944 the ABT, which had a quarter of RIBA membership, had six of its nominees elected on to the RIBA Council out of ten members elected that year (A. Jackson 1970: 161).[26] By 1953 of some 18,000 registered architects over half held salaried positions in public, commercial or private offices (Jenkins 1961: 239). In 1955 a committee was set up to find ways by which salaried

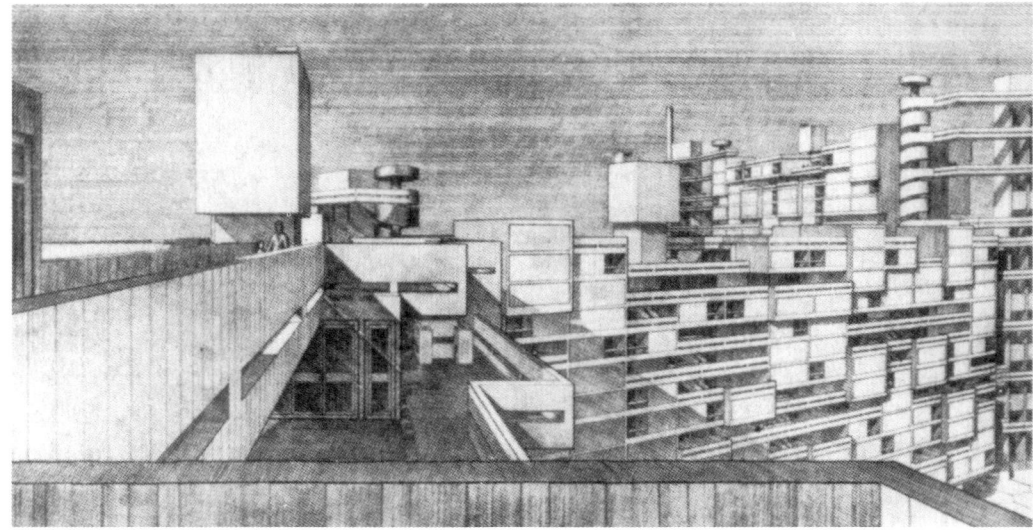

44 Dalton, Eardley, Knott, and Frazer: high-density housing, Paddington – AA fourth-year project (1956)

members could be better represented, but only after 1958 did the RIBA begin to redistribute membership after dismantling the Allied Societies which had retained their Council representation despite falling numbers of independent private architects (A. Jackson 1970: 198–200).

There are at least two forms of conspiracy theory in the interpretation of history. One is soft and general: the belief that events come about because groups of people desire a certain end and work towards it but that this activity is only one factor amongst many. The other is harder and more specific: that people covertly plot together and decide on tactics according to a bigger strategic plan, and that their success at this is why certain events occur. Whatever the dangers of the second form of conspiracy theory it can sometimes serve as one form of corrective to the historicist view that all change is the result of inevitable forces or some natural law. It may help, for example, to describe this new Official System in terms of conspiracy as a way of challenging the still accepted view that it was an inevitable emanation out of the conditions of modernity. If it emanated at all it was out of a myopic vision of what these conditions were: a vision that saw society as existing in a state of rapid and increasing flux and therefore wanted an education that trained for change; a vision that consequently elevated research in building science to a central role in schools, that believed in foisting the results of social surveys on an inert body of secondary clients, and that saw the machine aesthetic as all-pervasive, while it also espoused a belief in artistic self-expression in reaction to these conditions (44).

It was in a two-year period, from 1954 to 1956, that out-and-out modernists became an overwhelming force within the RIBA and its various committees. In part this was a generational change, especially in the case of the Board of Architectural Education, whose membership was always changing anyway. Some members of the older generation, such as Percy Thomas and Howard Robertson, were largely sympathetic to the planned campaign of the younger modernists. Others like Donald MacMorran and Rowland Pierce tried, as we have seen, to stage rearguard actions. It is also important to say that the modernists who acquired power in the the 1950s had several characteristics in common that distinguished them from the members of the 1930s MARS Group. In particular, most of the RIBA modernists had been educated at the AA or Liverpool in the 1930s. They had worked on systems building (particularly for schools and housing) and had conducted rigorous, if perhaps narrowly defined, research programmes. Several had experience in town planning and, as we have shown, many had worked for large public offices. Such characteristics also distinguished these campaigning modernists from most of the modern architects who had been elected to the RIBA Council in 1950, the first year that the majority of its members were modernists (A. Jackson 1970: 176).[27]

According to personal accounts, one of the catalysts for this take-over by campaigning modernists in the mid-1950s, and thus for a unified modernist policy on education, was Stirrat Johnson-Marshall (W. Allen and E. Mills, pers. comm.). Johnson-Marshall had been the most important architect behind the Hertfordshire Schools systems building, and in 1948 had joined the Ministry of Education. Apparently, however, the RIBA Council took a dim view of a Ministry chief architect designing buildings and when Stirrat was elected to the Council in 1953 he began stirring things up. Already Edward Mills and William Allen had been invited to organise the RIBA's annual conference in 1953, and this was arranged in a radical format, namely, a single paper on materials and techniques, with a strong emphasis on the immediate importance of technological development for practice, which formed the subject of discussion for the whole of the conference's two days. With figures like Robert Matthew, Donald Gibson, Leslie Martin, Richard Sheppard, as well as Peter Shepheard and Lionel Brett on the Council, the modernists now 'deliberately set about a revolution' (W. Allen and E. Mills, pers. comm.). Donald Gibson apparently wanted to set up a central architectural body to do all the major government work; a vastly expanded Office of Works even larger than the Architects' Department of the LCC, then the biggest architectural office in the world and treated by many as a kind of postgraduate department. Others wanted the RIBA to extend its purview to encompass planning and industrial design (E. Mills, pers. comm.)

Several members of this coterie held the view that power had to be gained within the RIBA before attainable objectives could be set. When C. H. Aslin, Stirrat Johnson-Marshall's superior at Hertfordshire, succeeded Howard Robertson as President in 1954, one of his major declared aims was to rejig the system of education that had been established some fifty years previously, in order to take account of the number of architects working in public offices, to clarify the distinction between architects and assistants, and to combine practical experience with theoretical training (Aslin 1954: 3). Aslin, Stirrat Johnson-Marshall and William Allen often dined together to plot their next moves at this time: 'We were', as Allen has recounted, 'determined to remake the profession as a profession of modern architects'.[28] They were backed by Everard Haynes, the Secretary to the Education Board, who, in Edward Mills's view, 'did more for architectural education than any other person' (E. Mills, pers. comm.). Reviews of research, office practice and education, and the appointment of modernists who had worked for public authorities as heads of key schools in the 1960s were all connected events brought about by this coterie. It was Allen, for example, who was the prime mover in drawing up the format for the 1958 Oxford Conference (RIBA Archives 7.1.1., 1956). Thus the recommendations of the Oxford Conference, the influential RIBA reports of the early 1960s, and the form of the model modernist schools of the 1960s – all to be discussed shortly – were part of this long campaign. The RIBA even abandoned its Eric Gill-designed badge in 1960 and the *RIBA Journal* adopted a sansserif typeface. We have called the network and policy of education that was set up by these technocratic modernists the 'Official System'.

By the end of the 1950s, then, with the establishment of a modernist hegemony at the RIBA, the schools were increasingly forced into line. By the early 1960s the educational models for this hegemony, both in terms of products and procedures, had been established. Before our attention can turn to this phenomenon we must backtrack a little and see how the vestiges of traditionalism were driven out.

6. Policy of even-handedness in the early 1950s

To summarise, the years around 1950 had witnessed an uneasy balance between the contending forces within the RIBA. Outside it some schools had taken on a clearly modernist outlook, while a declining number of schools functioned within the British Beaux-Arts tradition. Generally the policy of the Board at this stage was one of gentlemanly persuasion towards a middle line: when a Visiting Board inspected the AA in 1950, for example, it noted that there was an overemphasis on group work and that research and experiment (bywords for modernism) started early, but pressed for a 'corresponding responsibility to see that experiment does not get out of step with the student's knowledge, skill and experience' (RIBA Archives 7.1.2., 1950). There were still powerful advocates of the Beaux Arts in the RIBA, although some, like Howard Robertson, had simply converted many of its compositional rules into the forms of modernism. Martin Briggs, a historian and Honorary Secretary at the RIBA, argued for the retention of period designs and the teaching of the Orders. He believed that these practices still provided the best study of evolution, introduced students to aesthetics, and were necessary because much work was concerned with extensions and modifications to existing historical buildings (*RIBAJ*, 58, June 1951: 301–4). Those opposed to him questioned whether this training was of any value once students had passed their examinations (*AJ*, 7 June 1951: 725).

Briggs was a lecturer at the Bartlett (the new name for the architectural school at University College), the last architectural school to retain Beaux-Arts approaches as its guiding rationale. The Bartlett came under great pressure from Visiting Boards during the 1950s as they became more thoroughly modernist. Their remarks exemplify the ways in which modernist attitudes hardened towards a recalcitrant school.

At first, however, just as the Board had held a middle ground over the AA, so it attempted even-handedness towards the ultra-conservative Bartlett. In 1953 the Visiting Board remarked that the Bartlett's intense coverage of history, to which the Board was 'not by any means unsympathetic', crowded out essential studies in the fourth year, such as building materials and construction, specifications and properties. Furthermore, there was an over-strong emphasis on 'draughtsmanship and presentation and on the study of "classical forms"' (RIBA Archives 7.1.2., 1953).

In response the Bartlett's head, Hector Corfiato, pointed out that the Board's recommendations were not to be found in the report it made after its visit in 1947, and therefore it seemed that the Board had changed its policy. His main defence against the point that the school did not give sufficient attention to a training in technology was to argue, as indeed many heads argue today, that the university was not interested in training employees and instead 'endeavours to produce cultured and scholarly architects'. The Beaux-Arts-trained Corfiato believed that the Orders were part of the study of precedent required by all subjects, and that to give a project for a small building in the first year, as the Board suggested, was to put the cart before the horse; students needed to learn the 'ABC of architecture' first before designing (RIBA Archives 7.1.2., 1953).[29] In these points he was supported by the chairman of the Bartlett's Board of Studies, who saw the stress on technology as threatening to 'reduce university education to the standard of a technical school', and considered that the Visiting Board's remarks about the Orders expressed 'a fashion or mood of a section of the profession' (RIBA Archives 7.1.2., 1953).

When it returned to the Bartlett late in 1958, the Visiting Board's attitude had hardened considerably. Indeed from all accounts Corfiato's own attitude had slipped to one of lazy dilletantism – the Bartlett's declining years did not supply an example for any traditionalist. Early in 1958 Bartlett students had themselves begun to co-ordinate their complaints about Corfiato's regime. Some of them sent a letter to the Board urging it to investigate the school's decline: 'we believe', they wrote, 'that a thorough investigation would reveal that the general principles governing contemporary architectural education, as enumerated, for example, by Professor Gropius in his "Blueprint for an Architectural Education", have never taken root in the Bartlett School'. A petition was signed by 108 of the 110 members of the second, third, fourth and fifth years, complaining of the school's 'outmoded' nature and demanding an investigation (RIBA Archives 7.1.4., 1958).[30]

Unsurprisingly, the judgement of the 1958 Visiting Board was damning. The Bartlett, it reported, made little reference to the study of materials, building science or services. In its history courses there was little study of twentieth-century architects, buildings or theories. Its studio work was 'dull and uninspired', with an unrealistic approach; it was heavily biased in favour of traditional building, which was insufficiently understood: for instance, its 'working drawing dealt too often with methods of construction rarely in use today'. In general 'this traditional approach appears to be a negative one, based on a dislike of what people are doing today rather than on a love for the past' (RIBA Archives 7.1.2., 1958).

Armed with this report the Visiting Board threatened to withdraw recognition from the Bartlett. William Holford, who in 1949 had succeeded Abercrombie as Professor of Town Planning at the Bartlett, became a useful mediator. A solution was found by suggesting that a Professor designate should be appointed to succeed the retiring Corfiato, in order to 'overhaul the whole curriculum' (RIBA Archives 7.1.2., 1958). Richard Llewelyn Davies, one of the prime movers behind the Oxford Conference and one of the leading modernist students at the time of the AA's 1938 crisis, was soon appointed to this position (45).

The Bartlett was the most resolutely traditional of all the schools in the 1950s. But others had vestiges of the Beaux-Arts system which were increasingly squeezed out by the Visiting Boards. Northern Polytechnic, for example, had the extent of its classical designs carefully regulated by the Visiting Board in 1954 (RIBA Archives 7.1.2., 1954). Liverpool University's working drawings were said to be too elaborate and too detailed to meet modern office needs (RIBA Archives 7.1.2., 1956). The Visiting Board advised the Scott Sutherland School in Aberdeen to replace its formal examination in sciagraphy and perspective with additional studio exercises (RIBA Archives 7.1.2., 1957). At Oxford Polytechnic, however, the Orders continued to be taught until the late 1960s.

45 Richard (Lord) Llewelyn Davies with Henry Moore (*c*.1965)

The Oxford Conference of 1958

It has been crucial to modernist educators to emphasise the Oxford Conference's significance as a watershed; before there had been chaos, after there was order. It is often claimed that at Oxford in the space of three days modernist architects and educationists laid the groundwork necessary to impose the kind of training they desired throughout Britain. Most fundamentally, the conference has been perceived as marking a change in the vision of architecture from an artistic one to a scientific one. But in fact, as we have seen, important changes had come about at the RIBA in the twelve years since the 1946 report, not least of which was the eclipse of the Beaux-Arts tradition, and indeed of non-modernist architecture generally, by the delayed but now rapidly rising sun of modernism. However, there was still no sense of a coherent and consistent policy towards education and it will be argued here that the real result of the Oxford Conference was to consolidate the changes that had been taking place and to achieve a coherent policy throughout all the architecture schools recognised by the RIBA.

The idea for a conference on architectural education was hatched at the Board of Architectural Education in 1955 by those modernists who had recently taken control. Traditionalists realised, quite early in its organisation, the intent behind the conference; for example, Stephen Welsh, head at Sheffield, attacked it in 1957 for its 'narrowness of outlook', and complained that speakers and topics from 'another "lodge" or school of thought would not be welcome' (RIBA Archives 7.1.2, 1957). The conference was indeed carefully organised; lists of speakers were vetted, preparatory papers circulated, and attendance restricted to fifty-three invited guests and speakers who would meet for three days in April 1958 at Magdalen College, Oxford. Save for one or two traditionalists like Raymond Erith, almost all of the participants were modernist reformers, including all the key figures: Leslie Martin, Richard Llewellyn Davies, Percy Johnson-Marshall, William Allen, Richard Sheppard and Robert Matthew. It was decided to have three sessions, one to deal with professional needs, one to deal with routes of entry, standards and means of education, and one concerned with the development of advanced training and research.

In the absence of surviving minutes we are largely dependent on Leslie Martin's official report for an account of what actually went on at the conference (Martin 1958: 279–83). The number of candidates still taking RIBA examinations was a topic of discussion, as was the wide range of institutions teaching architecture: there were twenty-one fully recognised schools, five recognised up to Intermediate level, and forty-one that could only offer coaching for the RIBA exams (nine listed, and thirty-two facility schools). Attention was drawn to the different aims and standards amongst these schools. Much discussion seems to have focused on ways in which standards of entry could be raised while still providing diversified practitioners, and this was linked to ideas about the best places for education. Unrecognised schools and part-time courses received scant praise from this band of modernist professionals. Furthermore, the importance of research, that key word for British modernists, was emphasised, especially through a paper given by Richard Llewelyn Davies entitled 'Deeper Knowledge: Better Design'.

At the end of the three days, six 'recommendations for action' were decided upon:

1 Entry should be raised to a minimum of two 'A' levels
2 Courses based on RIBA examinations would be progressively abolished
3 Recognised schools should be in universities or similar institutions
4 Courses should be either full-time or sandwich

5 Other forms of training not leading to an architectural qualification would have to be devised

6 Postgraduate work (i.e. research) is essential and should be expanded

Amongst these, the most important recommendations made by the Oxford Conference were the raising of the standards of entry into architectural schools to two 'A' levels and the linked recommendation that courses should be full-time or sandwich and held in universities or similar institutions. At one stroke a policy had been adopted that would bring about the emphasis on full-time academic education that had been so strongly desired both in 1924 and 1946. Whether the intentions in 1958 were quite the same as on those occasions is doubtful. Following the 1946 report, for example, the RIBA had supported training within a diversity of architectural schools. As well as schools recognised for exemption from RIBA examinations there were also 'listed' schools (that provided full-time education without exemption) and 'facilities' schools (whose part-time courses were also not exempted). Although the number of schools exempted from the Intermediate examination had risen steadily in the previous twenty years, nevertheless many students in the 1930s had qualified by attending part-time courses and taking RIBA external examinations. Edward Mills, who qualified in 1937, worked as an office boy in the day and attended Regent Street Polytechnic in the evenings. The Polytechnic charged thirty shillings a year although it was subsidised by the LCC (E. Mills, pers. comm.). Part-time training, which really meant part-time academic education, enabled many people who had not had the privilege of full-time education to aspire to be architects. The numbers were still high in 1957, when 486 students qualified through recognised schools and 417 took RIBA external examinations (Musgrove, 1983: 107). And even by 1960, before the Oxford recommendations had come into effect, only 22 per cent of students were doing full-time architectural courses at universities compared with 63 per cent at art or technical schools (*AJ*, 135, 20 June 1962: 1377).

The 1958 conference also decided to place an overriding stress on university-level schools, much as had been already established in the USA. In the view of Elizabeth Layton, who was appointed Secretary to the Board of Architectural Education in 1962 in order to carry out the conference's recommendations, the raising of entry requirements entailed a new 'intellectual standard' for architectural courses (Trombley 1983: 90). And it seems that she saw this recommendation as implying that *all* architectural education should be in universities (E. Mills, pers. comm.). Indeed the issue seems to have been the only one that generated some dispute at the conference itself, as well as later on. Leslie Martin, apparently, wanted to split architectural education into three years at *university-level* institutions, followed by two years of training elsewhere. Later, Layton and others wanted to have a watertight system *entirely* based upon the universities. A compromise seems to have been worked out by William Allen and Edward Mills whereby 'university-level' meant colleges, universities and polytechnics, and a sandwich system meant three years in, one year out, followed by two years in and one year out – the system that generally prevails today (E. Mills, pers. comm.). Since most of those who attended the conference were modernists it is worth considering their previous position on this issue as well as the implications of their stress upon it.

In the late 1940s the MARS Group in particular had taken a close interest in the numbers of those educated outside the schools through a combination of external examinations and pupillage.[31] As 'hard' modernists, MARS members had seen a way to break the continuing hold of the RIBA exams by publicising the numbers who still took them and by advocating the raising of entry standards into the profession so that training would take place almost exclusively in the schools. The schools rather than pupillage would now be the ideal place for modernist initiatives, especially those versions of the Bauhaus method which were inconceivable outside them; this contrasts with Lionel Budden's reasoning in 1945 that university education would actually form a bulwark against too rapid change. The implication of the 1958 recommendation to locate training exclusively in the university-level schools, therefore, was that they were best suited to enforce the modernist ethos. Moreover, the new entry requirements would encourage the faculties of environmental studies advocated by Percy Johnson-Marshall and others, and stimulate the teaching of building science. They would also considerably lessen the time and importance given to drawing, which was not seen as a university subject. The new academic students were expected to be faster workers. Architecture would be regarded rather as an academic than a practical discipline with design more rigorously underpinned by theory, and the architectural profession would gain kudos amongst the other professions for being the first to demand such a high level of entry.

From this period the universities in turn seem to have become very interested in architecture as an academic subject. When the new policies advocated by the Robbins Report (1963) were eventually added to the higher entrance requirement levels, architecture seemed to resemble an ideal generalist subject, merging the arts and sciences – the Two Cultures – and with an applied element to boot. Although this notion was never carried into effect it closely matched many architects' desire to place architecture within faculties including all the building professions and involving specialist teaching staff from the sciences and social sciences; for this, university-level institutions were essential. And of course with these professional liaisons established in higher institutions, the Lethabitic or Ruskinian ideals were even more marginalised.

Looking forward, the situation envisaged in 1958 was ideal for experiment and expansion. Faculties of environmental studies or groupings very similar to them had been set up at Liverpool (1953), and in the 1960s it was joined by Regent Street (1960), the Bartlett (1965) and Sheffield (1965), amongst others. Problems arose from this at the Bartlett and Bristol, which both stipulated maths and physics 'A' levels. These schools were run by leading members of the Board of Architectural Education (Llewelyn Davies and Douglas Jones) and both ran into difficulties with their introduction of new specialists and their emphasis on building science at the expense of older skills. Practitioners found that graduates from these schools in the late 1960s were notably poor in drawing and design. The scientific bias of the leading theorists in architectural education encouraged many other schools to demand at least one science 'A' level.

The conference's attitude to examinations was linked to its advocacy of full-time courses and of university-based departments. Its discussions about RIBA examinations clearly expressed the growing sense that they were inappropriate and out of touch with contemporary needs; that an attempt to assess students' acquisition of a static body of knowledge was incompatible with the flux of the social and technological world. The continued existence of RIBA examinations might also enable many schools to remain relatively immune from reforming policies. Examinations also enabled the continuation of pupillage with all its accumulated associations with the *ad hoc*, and its myths of neglectful and corrupt practices. It is interesting that where the nineteenth-century utilitarian radicals had called for examinations in order to control entry, those very examinations were now seen as supporting the continuation of a practice that excluded the range of modernist interests and forms of training. The accumulative, skill- and knowledge-based aims of pupillage were anathema to these bureaucratic and academic modernists. But although they have succeeded in reducing the centrality of the examinations in RIBA policy, and hence in architectural training, they have never been completely phased out. The reason for this is quite simple, although it seems to have taken much work by Everard Haynes, the Secretary to the Board of Architectural Education until 1962, to convince the modernists of it. If the RIBA had stopped its examinations then it would have been possible that the other groupings on ARCUK could press for that body to hold examinations, and thus the RIBA would lose its control of entry into the profession. It was better for the examinations to continue but with less influence.

The conference had debated the issue of whether a class of architectural technicians should be formally created. Its conclusions were to some extent pre-empted by a paper that William Allen had presented to the Board of Architectural Education in 1956, entitled 'Training for the Profession as a Whole' (RIBA Archives 7.1.1., 1956). At this time most general office work was done by unqualified or newly-qualified architects; work such as site investigations, working drawings, details, tracing, drawing up contracts and so on. With the conference's proposal to abolish pupillage and part-time courses and the recommendation to raise the level of entry into the profession, the old sources of technicians would dry up. If these did not come from the old external examination students then they must come from a new source. In effect two tiers would have to be created each with their distinct methods of training and qualification; one to have practical skills, the other to control design. This also accorded with the attempts of the Association of Building Technicians, well thought of for their support of modernist policies (and usually represented on the Board of Architectural Education by a modernist such as Percy Johnson-Marshall), for greater recognition. In 1965 the Society of Architectural and Allied Technicians was formed. The training for these technicians was strictly tested by the ONC and HNC examinations which from 1964 were largely controlled by the RIBA. Their curriculum included geology, soil mechanics, theory of structures, structural design, law, finance and management (RIBA Archives 7.1.2., 1959). To keep the boundaries between the categories clear the technicians were given instruction in design appreciation rather than actual studio work. The paradox here was that out of this recommendation the technicians were eventually given a system which included day release, evening classes and recognized exams (from the age of sixteen), many of the items that were being phased out for the architects. The recommendation to create the new class should also be seen as one aspect of the many ways in which the profession continued to tighten its boundaries and augment its control over the building trade. Its formal separation of architectural categories was directly in line from the ideas of Cockerell and Kerr a century before (Saint 1983: 61).

When the Oxford Conference advocated research it did not mean the rather loose sense of that term as practised by pre-war MARS Group members. Instead, the new notion of research took off from the Rowse–Geddes tradition and the experiences of war work and was exemplified by the Hertfordshire Schools programme, by the Ministry of Education development group, by the work of William Allen on day-lighting at the Building Research Centre, by Leslie Martin's study of building densities and by the work of Richard Llewelyn Davies on hospitals for the Nuffield Foundation. In other words research was to investigate the possibilities of industrial production and the best environment for the physical needs of users, and it was to do this using the procedures of the physical and social sciences. This attitude to research was often consciously inspired by the specialised activities of modern science; in Andrew Saint's words, a group working on research regarded itself as 'a vanguard removed from everyday tasks to find some radical solution of general applicability to a pressing technical problem' (Saint 1987: 116; Allen 1953).

At this point it is worth broadly signalling the consequences for British architecture of this emphasis on a particular, and apparently innocuous, notion of research. It was not, of course, an idea limited to postgraduate work, but permeated the ideology of modernist architectural education. As Leslie Martin put it,

> Post-graduate research could provide an operational framework for clarifying the issues that are involved and parcelling out the problems to be solved . . . an area of study carried out by research students at the level of 'Strategies' could be broken down into sections of decreasing complexity capable of development at the 'Tactical' level by students from the second year onwards (Martin 1961).

This necessitated the recruitment of specialists who could teach a range of non-architectural subjects as a grounding for future research. This in turn had the effect of limiting the time spent on design as well as on professional, drawing and building skills in favour of an orientation towards new subject areas in the pure and social sciences. Such a conception of research picked up on the Bauhaus notion that all assumptions should be questioned and researched as if no satisfactory solutions had been reached previously. This led to that most airily 'systematic' of 1960s pursuits, systematic design methodology, in which the inductive methods of science were to be applied actually as methods of design.

Rather than a watershed, the Oxford Conference should be seen as a significant step in consolidating the march of modernism through the institutions of architecture. Its conclusions were certainly controversial, but its supporters had already gained such institutional leverage within the RIBA, the architectural schools and the Ministry of Education, that it could hardly be resisted. Critics of the conference's recommendations pointed out that its two-tier system threatened to limit the chances of working up through apprenticeship, to create a strong divide between 'long-haired architects and short-haired technologists', and to take away the chances of those who depended on part-time education in the interests of the full-time educators, who were overwhelmingly represented at the conference.[32] But there was in general, as the *Architects' Journal* put it, 'no effective opposition by reactionary architects to extending and developing the school training system' (*AJ*, 17 April 1958: 563). The Oxford Conference was a rubber stamp making official the modernist changes that had already gathered strong force in the post-war years. Broadly, it moved education from a largely professional to an entirely academic basis, ostensibly offering a purer sense of 'necessary knowledge' rather than 'professional knowhow' (Maxwell 1983: 113).

Thus it left questions about the forms and standards of education, and especially of the content of the curriculum, unspecified and simply offered the framework within which architectural knowledge could be imparted and advanced. It may have been this that prompted MacMorran to say in 1958, 'To obtain a university degree in architecture today it is necessary to appeal to the personal taste of the design examiners' (RIBA Archives 7.1.2., 1958). The reason for the absence of these topics was threefold. First, there was the fact that the teaching of modernist architecture had already taken over almost all the schools. Second, there was no consensus about approaches to design amongst the modernists, except for the negative one that no one wanted the old Beaux-Arts approach to design.

The third and most important reason can be found in the idea, often adopted by modernists, that the modern world is a place of continuous change and, accordingly, no system or approach, let alone a style, should be fixed. Education would both encourage change and equip its students with the attitudes that would enable them to expect and cope with this change. Accordingly the framework would enable flexibility within it subject to the discretionary powers of its managers, or in this case of its teachers, heads of school, and RIBA Visiting Boards.

The RIBA and architectural education in the 1960s

By 1964 William Allen could finally declare that this new educational system was in place and that the modernists had won (Allen 1964). In the 1960s the RIBA and its Board of Architectural Education became the heart and leading edge of educational change in a way that it had not been since the Board was first set up in the early years of the century. Its renewed influence was partly the result of internal reforms and new personnel, and partly of a fundamental change in its relation to education. The leading personnel at the RIBA now consisted of those architects who had been most active in applying the ethic of progressive paternalism through public service architecture in the 1940s and 1950s; men such as Alex Gordon, Hugh Wilson, Richard Llewelyn Davies, Henry Swain and Bernard Adams. From 1960 there was a succession of Presidents who had worked in public offices; William Holford, Robert Matthew, Donald Gibson and Lionel Brett. Intellectual direction was supplied by figures like Llewelyn Davies, Leslie Martin and William Allen, who were all in good positions to influence others in architectural schools, research establishments and public offices. Following reforms advocated by the Oxford Conference Committee, the Board of Architectural Education had a new cohesion and purposiveness about it (46). Many of its members had gone through the LCC and the Ministry of Education and their ideals were based on anonymous service and control over such public resources as housing and planning. As we have seen, some of them had infiltrated the establishment through stealth, coups and caucus meetings. Now they held the reins of power.

These people brought a new energy and an infectious dedication to the Council and they were particularly determined that the new framework for education should be a success (E. Layton, pers. comm.). They came from civil service departments such as the Ministry of Town and Country Planning to an

46 The RIBA Board of Architectural Education in session (1969)

organisation that was reforming itself on quasi-civil service lines to become a kind of Ministry of Architecture dominated by a managerial culture. Of the most influential new officers, Gordon Ricketts replaced the long-ensconced Ian MacAllister as Secretary to the Council and Elizabeth Layton replaced the even longer-established Everard Haynes as Under-Secretary to the Board of Architectural Education in 1962. The new officers not only had the same values as the Council, they also had a more energetic and prominent conception of their role; Layton, for example, had worked with the legendary Dame Evelyn Sharp at the Ministry of Health during the war, and was employed by the New Towns Development Corporation, working closely with Frederick Gibberd at Harlow New Town and writing a study of how local authorities ran their building departments (*Building by Local Authorities*, 1961). In the 1960s these officers were supported by a considerably expanded staff.

The RIBA's new attitude to education entailed a revamping of the Visiting Boards and, following the recommendations of the Oxford Conference, an emphasis on research and a considerably reduced interest in the external examinations. Research, as recommended by the Oxford Conference, was fostered both in the schools and in the RIBA itself. Bill Hillier, Alex Gordon and Richard Llewelyn Davies were on hand to help the RIBA to guide research in the schools, especially research into subjects of a social scientific or technological bias. If it had become rather a form of civil service department than the trade union that John Summerson had wanted in 1942, the RIBA had at least now become 'a centre of, or at any rate the mouthpiece for, technical research' (Summerson 1942: 237).

[145]

The earliest results of the RIBA's own research were *The Architect and His Office* and Elizabeth Layton's *Report on the Practical Training of Architects*, both published in 1962, having been produced across the corridor from each other in Portland Place. They had important implications for architectural education. Like the raised standards of entry, *The Architect and his Office* did much to elevate the status of architects in relation to other professions. Here architects were seen to be examining their practices in a rigorous and public manner. There were sharp criticisms of the way many private offices were run, particularly the smaller ones. Much of the reason for this, the report argued, was because the business aspects of the profession were neglected by architectural education. Furthermore, architectural education should be diversified by allowing students to specialise in one of eight technical aspects: management, work study, ergonomics, 'psycho-physics', services, structures, building economics and production engineering.

In the Layton Report the remoteness of students from the realities of the architectural profession was compared unfavourably with medicine and engineering. Layton advocated the urgent adoption of the two-year practical training period that had been recommended by the 1955 MacMorran Report, and a more varied range of training involving experience with builders, manufacturers, engineers and quantity surveyors. Layton wanted more management training in the schools and more closely defined and supervised practical experience with schools taking on the main responsibility for co-ordinating training. To assess progress she argued for the use of log-books and an index of those architects' offices that offered the best opportunities for training.[33] The new rigorous approach to practical training, together with the reorganised relationship between technicians and architects was to sound the final death-knell of the pupillage system. The Layton Report, like the *Architect and His Office*, also helped to promote a new belief in the values of a managerial and entrepreneurial outlook that has gradually taken over the older professional ethos (see Saint 1983).

Although a committee had been set up immediately after the Oxford Conference to implement its recommendations, movement was relatively slow. Of 842 new students in 1962, 618 had two 'A' levels and there were insufficient university-level schools to house even this number (Startup 1984: 83). When Elizabeth Layton was appointed she was specifically charged with putting the recommendations of the Oxford Conference into effect. Thus things began to move more quickly. The Visiting Boards were overhauled and the system of examinations and Testimonies of Study was run down. Visits were expanded to two days, more information was requested from the schools before visits, and reports became longer and more detailed. The Visiting Boards now became the main plank in the RIBA's new policy towards education. The external examinations and Testimonies of Study had previously been regarded as the models by which education in the schools should be shaped. They had changed slowly over the years and by the early 1960s it was apparent to most at the RIBA, as it had been clear to the majority of the schools, that they were 'archaic and inflexible – too arduous and too limited' (E. Layton, pers. comm.). Testimonies of Study were regarded as time-consuming set pieces requiring little imagination and were finally abolished in 1967 (see Appendix), while examinations were seen to foster a crammer's attitude to education. The rejection of a system that had provided at least a sense of a core curriculum to the schools was accompanied by the considerably increased significance attached to the Visiting Boards. What had happened in effect was that a system of prescribed syllabuses, curricula and procedures was deliberately neglected and largely replaced by one based on the discretionary powers accorded to an appointed group of experts. We must state this carefully. Others certainly had a say in architectural education, including ARCUK, university examination boards and external examiners, and, from 1965, the architectural board of the CNAA. Yet none of these had such a grasp on policy and such a guiding hand on the link between training and practice as the RIBA and its Board of Architectural Education. Even the most ardent Beaux-Arts supporters had not envisaged this degree of control.

How was this new discretionary system to operate and what policies did it advocate? The Visiting Boards consisted of two practitioners and two teachers chosen from a panel of twelve. This panel was intended to be a cross-section of the best from the architectural firmament and inevitably this meant that they came from the schools with reputations for innovation and the most renowned public practices. Their members met and worked out policies but they also learnt from the experiments of the schools. They had no explicit terms of reference because these would have contravened their discretionary nature. Instead, according to Elizabeth Layton, they were concerned with standards, they advocated what was appropriate to 'the climate of the times', and they encouraged the ideas of the RIBA by putting pressure on the schools.

Changes were intended to come about 'by evolution rather than programmatically', because the ideal relationship between the Visiting Boards and the schools was one of 'discretion, tact and enlightenment' (E. Layton, pers. comm.). Where, however, an architecture school was still basing its curriculum on the external examinations and providing largely part-time courses, it was closed down; this was the fate, for example, of the Bournemouth School of Architecture and of the departement at Southend College of Art in the late 1960s. Elsewhere the Visiting Boards worked more subtly. They might suggest, say, that more research should be done or they might encourage more building science. Although individual members of the Visiting Boards might enjoy measured drawings, for example, they did not insist upon these being undertaken and so they faded in importance. Towards the end of the decade the

Board of Architectural Education became concerned with resisting the proliferation of new schools because they did not think they had sufficient specialist teachers for the kind of departments they desired.[34]

As with many other policies, such a system relied on having the right personnel in the right positions. In other words a Visiting Board could press for change, as they had with the Bartlett in the 1950s, but this would have minimal effect unless sympathetic principals and teachers were already in place.

Key Official System schools

The most influential schools during the 1960s were those most closely linked to the personnel at the Board of Architectural Education and its Visiting Board panel. Bristol, under Douglas Jones from 1962, took on a strong scientific bent emphasising engineering and building science, and especially a bias towards 'mathematical analysis' (*Architect*, 4 July 1974: 40). In 1961 William Allen was appointed Principal at the AA specifically in order to improve the technological side of education there (47). But the two flagships of the Official System were undoubtedly the Bartlett and Cambridge.

The Bartlett underwent the most dramatic change of character when Richard Llewelyn Davies replaced Hector Corfiato as head of the school in 1960. As a prominent member of the Board of Architectural Education, Llewelyn Davies brought with him their intention 'to overhaul the whole curriculum' (RIBA Archives 7.1.1., 1958). As we have seen, Llewelyn Davies already had a reputation as an ambitious leader. He had taken a degree in engineering and been a prominent student radical at the AA in the late 1930s. His inaugural lecture at the Bartlett presented a kind of manifesto. His stated aim was to bring science and art together after their separation by the Beaux-Arts tradition (Llewelyn Davies 1961: 3). By 'art' he meant neither artistry nor a learned compilation of sources, but rather an unsullied talent, and so the new Bartlett course was to have its first six months devoted, like the *Vorkurs*, to freeing the student 'from all pre-conceived ideas about form . . . helping him to use first hand experience' (Llewelyn Davies 1961: 6). There would then be parallel courses in the school workshops and in design, the first being aimed at a 'direct feeling for form and material', while the second was studied in tandem with the psychology of vision and the physics of light (Llewelyn Davies 1961: 7). Models were constructed so that 'allometry, semiotics, Markovian process, sensory thresholds, self-regulating systems, Boolean algebra, theory of measurement or the theory of limits' could be examined (48; Latourell 1969: 91). Llewelyn Davies saw the first year as the time when the fundamentals of a range of sciences and social sciences should be taught, in order that environmental and social factors should be seen as inherent to the process of design.

To implement this new education experts in technology, science, planning

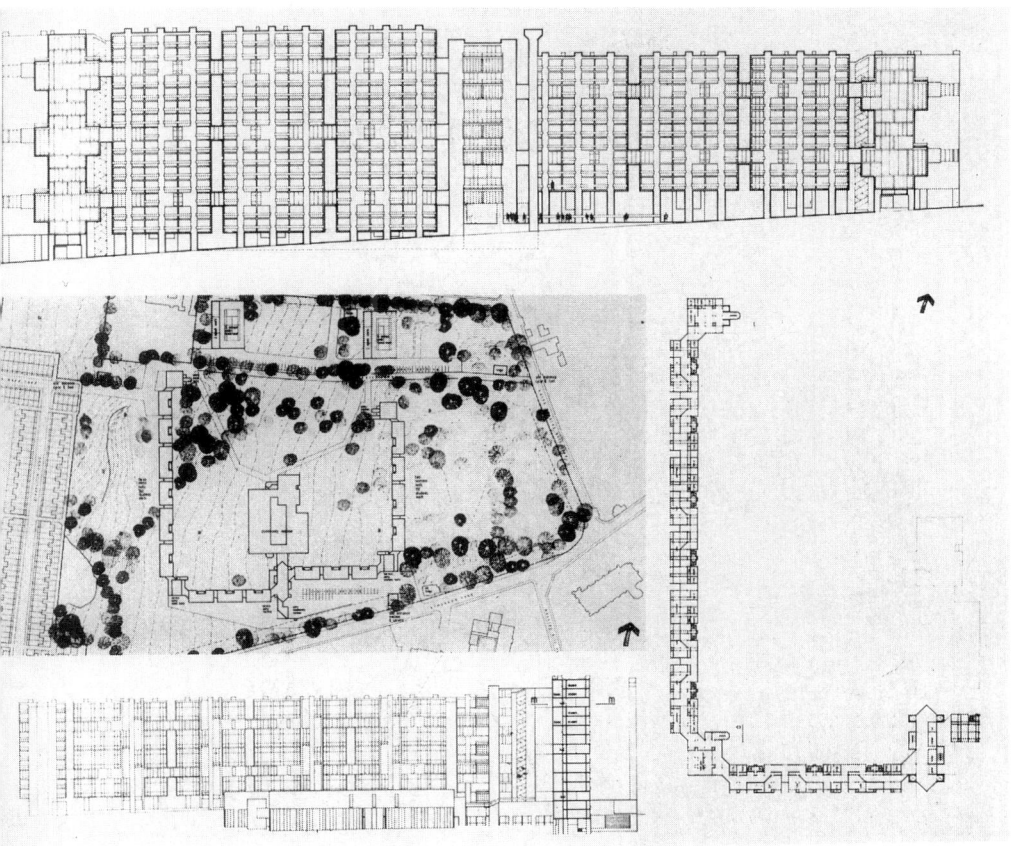

47 Michael Macrae: 'Carnatic Community' – fifth-year thesis, AA (1962)

and the social sciences were brought in (49). Research would be the dominating idea and the way in which teaching, theory and advanced practice would be joined together (Llewelyn Davies 1961: 10). History would be taught as the understanding of how architects in the past had dealt with certain problems: methods and principles of enquiry would be learnt rather than the forms taken by past buildings (Llewelyn Davies 1961: 11). Design was still central, but now it could be presented through writing, speech and other communication as well as through drawing. In teaching design the aim would be to free the student from preconceptions. The architect, stripped of acquired culture, would be able to confront nature (the 'problem') afresh. Once this was achieved in the first year the student would move on to increasingly larger and more complex subjects and design problems in the succeeding years. In this way students would be given an education that would not just equip them for

48 Bartlett School: allometry model (*c.*1965)

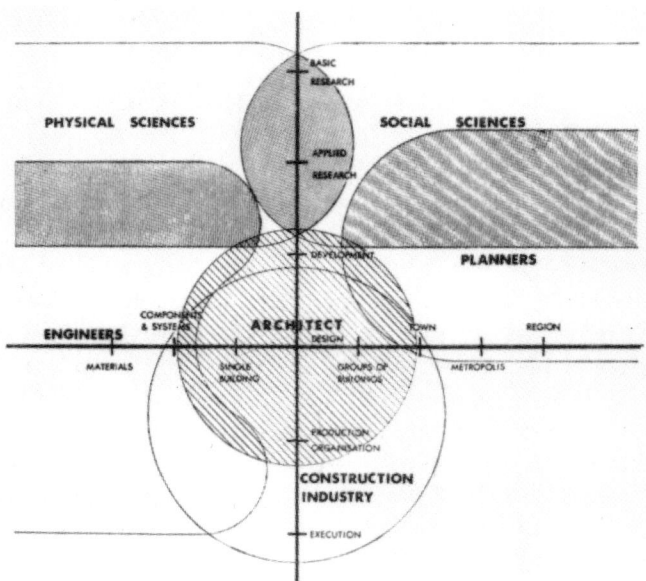

49 Richard Llewelyn Davies: diagram showing the architect's relation to other professions (1967)

50 Le Corbusier and Sir Leslie Martin in front of a drawing by Henry Moore during
Corbusier's visit to the Cambridge School in 1959

change, but would also, Llewelyn Davies hoped, enable them to initiate change
in society (Latourell 1969: 88).

When Leslie Martin took over as head of the architecture school at
Cambridge in 1956 he already had experience as head of the school at Hull
during the late 1930s. There he had the scope to introduce modernist teachers
and ideas but not the power to find a suitable curricular and institutional
embodiment for them. At Cambridge Martin established a degree course in
1958, in 1959 building science was introduced, and by the beginning of the next
decade he had set out the structure that has largely been maintained by his successors (50). As we might expect from the man who chaired the Oxford
Conference, the course typified the Official System. It had a three-tiered structure consisting of basic training, a period intended to extend the student's
range, and finally research. The 'strategy' of the research level would be broken
down to be dealt with at the 'tactical' level by students from their second year
onwards (Martin 1961).

The first year was intended to reacquaint students with their sensory or pre-
cultural judgements through basic draughtsmanship, perception and colour
studies (using Gestalt theory and the Munsell system of colour measurement),

and to re-equip them through building science, mechanics and a range of other 'objective' subjects. A wooden model was made of a simple building with a large-scale model of one portion of it. There were exercises with abstract reliefs, and a spatial problem was set involving a simple brick construction on a modular base.

The course was itself modelled on an ideal vision of design as a rational process of research. Having isolated the parts and broken down the problem in the first year, the following years were devoted to the re-fusion of these parts. Studio projects became larger and more complex, paralleling the greater difficulty of the subject teaching. The degree course was intended as an intensive basic training, teaching – in a memorable metaphor borrowed from Colin St John Wilson – the 'jungle-fighter's' self reliance in a hostile environment' (Martin 1961; 1970). Design projects were usually flat-roofed, small-scale, with a marked use of wood amongst their generally mixed materials. In their fourth and fifth years students did more technical and specialised work, which might be connected to the research done in the Centre for Land Use and Built Form Studies (set up by Martin soon after starting at Cambridge and later renamed after him). Theoretically, then, research on families and housing, daylighting, and the growth of 'restrictive' legislation, actively aided by the teaching of sociologists and economists, could be directly fed into the students' detailed work on projects for housing. Ideally this research would enable an open choice between fully-explored options (Martin 1961).

Some key beliefs of the Official System

The most salient policy issues in architectural education in the 1960s were also those advocated by the RIBA. The five most notable were architecture at university level; faculties of environmental studies; building science; practical training; and research. These overlapped and proved to be mutually facilitating, and the often repeated trinity that guided this new educational consensus was 'diversification, specialisation, integration'. In some ways this may appear no more than the evolutionary outcome of the calls for academic education and for breaking the barriers between practice and education that had been a common theme in every conference and committee on architectural education since at least 1904. But if these appeared to be similar themes they only thinly disguised a different consensus. Throughout, the emphasis was on integrating rational or scientific practices into a discipline whose outlines were becoming both more blurred and more all-encompassing just as its particular procedures and experiences were being emphasised. Thus, for example, a major focus was upon the manipulation and cognition of architectural space. But this was to be taught not by architects but through bringing in psychologists and sociologists to teach its human aspects and scientists specialising in acoustics, heating and lighting, to teach its environmental aspects.

This twofold movement of the teaching of architecture, outwards and inwards, needs explanation. Just as modernist theory in the arts in general had concentrated upon the qualities and possibilities inherent in and unique to the medium, so in architecture those experiences and procedures that were considered peculiar to buildings were those upon which attention was focused. Hence courses were devoted to materials, colour, space, construction and the various building sciences. These subjects were abstracted from past rules and from their acquired meanings. Architecture was seen, of course, as an undeniably social art but its very 'realism' was to be dealt with by using the newly-related specialisms to re-examine the activities that it served, discarding the lessons of precedents, traditions and conventions. These were replaced by a study of needs and the exhibition (or 'honesty') of use and construction. Similarly it was a basic premise of much of the research that was fostered by architectural departments that it should go back to first principles and consider every problem anew as if there had been no inherited body of knowledge and practice. Just as with research so with the individual student a process of clearing away the detritus of culture would take place, thus supposedly returning him or her to the inherent creativity of the child. The old Romantic notion of free creative individualism was now to be linked to the lessons of certain kinds of art education and psychology, and some of the modes of avant-garde activity in art. Typical of this were the words placed adjacent to a photograph of a child cutting paper by the head of the Nottingham School of Architecture in 1962:

> We do not get the best from students. Blockages in the desire, or ability, to work or think can only be tackled from the point of view of therapy. (Discipline as imposed by those who are in authority, having been thoroughly discredited as a method for our times 'should' is replaced by 'why does he not?') To provide opportunity for working the rough complexes, inhibitions and fears (basically the fear of freedom and pleasure) becomes a real need in architectural education (Ritter 1962: 942).

The familiar assumption was that society was in flux, that what had been learnt from history or personal experience was profoundly flawed, and that the answer lay in a process of purification.

Conclusion

There appeared to be much good in the attitude behind the Oxford Conference and the Official System that it helped to set up. It questioned the system of beliefs of a particular entrenched set of values, embodied by the Beaux-Arts tradition with its claims to universality and to a continuous tradition of good practice. It aimed at maximum flexibility in order to adopt technological changes as they occurred, to the benefit of a changing society. Technological and social interests, it was hoped, would fill the vacuum created by the abolition of the Orders and other Beaux-Arts paraphernalia. In effect, despite the rhetoric of functionalism, the space was filled by the discretion awarded to teachers within the studio. Design, emptied of culture or notions of tradition, became the result either of abstractions from manifold reality or of personal expressive impulses. The obvious and to some extent admitted casualties of this were a marked diminution of interest in established notions of sound building, as well as in practical building skills and drawing ability.

The Official System had a much closer relation to political systems and institutions than the British version of the Beaux-Arts tradition. It grew up in the immediate post-war years when national resources were keyed to reconstruction. Its leading lights – Robert Matthew, Leslie Martin, Richard Llewelyn Davies and Percy Johnson-Marshall – all moved, around 1960, from powerful public offices to university chairs of architecture or town planning. These figures had all proclaimed leftish leanings in the 1930s and by the 1950s had identified themselves closely, to the point of anonymity, with the workings of the welfare state and its progressive paternalism. Similarly the RIBA was gradually reformed until it became in the 1960s a kind of crypto-government department with a succession of ex-public service architects as its President. In many ways modernists tried to present the architectural spectrum as having similarities to the political spectrum, with the Beaux-Arts on the right and official modernism to the left. However, this analogy with overt politics was always superficial.

Yet the Official System can also be seen as having great consistency with certain Beaux-Arts ideals, refining and taking some of them to an extreme. A state system both of architecture and of architectural education had been put in place. The great movement towards institutional control that had been inaugurated by the establishment of the RIBA in 1834 and received impetus by the importation of Beaux-Arts policies in the late nineteenth century had finally come to fruition in the 1960s. Training for architecture was firmly established in one kind of academy (university-level institutions) where the design project dominated the curriculum. This training was ruled over by a central authority, and closely linked to the production of public architecture. The variety of routes into architecture that we analysed in the period before 1830, several of which had survived even into the 1950s, had been transmuted by the 1960s into a uniform academic system. Thus modernism in Britain did not destroy the academy, it perfected it.

Notes

1 This account of the Bauhaus is largely based on Frampton 1985; Benton 1975; Banham 1960; Rykwert 1982; and Saint 1983.

2 The 1919 Programme for the Bauhaus is republished in Conrads 1971: 49.

3 See Marcel Breuer's comments in *A & B N*, 194, 10 December 1948. 493; Dearstyne 1986: 198.

4 Itten's *Design and Form* was only published in English in 1964.

5 *RIBAJ*, 41, 19 May 1934: 668. Gropius's lecture appeared in *A & B N*, 138, 18 May 1934: 198.

6 RIBA Archives 7.1.1., 1938. It is interesting to see how some dealt with these examinations. Douglas Jones, head of Manchester Architectural School in the early 1940s, told his students to prepare Testimonies of Study in their own time and for the design exams gave his students one-day designs every week for six weeks prior to the exam. (D. Jones, pers. comm.).

7 *Focus*, 1, summer 1938: 1. The prime movers behind *Focus* were Anthony Cox, Leo Desyllas and Blanco-White.

8 Pattrick 1958: 150. These suggestions are unsurprising in the light of Robertson's use of the Einstein Tower in his *Principles of Architectural Composition* of 1924.

9 Many reports, however, show that the functioning of any atelier relied upon a great deal of learning from peers through the informal collaboration of students (e.g. Gowan: 1975 19).

10 The committee consisted of Anthony Cox, R. F. Jordan, A. F. Anderson and J. H. Forshaw.

11 Students lost their vote in AA affairs late in 1938 (*Focus*, 3, spring: 1939 107).

12 He was canvassed as a possible successor to Reilly in 1935. He also gave talks at student exhibitions (see Gropius 1936).

13 *A & B N*, 200, 26 July 1951: 100; Philip Jebb's lecture at the Prince of Wales Summer School, 1990.

14 Startup 1984: 72 – she sees this as a deliberate policy of two-tier 'gentleman and players' training.

15 See CIAM 1951, where Gropius said, 'I wish we could be closer to the test laboratories of some industries.'

16 See, for instance, the *Journal of the Indian Institute of Architects*, July 1943: 22.

17 Percy Johnson-Marshall, pers. comm. The faculties would be in the form of Technical Training Centres including an art school, a school of architecture and regional planning, a building school and a planning and building research station. Students would progress through a syllabus of three stages: a two-year basic design course, including basic coverage of the knowledge needed to understand the environment, followed by a five-year architecture course working from small to large, and completed by a two-year postgraduate course in architecture and regional planning (Johnson-Marshall: 1944).

18 Johnson-Marshall and Tatton Brown also devised a National Plan for Burma, inspired by Patrick Geddes's in India thirty years before and the more recent New Deal planning of the Tennessee Valley Authority which had attracted much attention in wartime Britain as an exemplary state planning project. The Burma Plan included a detailed scheme for the destroyed city of Prome on which it was intended to employ students of architecture, town planning and engineering who belonged to SATO (*AJ*, 103, 2 May 1946: 339–44).

19 Johnson-Marshall 1957; 1965. For the influence of this article see *A & B N*, 213, May 1958: 189; *AJ*, 134, 27 December 1961: 1279–86.

20 These and other references to the 1947 Act can be found under Acts 10 and 11, Geo VI, Chap. 51, Sect. 5 (1).

21 RIBA Archives 7.1.1., 1948. By contrast the Final examination syllabus had, since at least 1939, included recognition of some modern developments (RIBA Archives 7.1.1., 1939).

22 RIBA Archives 7.1.1., 1957. On this issue see also Banham, Pevsner *et al.* 1959.
23 Design was defined as 'The embodiment of plan, construction and equipment in unified, appropriate and expressive form' (RIBA 1946: 18).
24 *RIBAJ*, June 1951: 301–4. For another expression of this compromise position see Mills 1945 (a book intended to attract architects from the armed forces).
25 Douglas Jones was one of the most persistent members advocating student work on sites.
26 The Council was composed of seventy people, only thirty of whom were elected by national balloting, while a third were elected by local Allied Societies.
27 The modernists were Frederick Gibberd, A. M. Chitty, C. G. Stillman, D. Clarke Hall, Lionel Brett, Peter Shepheard and Robert Matthew; but the member who garnered most votes in 1950 was the eclectic and long-established George Grey Wornum, architect of the RIBA building in Portland Place.
28 William Allen, pers. comm.; cf. Saint 1987: 245–6. See also Allen 1964: 211; Esher 1981: 65.
29 Interestingly, the final revised Visiting Board report edited out its earlier comment about the needs of future employees.
30 Another channel for these students' views was the magazine *Outlet*, which they started in 1959.
31 *Builder*, 175, 29 October 1948: 491–2; on the RIBA's response to this see *RIBAJ*, 59, January 1949.
32 *AJ*, 130, 15 October 1959: 344; *RIBAJ*, 66, September 1958: 391–2; *RIBAJ*, 67, January 1959: 99–100; *RIBAJ*, 67, February 1959: 132–3; *RIBAJ*, 67, April 1959: 218; *RIBAJ*, 67, December 1959: 63.
33 These recommendations were quickly put in place by the RIBA Practical Training Scheme of 1963.
34 E. Layton, pers. comm.; see also Layton 1970: 404, where she talked of having only twelve schools in 'advanced seats of learning'.

CHAPTER FOUR

The triumph
of the paradigm

'The profession in Britain is already in a relatively influential position, responsible for by far the largest sector of fixed capital investment in the country'
(Allen 1966: 223). This crow of triumph was uttered by William Allen in 1966
at the end of his stint as Principal of the Architectural Association. At the time
it could well appear that the architectural profession led by the RIBA had at last
been victorious in its long-running struggle with the construction industry
and that the architect was fully established as the leader of the building team.
This had finally come about as a result of the huge increase in public sector
building both pre- and post-Second World War in the establishment of the
Welfare State, so that local authority and ministry architecture departments
were in a position to determine the specifications for schools, housing, hospitals and public sector offices. Public sector architects, particularly in housing,
were effectively the developers as well as the designers of buildings, enjoying
huge budgets and therefore in a strong position relative to building firms.

In addition, through the appointment of senior architects as Chief Planning
Officers in several large cities during the 1950s and 1960s, public architects were
able to determine the effective planning policies for large areas of the country
and hence to control the overall nature of private architecture too. Moreover,
through the appointment of architects to key ministries and as government
advisers the profession was able to exert influence on the reshaping of the construction industry into fewer large-scale firms better equipped to implement
modern industrial systems of building using prefabricated units.

No wonder then that Allen listed the three functions of architectural education as

1 Preparing 'people for the making of physical environment at all scales and
  in all situations'.
2 Developing 'the ability to harness with authority the available scientific and
  technological resources of a country'.

3 'To put into the hands of students *the power to reach the highest level of national decisions about policy for building and planning*' [our italics]

In his view the highest ambition of an aspiring architect, therefore, was not to design great or good buildings, it was not even to design buildings at all, but to stalk the corridors of power determining and implementing policy at 'the highest level' – hence the third and most important of these functions of professional education. Allen was quite explicit:

> For me architecture and planning is not just a design but a major social, spiritual and economic activity; not just a question of designing what we are invited to design, but of participating in all sorts of ways, activist, governmental, economic, industrial and what you will, of deciding what a country *should* build, *where and how*. (Allen 1966: 223)[1]

Where the nineteenth-century architect seeking high professional status wished to distance himself from the act of building, the Official System seemed on the verge of distancing the architect from the drawing-board activity of architectural design itself! This may be an extreme view but it does epitomise an important element in Official System thinking. For many of those active in the RIBA and instrumental in setting up the Oxford Conference, for Allen at any rate, and for others like Llewelyn Davies, Stirrat Johnson-Marshall and perhaps Leslie Martin, such considerations dictated the curriculum. They help to explain why, at the height of the Official System's influence in the 1960s and 1970s, students of architecture were often discouraged from producing anything so banal as an architectural design for their projects and were expected to produce written reports instead.[2]

Let us remind ourselves of the fundamentals of this Official System. Architects should be educated full-time in university-level institutions, with two 'A' levels as the minimum level of entry qualification. An architect's education should, in other words, be academic rather than practical and pupillage should disappear, to be replaced by two years working in an architect's office as part of the requirements for qualification. Ideally these schools of architecture should enjoy similar links with the architecture departments of local authorities as medical schools with teaching hospitals. The first aim of this training was to release students from the impurities of their inherited or lay culture rather than to supply them with basic skills, particularly of drawing. A limited concept of research into needs and technology, based upon the social sciences and building science, as practised in the Hertfordshire schools, became the basis for design projects, replacing established aesthetic criteria, building types and a historical continuum of practice. This conflation of research and design continued a legacy from the Bauhaus; the desire to reconcile scientific or rational procedures with subjective notions of creativity. But the arena for this was the Beaux-Arts studio system, which continued to dominate the curriculum but had lost its historical sensibilities. Indeed the content of the curriculum was not even specified, according to the basic premise that the world was in constant flux and that the best education was 'education for change', which must itself always be flexible enough to change with the circumstances of the time. Hence, in theory, the content of the curriculum was left to the schools to decide, subject to the discretionary control exercised by the powerful quinquennial RIBA Visiting Board upon whose report the school's recognition for exemption from RIBA examinations depended. Where possible architectural students would learn the attitudes of their fellow environmental professions in larger faculties of environmental design. Thus the architect was to be initiated into a powerful professional administrative world, not into a community of fellow-constructors – the very reverse of Lethaby's ideal and of the early Bauhaus's attempt to give craft training an equal role in architectural education. The system was locked into place by legal control over the title of architect and by a discretionary network of exemptions from RIBA examinations and Visiting Board reviews watched over by the RIBA.[3]

A single mould had finally been created for architectural education in Britain. The curricula and teaching methods of this mould were exemplified at Cambridge, Edinburgh, Liverpool, Bristol, the reformed Bartlett and the AA. Cambridge, the Bartlett and the AA also tended to produce those who went on to teach elsewhere. Schools of architecture in university-level institutions were now in effect the sole route to professional qualification, replacing a variety of routes and institutions. (We shall argue that that variety has been replaced by a different species of variety – of avant-garde experimentation within the schools.) Since 1958 the numbers of students qualifying in these schools has risen dramatically, from 54 per cent in 1957 to 97 per cent in 1984 (Transbinary Architecture Group 1984: 5). At the same time the number of registered architects has steadily increased and architects have, until very recently, enjoyed a growing dominance in the building industry, so that while in 1939 they were responsible for some 50 per cent of all new building, by the last decade they had become involved in approximately 75 per cent of such building work, although there has been a decline in overall construction in recent years.[4]

In this chapter we shall examine what has happened to the Official System in the thirty years from its inception in the late 1950s until the early 1990s. Has it continued unaltered, has it been totally superseded, or has it developed in a variety of ways?

At first sight it might appear that the Official System has been totally superseded, that the highly ordered and rationalist bureaucratic system envisaged by William Allen or Sir Leslie Martin, to educate the architect as a member of a highly disciplined elite corps – Colin St John Wilson's 'jungle fighter' – has been replaced by anarchy in which competing architectural fashions come and go through the schools. But although those people who devised the Official System cannot be happy when they view this stylistic anarchy, we shall argue that the key supports of the system survived in fairly good health and that the anarchy can be accounted for without presuming either fundamental change or an evolutionary development.[5]

The appearance of anarchy revealed itself most clearly in the visual appearance or style of students' work. In the course of our research we visited the student exhibitions of twenty-eight of the thirty-six architecture schools in Britain, most of them in two successive years, 1989 and 1990, and we must have seen the work of 6,000 students in passing. (There are about 7,000–8,000 architecture students at any one time in Britain.)

While there are several schools where all students show a broad stylistic consistency in the modernist idiom, such as Canterbury, Heriot-Watt, Kingston, Leicester, Manchester Polytechnic and University, Oxford Polytechnic, the Bartlett and the Royal College of Art, as well as Cambridge (where the distinctive graphic style of a single charismatic teacher suffuses every single drawing in an atmospheric play of light and shadow upon the cut-away interiors of buildings; 51), the remainder are highly pluralistic in their approach. But what this means in practice is that the styles of fashionable international architects whose work has been illustrated in the previous year in the architectural magazines crop up over and over again. One year it might be James Stirling, another year Nick Grimshaw, or Richard Rogers, or Peter Eisenman, or . . . depending entirely upon who has been in the limelight that year as the result of unveiling a major building. The head of one prestigious school was perfectly frank about this. Stylistic ideas were spread by the fashionable glossies. Style was what clients wanted, it was something to be bought, and from the point of view of the schools it was a fact of life. At one school, the AA, fashionable styles are not so much imitated as initiated; for the past decade and beyond their students' exhibition has been a showplace for the latest trends, developed by individual tutors running a unit, sometimes developing a style in their academic atelier before setting up with their former students in commercial practice. To a layman these exhibits seem to have far more to do with the wilder reaches of contemporary art than with building.

About a third of the schools therefore seem to be tied to the broad approaches established under modernism, while amongst the majority a somewhat market-oriented creative freedom seems to reign. At first sight, then, one seems to see the crumbling ruins of the Official System – it is hard to see more.

And yet when one starts to analyse the situation a certain pattern emerges. Though there is indeed a wide range of permissible fashionable styles there is an almost total absence of what could be described as traditional styles; Gothic, Classical, Arts and Crafts, and so on. In one year we counted twenty-eight

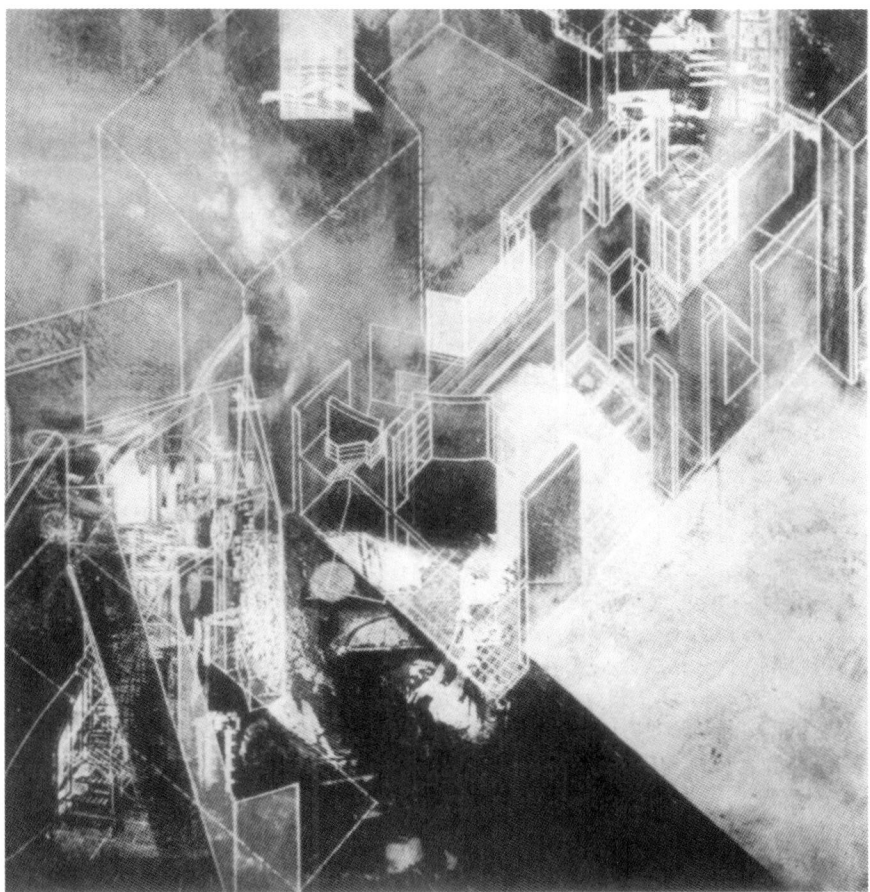

51 Christian Frost: 'Surrealist museum and ocean research institute', Cambridge School project (1990)

students (out of about four thousand) producing work in these styles, and many of them reported considerable opposition from their teachers.

It is not only unacceptable stylistic approaches that are excluded. The study of structures, construction and building materials, while being part of all courses, cannot be described as an integral part. All three subjects tend to be taught through lectures, with little classwork and no attempt to relate them to architectural design. The history of architecture, similarly, is taught through a weekly lecture and is frequently limited to the modern movement. Although approximately half the schools visited required students to produce at least one measured drawing of a historic building (a fundamental means, if done thoroughly, of learning to understand its design and construction), this exercise was in most cases a rather lifeless formality. Some four schools provided facilities for students to learn freehand drawing from the human figure and twice that number encouraged students to sketch buildings, but nowhere was drawing a compulsory part of the course and the overwhelming majority of students could not draw from nature. There was only one school, Newcastle, where students had any hands-on experience of any of the building trades like bricklaying or joinery. There were only two schools, Newcastle and Hull, where there was any emphasis upon community architecture, understood as the attempt to research and utilise the requirements and ideas of the users of buildings and of the general public and to involve them in the design of their surroundings. There were only two schools which included optional courses on conservation. In almost all courses the relationship between new buildings and their pre-existing surroundings was treated in a totally perfunctory way.

When we set these desiderata against the great variety of styles in which students are permitted to design a certain pattern begins to emerge: all the permissible styles – post-modernism, neo-rationalism, deconstruction – belong to the artistic avant-garde, to a fancy-dress parade of modernist art movements. They are part of and a response to the ever-changing flux of the modern world. The same goes for the approaches and styles which preceded them in the 1950s, 1960s and 1970s, the Independent Group, Brutalism, Archigram, High-Tech. Although changes of style may not have been what the serious founders of the Official System had in mind when they wished to establish a system of 'education for change', these movements did not fundamentally challenge either the Official System or modernism itself, but were part of a continuing debate within modernism.

When we examine the typical route through an architecture course, it becomes apparent that much of the Official System is still in force.

A typical route

An introductory first-year course is followed by two years in which projects are set for students to design for periods of four to twelve weeks. In addition there are lectures on the history of architecture, structures, construction and other subjects. Students spend a year out in an architectural practice after finishing their degree (three years in England, four years in most Scottish schools). This year of practical experience is a relic of the old pupillage system, yet, interestingly, it is a year that most architects regard as an essential part of their training.[6] Finally there is a two-year diploma course (one-year in the case of Cardiff and, for a while during this period, the Bartlett), in which students continue the pattern of the second and third years. In their final year they frequently have to design a complex scheme of their own choice for a real site. Some areas of this structure require more elaboration.

[162]

The first year is devoted to the rudiments of architecture and is in effect an induction into the modernist way of thinking, Bauhaus unlearning or deschooling and the design of the small autonomous object. These courses are all still based to some degree upon the Bauhaus *Vorkurs*, but all differ and tend to change as tutors change. The course at the Mackintosh School of Architecture in the year 1988/89 is representative of this common core. The year was based around three design projects of increasing scale and programmatic demands. The first, a personal statement designing an object using the regular geometric solids, was an exercise in abstraction and the manipulation of pure forms and space, three-dimensional pattern-making without regard to practical requirements. The second project, designing a labyrinth, required students to arrange spaces and paths through a building in a beguiling and even poetic fashion; it also introduced the idea of a programme and the notion that a building can tell a story, though it may not have been the best introduction to planning a real building. The third project, a home and workspace for a young couple who are professional photographers, involved the arrangement of spaces within a shell of fixed volume for a client with practical requirements and artistic tastes, but did not consider the external appearance of the building. Once these had been completed students designed a small house and a small shop. But the central feature, here as elsewhere, was the progression from an imaginary structure using basic abstract forms through the design of interiors to that of a house, with the emphasis upon architectural design as the manipulation of sculptural form and space, based upon the personal creativity of the designer and upon the creation of interiors around the functional needs of the client. While 'observational drawing' is included it is not actually taught and is focused to a considerable degree upon industrial objects and structures. Structure is limited to a trussed structure.

Studio projects. The heart of modern architectural education, and the part of it that is least questioned, is the design studio, which usually takes up between 60 per cent and 80 per cent of the total time and thus is as central to the system as it was in the Beaux-Arts tradition. No such studios existed either in pupillage or in the building lodge, where learning to design was an integral part of learning to draw and the other functions of an office apprenticeship. As we have seen, studio projects generally grow in complexity and scale as the course progresses, ending with the most complex, the final fifth-year project, which is a kind of 'masterpiece' very much like the final Beaux-Arts project.

To simplify, the act of designing is ideally seen as an oscillation between individual creativity, scientific method (particularly in the 1960s) and a set problem, during which the student works imaginatively and analytically from a simple generative idea (which is rarely changed, despite contradictory information) to the complex embodiment of that idea. Precedent studies, generally meaning recent typological precedents, may be used on the way, while historical pastiches are strongly discouraged unless they are modernist or avant garde (as most of them are).

But it is notoriously difficult to describe this process of learning to design in the modern system and, as modern architectural educators have found, to describe and defend it to lay people.[7] Perhaps this is because of the design studio's subjective (particularly since the 1970s) and discretionary basis, perhaps because of its frequently unstructured workload, and perhaps because it does not obey the rules of other disciplines and their methods of teaching. Indeed in Llewelyn Davies's inaugural lecture at the Bartlett in 1961 he stated this explicitly:

> We must recognise that training in design is not a form of teaching, but something quite different. Teaching involves facts and knowledge which are imparted to the student by a teacher. There are no facts about design.

Therefore he recommended that

> Instead of trying to teach design we must go back to the lessons of the Bauhaus, and consider how best we can free students from the things that stop them being able to design. We have to clear away preconceptions, clichés, a whole mass of accretions, which prevent them seeing their problems freshly (Llewelyn Davies 1961: 13–14).

When asked, in a questionnaire devised for this report, how they learnt design, architects educated in various schools over the last thirty years answered in a number of ways. Some, it should be said, found the question simplistic, obvious or impossible to answer. Others answered thus: by doing it, by emulation of peers and 'masters' (cribbing and osmosis), by trial and error and personal discovery, by reading books and by intuition. Others frankly admitted that they were told by their tutors to see what was being done in the glossy magazines. Most of them implied that an iterative dialogue with the teacher together with formal criticisms (a relic of the Beaux-Arts approach), had been the most important method of learning design. Without the formal rules of the Beaux-Arts tradition, or indeed any overt analysis of aesthetic principles, the modern studio system thus depends to a great extent on the discretion and subjective judgements of teachers and hence on the nature and quality of their relationship to the current architectural culture. This explains, to some extent, how rapidly visual and pedagogic fashions pass to and from these studios.

If we now look back to our earlier description of the components of the Official System we see that almost all of them remain operative, with the exception of the teaching link between local authority architecture departments and local schools which has been eroded by the decline in public sector work over the past decade. None the less there are places where even this was successfully established and still survives, as in the link between Portsmouth and

Hampshire Architects' Department, whose head became Professor of the Portsmouth school.

Above all, the parade of styles, while not what the founding fathers may have envisaged, is none the less totally permissible within the general underlying premise of the world being in dynamic movement. The approaches and subjects which are excluded, such as measured drawing or exercises in traditional styles, however, are at odds with this premise or might seem to be.

Clearly, then, the Official System had remained substantially intact until the early 1990s, with certain changes. But how does one account for the fact that these changes appeared to be in one direction rather than another, towards the avant garde? We think that to explain this as an evolutionary change in response to changing external circumstances is too weak and does not really account for the resilience of the system during a period in which almost everything the founders stood for has been subject to overwhelming public criticism. We will borrow an idea from the history of science as a basis for our own explanation.

The Official System as a paradigm

The Official System can be understood as a paradigm, in the particular senses of that word (which we will explain shortly) employed by the historian of science Thomas Kuhn. Some aspects of Kuhn's thesis are particularly useful for an understanding of the success that the Official System achieved in establishing and maintaining itself. However, as we will explain later, we do not follow it as a theory of history but rather as an exemplification of certain historical attitudes. Kuhn's theory was conceived in the late 1940s and appeared fully articulated in 1962 in his *The Structure of Scientific Revolutions*.

Kuhn uses the word 'paradigm' to describe all the different aspects of a particular scientific approach – scientific law, theory, application, instrumentation, and most important of all, the professional and social aspects as well – established by works such as Newton's *Optics*, Einstein's *Theory of Relativity* and so on. Works such as these (nowadays they would probably appear as papers rather than books) define the problems and methods of a particular field of research for the succeeding generations of practitioners. In other words, once they are established they make a sharp break with the pre-existing paradigm and at the same time they leave all kinds of problems for the next generation of scientists to investigate; they establish a research programme. But at the same time they play a crucially important professional and social function. A student scientist is initiated into membership of a particular branch of science by studying the current paradigm, and the activity of the professional community will be organised around the continuing researches which the paradigm provokes. A new paradigm comes about not through gradual evolution but because there is some anomaly which the old paradigm simply cannot explain or account for, and which a new theory seems to be able to solve. In other words the old paradigm breaks down, and when this happens the scientific community in question has to reconstitute itself. This is often a very painful process because of the social as well as the intellectual disruption that is caused.

Once the new paradigm has been firmly established many features of the old one will be ignored, often ridiculed and excluded from the serious study of the subject. Any individual scientist who abides by the old paradigm (such as Philip Gosse, the natural historian and father of Edmund Gosse) or changes to it will suffer isolation and exclusion from the mainstream scientific community.

But not only did Kuhn discuss the shift from an old paradigm to a new one, he also considered the formation of new paradigms where none had previously existed. The example he gives is that of electrical research in the early eighteenth century, when there were as many different concepts as there were experimenters. Only the work of Franklin provided a theory which accounted for all the known effects, and this became generally accepted amongst scientists and provided a common paradigm for research. At the same time it also brought into being the specialist field and community of electrical science. Franklin's work, therefore, ushered in the first paradigm in the study of electricity.

One must be wary in transferring a concept derived from the history of science to the history of architecture, from a science to a profession, but Kuhn's notion of a paradigm does seem to throw some light upon the Official System and its recent development as well as upon the wider subject of this book – the establishment of the architectural profession and its methods of training.

The similarities between this notion of a scientific paradigm and the Official System should be clear. The modified British form of the Beaux-Arts tradition that was in operation immediately after the First World War did not seem to account or provide for modern developments, which the Official System seemed to do by emphasising certain technological, artistic and sociological concerns within a new academic framework and centralised system for the subject. We say 'seem' here because, as we demonstrated in the previous chapter, the presence of the Official System had more to do with ideology and fashion than inevitability, in any sense. The period from the 1920s to the 1950s can be seen as a period in which an old paradigm, the Beaux-Arts paradigm, was being replaced by a new one, with frequent debates amongst modernists about methods and problems in architectural education as well as in architecture itself. The final establishment of the Official System fundamentally shifted the way that architectural education was conceived of and practised towards a tight system incompatible and incommensurable with the old paradigm.

[166]

We can see Kuhn's 'paradigm' at work in the formulation and establishment of the Official System within the architectural schools, the RIBA, and amongst a group of educationalists, bureaucrats and architects. Like scientific education, as Kuhn describes it, this new architectural education is a process of professional initiation which prepares the student for membership in the particular architectural community.

Indeed, in a curious way, although Kuhn's book was not published until 1962 one feels that the founders of the Official System were almost self-conscious in their endeavour to change the paradigm, by arguing and demonstrating, as a scientist might do, that the old paradigm, in the case of architecture, simply did not fit the facts of modern life; transport, science and technology, and particularly its exponential rate of change. Moreover in establishing their new paradigm they also sought to act like scientists in adopting a research-based and problem-solving approach towards their subject, intending that the reshaped professional community would explore and solve problems of building density, economics, daylighting, flexible planning and so on.

Just as Kuhn describes it in science, so in architectural education the establishment of this paradigm was only fully possible with a generational change amongst the most influential educationalists. Its success was measured in the way it reproduced solutions to modernism's particular conception of the dynamic conditions of modernity. The Official System used exemplary modernist achievements (the Hertfordshire schools, LCC housing, Leslie Martin's researches, Llewelyn Davies's hospital researches and a number of classic modernist buildings) and, in a way typical of a paradigm, it adopted certain rules, methods and principles that were not learnt abstractly or by themselves, but were displayed in the process of learning design, guided by the discretion of individual tutors. Hence the centrality of studio projects, hence also the unwillingness to lay down or define the content of architectural education (Kuhn 1970: 46–7).

So much for the recent past; it is also possible, however, to apply Kuhn's ideas to give insight into the process and events of the nineteenth century as described in Chapter Two, whereby the architectural profession attempted, successfully as it turned out, to separate itself from the world of building by defining the paradigmatic activity of the architect as that of design – the architects, in short, created a new paradigm. In this light, the earlier period of the late seventeenth and early eighteenth centuries, discussed in Chapter One, with its many different routes into the activity of architectural design, and the ill-defined nature of the architect's metier, can be seen as a pre-paradigmatic period. Moreover the position of those like Pugin, Ruskin, Lethaby and the members of the Arts and Crafts Movement can be understood as a rear-guard action by those who wished either to preserve the real virtues of pre-paradigmatic practices or to incorporate them, as far as possible, into the paradigm.

Real history is never quite so neat as a general theory, and certain features of the pre-paradigmatic period like pupillage and remnants of the multiple routes of entry survived the establishment of the first paradigm and even its clear definition around 1900 and only finally disappeared with the establishment of the Official System, itself the second architectural paradigm. Even so, the remnants of pupillage survived both paradigms.

Looking at the Official System from the point of view of a shift in the professional paradigm certainly seems to help to describe, if not to explain, features of the Official System in its original form. But it also helps to explain, we feel, how the system has incorporated a succession of avant-garde approaches without any further change of paradigm. This we shall examine in the next section of this chapter, and in the final section we shall explain the reasons for the continuing exclusion of certain other features and approaches.

Inclusions – The institutionalised avant-garde

The Official System paradigm is flexible enough only to allow certain questions to be asked within it and of it while excluding others. An internal modernist 'avant-garde', quite unlike the anti-establishment avant-gardes of early modernism, has developed since the 1950s that asks questions that are only comprehensible, indeed perhaps only conceivable, within the paradigm. The avant-garde starts off with the concepts and principles taken for granted in the Official System and its gestures of challenge are gestures allowed within that system. Furthermore, it is often germinated and spread within the culture of the architecture schools – through teaching, peer contact and the student magazines that multiplied after 1955[8] – and it provides the system with profuse design theories for its voracious studio system.

A good example of these shared concepts is the belief in architecture as an exemplum of technological utopia in a state of flux. Here the line of development might follow the engineering aesthetic of the 1950s embodied in the Festival of Britain (some of whose architects were the mould-makers of the Official System) or the systems building of the Hertfordshire schools, through the robot-like architectural projects of the Archigram group and their followers in the 1960s (52, 53), to the technological aestheticism of High-Tech – the work of Richard Rogers and Norman Foster. The technicism of post-war British modernism can be seen to have had roots in the technology of the war effort, although where William Allen, Richard Llewelyn Davies and Stirrat Johnson-Marshall had been backroom boffins researching the new military technology, Reyner Banham and several of the other Independent Group members actually serviced or operated military hardware.

It was also crucial to the avant-garde, as it was to those who established the Official System, that popular life and popular tastes should be seen as revolving around a machine culture of aircraft, cars, the radio, television and cheap scientific magazines. Although the Official System might be sceptical of its consumerist aspects, both favourably compared this mass technicist culture to a polarised notion of the popular as an artisanal culture of pre-industrial skills and folk customs (as was seen in the 1951 Exhibition of British Popular and Traditional Art). The new idea of the popular was also linked to an aesthetic of rapidly evolving, rapidly consumed and thus expendable objects. Here was an ideology, shared by official modernists and avant-gardists alike, that was ideally suited to the government policies of accelerated consumption and military-industrial growth of the 1950s (Mellor 1990).

Of all the avant-garde groups the Brutalists have probably had the most exemplary and pivotal relationship to the Official System. Led by Alison and Peter Smithson, the Brutalists emerged in the early 1950s proclaiming the need to return to the 'heroic' modernism of the 1920s in reaction to what they perceived as a compromised official modernism, and inspired both by the consumerist fantasy and by an anthropological image of archetypal social patterns and symbols.[9] For many students of the 1950s and 1960s the Smithsons replaced Leslie Martin as role models, and the archetypal habitat or the futuristic technologically serviced mini-environment became a common inspiration in studio projects. Their models were the Independent Group's *Patio and Pavilion* and *Fun House* exhibits at the 1956 exhibition *This is Tomorrow*, as well as the Smithsons' *House of the Future* at the 1956 Ideal Home exhibition. Buckminster Fuller's Dymaxion car and Le Corbusier's Maisons Jaoul provided esteemed international foils for these works. While sharing its belief in industrial modernisation, the Brutalist members of Team X provided a critique of CIAM, the group of international modernists whose activity and theory were important to the tentative post-war British modernism. As modernist apostates Team X replaced CIAM's functional concepts of city life which had been embodied in their 1933 Athens Charter (work, dwelling, recreation, transport) with its own concepts (house, street, district, city). But they needed the conceptual framework of modernism to make their own position architecturally pertinent. In such ways are paradigms shared by members of a professional or scientific community.

Architectural post-modernism also fits well within the paradigm. Colin Rowe's teaching at Liverpool immediately after the war stimulated many students' divergent explorations of modernism treating it as a locus of classical proportions, a historical source (eventually influencing the work of James Stirling; **54**), or as a vehicle of expendability (influencing that of the Smithsons) either of meaning or of objects. Rowe at Liverpool, Reyner Banham at the Bartlett and Charles Jencks at the AA can all be seen as incubators of the post-modernism that first emerged in the late 1960s, with its free historical allusions and inclusiveness, propped up by the idea of uncontrolled development ('non

plan') and, once again, inspired by 'the cybernetic revolution; the mass afflu-
ence revolution; and the pop/youth culture revolution' (Banham *et al.* 1969:
442; Jencks and Baird 1969).[10]

The aim of 'non-plan', which appeared in 1969 in an article by Banham,
Peter Hall, Cedric Price and Paul Barker, was to extend the discretion accorded
to the planner in the Town and Country Planning Act of 1947 into a planning
freedom regulated only by the market. There are close links between Llewelyn
Davies's involvement in developing Milton Keynes and the idea of non-plan.
He and John Weeks had developed a theory of endlessness or 'indeterminacy',
arguing that a building's potential for growth and change should be encouraged by its design, and this theory was also behind the 'indeterminate plan' of

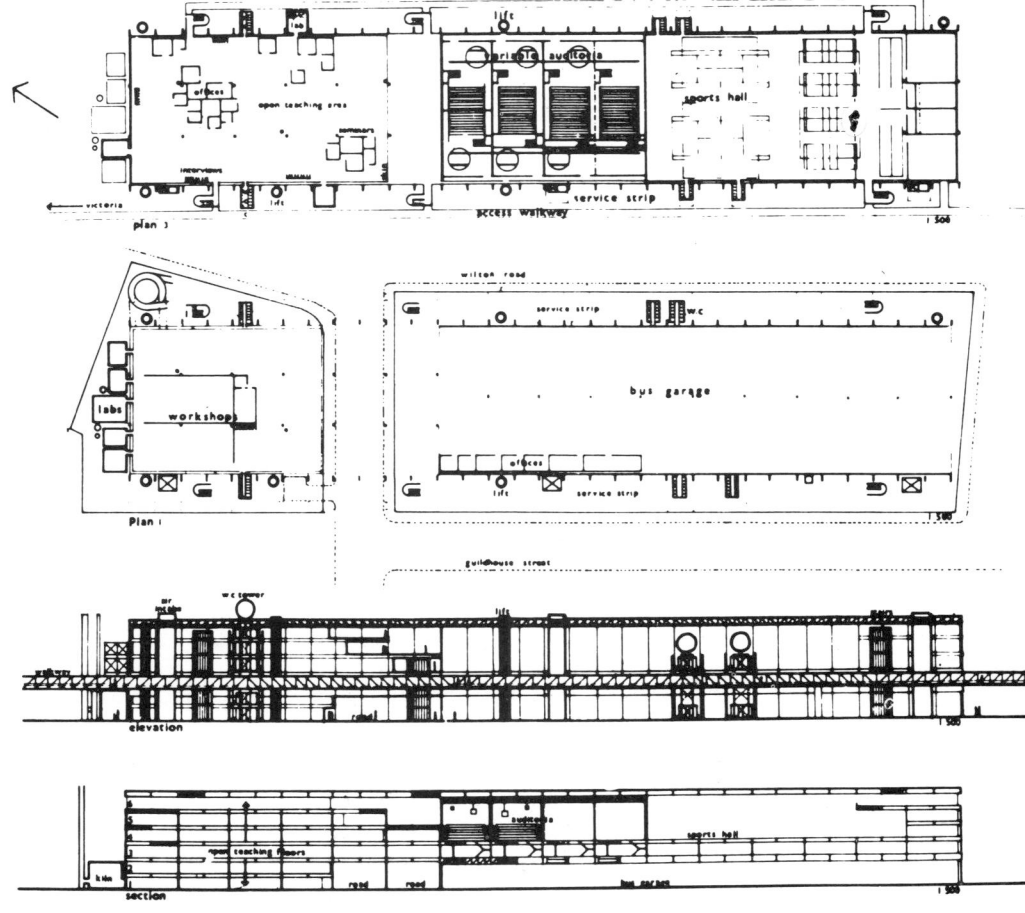

52,53   C. Abel and C. Dawson: school project, Pimlico – fourth-year project AA (1967)
and (*facing*) mobile learning station

Milton Keynes. Banham was one of the first admirers of this theory; he saw the links between it and the clip-on concept of Archigram (Banham 1965; 1968), and he became an important member of the teaching team assembled by Llewelyn Davies at the Bartlett, where both Milton Keynes and Banham's own theories had an important role. Non-plan took the deliberately flexible planning of Milton Keynes and opened it to a complete freedom, governed only by the order of the market. The untrammelled planning allowed by 1980s Enterprise Zones within unelected Development Corporations is a manifestation of this theory, but so too is the free, market-led, notion of facade design essential to post-modernist architecture.

We can see in this confluence of post-modernism and non-plan a typical

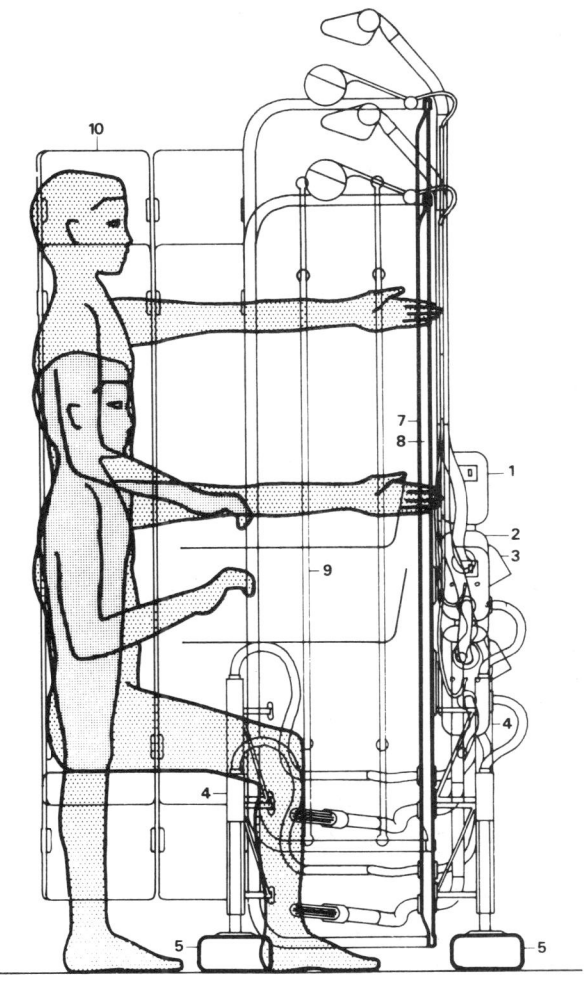

54 James Stirling: community centre, model – fifth-year thesis, Liverpool School (1950)

fusing of avant-garde and Official System interests, in which an architectural school became an important centre for testing and spreading ideas. But we would also go further and contend that the flimsy facadism and poor detailing of much post-modernism can be seen as wittily exploiting the Official System's disdainful attitude towards the rendering of detail and its lack of respect for historical styles.

Post-modernism emerged at the moment when modernism had not only taken over the system of training but also when it had become the 'official' form of architecture, yet post-modernism offered no new pedagogy or new system. This seems particularly strange in that many of those who supported post-modernism claimed that it represented a new economic order ('post-industrialism') and a new pluralistic social and intellectual condition. Yet it offered neither a fundamental analysis of, nor a real challenge to the existing paradigm. It did not seek to change the relation of the architect to the rest of the building team, nor to change the way architecture is produced, and certainly not to change the way that architects are trained. Post-modern plurality allowed everything except a deep institutional critique.

More recently the internal avant-garde, stimulated by post-modernism's metaphysic of pluralism, has introduced theories into schools – often from other disciplines – and upturned them with great rapidity; anything from deconstruction to chaos theory. Avant-garde culture is seen as offering an autonomous domain where ideas can be generated free of the demands for 'realism' and 'buildability' that periodically run through the Official System. The AA, particularly under Alvin Boyarsky's direction (1971–90), has played a crucial role here as a self-consciously avant-garde and cosmopolitan school, 'fostering . . . the conditions in which creativity can flourish' (C. Davies 1990: 14; Ruedi 1991: 22–4), and disseminating fashions and theories through the system by way of its very prominence as a market-led organisation as well as through its own graduates and publications. The AA was a more conventional Official System school in the mid-1960s when William Allen was head. Allen had been brought in specifically to improve the AA's technical side. The difference between Allen's and Boyarsky's regimes can be seen symbolically by comparing the small, grey prospectus for 1964/65 that expressed a technocratic vision of training with the prospectus for 1974/75, an A4 size booklet randomly mixing text and photomontaged images. The AA had moved from science laboratory to arts laboratory, with the unit system revived not to enable teamwork and research, but to foster the notion of education itself as an avant-garde activity (55) and a commodity.

Increasingly the verbal and visual language of these avant-garde fashions has become self-referential, wilful and obscure, and their manifestations fill the walls of many architectural schools' end-of-year shows. Indeed the traces of avant-garde fashions of the last thirty years may all be found reproducing

55 AA Unit 10: view of end of year exhibition (1983)

themselves somewhere in the present system. It is a curious development from what the Official System's founders had in mind.

Despite its ostensibly critical role, this internal avant-garde has rarely if ever offered any real antagonism and certainly no alternative to the system, indeed its iconoclasm helps to recycle and regenerate the imagery of modernism within the system. By concerning themselves with the institutional structure for education and leaving a hole for content at the Oxford Conference, the Official System reformers called their own opposition into being, on their own terms and at the very moment when they were perfecting the system.

The schools have become, perhaps even more than the architectural magazines, both a funnel for gathering avant-garde activity together and the fuel tank of that avant-garde. They are clearing-houses for the architectural culture, developing and disseminating new fashions. Thus, in an important containment of architectural discourse, the external variety of routes, institutions and learning methods, still just discernible after the last war, have been replaced by an internal variety of image-making and theory-production.

Internal avant-garde variety has also coexisted well with wider changes. These need only be characterised schematically: the rise of the developer – bohemianism provides fashions; the attack on the products of modernism in the 1970s – internal critiques of modernism; instead of technocrats, the technological aesthetic; instead of an International Style, an international avant-garde culture with international competitions, exhibitions and magazines; the move from an anonymous public authority architecture to a commercial architecture of rapidly changing fashions in which the avant-garde was able to fill some of the spaces left by the breakdown in public sector work and often to celebrate consumerist values; and the loss since the 1970s of the public architect as role model – from Nikolaus Pevsner's ideal of the anonymous building to the 'landmark' or signature building and the production of artistic statements.

Exclusions from the paradigm

All these novelties could be accommodated even if they were unforeseen or unwelcomed by the founding fathers, because they did not challenge any fundamental features of the paradigm. The emphasis may have been far more upon the aspect of individualistic creativity than upon rational problem-solving, but both the avant-garde and the founding fathers shared the premise, enshrined in the *Vorkurs*, that the fledgling architect needed to be thoroughly laundered of his or her lay culture so as to be able to set themselves throughout their future career against the likes and dislikes of ordinary people, because they had been initiated into a higher and more creative form of wisdom.

The laundering process is not only designed to separate the architecture graduate from the layperson, but also from the superseded Beaux-Arts para-digm, just as that excluded the activities and skills which an architect or builder or patron or artist might have combined in the seventeenth and early eight-eenth centuries and earlier – the time which we have called the pre-paradig-matic period. And indeed these older skills remain rigidly excluded from architectural education, perhaps even more strictly than ever, because their exclusion was an essential part of the separating off of the professional archi-tect from the craftsman or builder. (Indeed the process might well have gone one stage further if William Allen's concept of the architect as a policy-maker had held sway – then the true architect would have had nothing to do even with designing let alone building!)

Looking at these exclusions one at a time they will be seen to fit into a pattern.

Arts and Crafts

The establishment of the first professional paradigm during the nineteenth century perhaps explains the failure of the idea, championed by Lethaby and the Arts and Crafts movement, of training the building trades together (which itself derived from the older idea of the building lodge), because it challenged the fundamental notion of the specialised architect. It may also explain the failure of that aspect of the Bauhaus teaching which attacked the tyranny of paper designing and sought to bridge the divide (Gropius 1951b: 41–6).

Structures, construction and building materials

Related to this earlier separation is the somewhat distanced approach to the technical aspects of building such as structural engineering.

It was during the nineteenth century that the argument raged on these issues and was resolved with the triumph of the Beaux-Arts system. But while build-ing construction remained fairly traditional an architect could acquire a good working knowledge of the necessary science and did so. The attitude of the Official System, as spelled out in Llewelyn Davies's inaugural lecture, was to criticise the Beaux-Arts system for evading the problem, and to argue that stu-dents needed to gain a mastery of the mathematical side of engineering design. But Llewelyn Davies was adamant that what teaching of 'applied structures' survived should be reduced on the grounds that 'no architect today designs his own steel frame, and no point is served in trying to train him to do so' (Llewelyn Davies 1961: 12). Similar arguments were applied to building construction and materials.

The result is that these subjects are nowadays taught, as they were in the Beaux-Arts system, largely through lectures. This system was heavily criticised by those who answered our questionnaire on the grounds of its being totally remote from reality and from the process of design. Students rarely learn to design within realistic budgets. Furthermore, it may well be true that no architect does design his own steel frame, but learning to do so will surely provide a deeper understanding of its possibilities than not learning to do so. In a group of twenty-six advanced architecture students one of the authors of this report found that none of them knew the approximate depth and width of concrete footing required for a six-foot masonry wall! Whether this knowledge is learnt in practice or not is irrelevant; the point is that an understanding of structures is not linked to design ability at a formative stage. The notion of transferable skills seems to have been forgotten by the Official System.

Drawing from nature

This used to be an important part of an architect's education. It was considered necessary for many reasons including that of enriching the understanding of existing buildings as well as being able to sketch out ideas quickly and being able to communicate to clients and others without resorting to the apparatus of the drawing board. Drawing exercises the powers of observation, it is an analytical tool, and a means of assigning perception to memory.

The drawing methods marginalised or abolished in the 1960s – drawing the Orders, life drawing, and drawing historical styles and details – should be understood in these terms rather than as just the copying of a particular style or the adoption of a conventional technique, useful though these might be. These skills should be distinguished from formal drafting techniques which are largely instrumental and thus may change and adopt the latest technologies.

Architectural history

As this is taught at present it is either restricted to the modern movement, and therefore assists in a very direct way in establishing the paradigm, or if earlier periods are studied they are treated as being the unique productions of their own time and place, of their own *Zeitgeist*, in Hegel's terms. The result of this is to create a huge gulf between the works of the past and those of the present, the former to be admired, surely, but never to be learnt from in such a way as to inform the architecture of the contemporary architect or student.

Community architecture

We define community architecture, at least in regard to architectural education, as a principle rather than as a movement. Put simply it is the attempt to teach students how to consider and consult the 'secondary' clients – users, passers-by, neighbours and society as a whole. Because this might help to demystify architecture and deprofessionalise control over design – thus challenging the emphasis on originality in the design studio – it offers a threat to architects.

[176]

Context and designing to meet by-law-type controls

Last and perhaps most important of all the architectural profession remains adamantly opposed to any change to the 1947 settlement, as one might call it, opposed therefore to the statutory introduction of aesthetic controls, building codes, by-laws or the like. A speaker at the 1991 RIBA Conference on Architectural Education observed that contextualist approaches blocked the inventive potential of students. He suggested as an exercise to loosen up Diploma students (who had presumably been contaminated by their contact with the real world of planning during their year out) and to get rid of their fear of touching a historical ensemble, to give each of them a photograph of a city square and invite them to black out buildings with gestural action marks. A year-long project for the final year of the Diploma at the Bartlett in 1989 involved the thirty-eight students working as a group to replan a large area to the south of King's Cross in London (56). Their tutor started with the statement 'I think the King's Cross area is a mess. Let's start by bombing it and ravaging every listed building on the site', or words to that effect. The students responded in spirit – one designed railway tracks over the roof of King's Cross Station; another proposed outlandish structures totally dwarfing St Pancras.

As we have argued in Chapter Three, the repeal of the hard-and-fast by-law controls on building and the introduction of discretionary controls in 1947, which essentially give the planners only the power to respond to ideas of the

56 Bartlett School Final Year Diploma Project: King's Cross (1989)

architect, were consciously designed by Official System architects to free themselves of all the obstacles to producing the most rational and creative solution to a particular site. Nothing is more essential to the current paradigm. As the Planning Officer of the City of London observed at a recent RIBA Annual Conference, if planning rules were to be imposed, then cities would have to be zoned for development and architects would no longer be able automatically to put up buildings where they wanted (*Building Design*, 31 May 1991: 3).

Notes

1 Lionel Esher and Richard Llewelyn Davies made a similar statement in 1968: 'the years 1940–60 saw a remarkable deployment of architects into new or greatly expanded fields: industry, construction, central and local government and public agencies of all kinds . . . architects began to see their collective strength in terms of a "thin, even spread" throughout the complex agencies through which society creates its built environment' (Esher and Llewelyn Davies 1968: 448–9).

2 One of the most public airing of doubts about this was probably at the 1970 Cambridge Conference on Architectural Education (*RIBAJ* 1970). In the Bartlett's 1970 syllabus design occupied a quarter of the time in the degree syllabus. Design projects included such matters as alien communications, the institutional set-up of the school itself, and service facilities on a motorway; it was seen as a method best approached through systems theory, cybernetics, information theory, decision theory and indeterminacy (Abercrombie and Hunt 1977: Appendix E; see also P. Davies 1974b: 45–6). But it should also be said that this did equip the community architects of the 1970s very well for some aspects of their task. Seventy-five per cent of architecture in a community technical aid centre may be devoted to organisational and research work (Wates and Knevitt 1987: 132).

3 The conscious manner in which the Oxford Conference has continued to guide decisions can be seen in the way that Visiting Boards use the recommendations of the conference as their framework and their point of origin (Fisher 1984; *RIBAJ* 1979).

4 Transbinary Architecture Group 1984: 6, 58; *RIBAJ* 1939: 898; RIBA 1992: 61–3. The compiler of the 1939 figures added 'if, however, speculative and municipal housing are excluded, the architect is responsible for at least eighty-five per cent of all other building work'. For 1992 figures see *AJ*, 16 June 1993: 30. These, however, do not separate new build from refurbishment by percentage.

5 This idea that there has been no fundamental change since 1958 is not in itself new, and indeed is shared by many of those who support the current system; see, for instance, Maxwell Hutchinson's speech at the 1991 RIBA Education Conference: 'Since [1958] we have shuffled about the pieces . . . never have we tried to rethink the form and pattern of architectural education'.

6 This is based on replies to questionnaires sent out to a hundred randomly selected architects.

7 This was a recurrent theme of the 1991 RIBA Education Conference, where the need to defend the design studio was frequently asserted yet never explained. See also Woolley 1991.

8 Steedman has counted four new magazines between 1935 and 1955, twelve between 1955 and 1965, and twenty between 1965 and 1970 (Steedman 1971: 40). He also noted that with this increase student magazines became more sectarian.

9 On the Brutalists' reaction to the versions of modernism in England see A. and P. Smithson 1954.

10 The non-plan ideal also appealed to Alfred Sherman, later to become economic adviser to Margaret Thatcher (*New Society*, 17 April 1969: 610).

Even as this book goes to press the crisis in architecture, and correspondingly the crisis in architectural education, intensifies. Few schools are sure about their roles as educators or trainers, there is uncertainty about the numbers of students that pass through them and what roles they might have when they leave. In the studio, current strategies seem increasingly subject to pastiche and their alternatives dogged by a self-doubting relativism. But the crisis also seems to represent a major historical shift. The 'Official System', which we call the second professional paradigm, has collapsed and with it many of the ambitions which motivated the architectural profession over two centuries. The consequences of this for the politics of the built environment as a whole, not just for the future of the architectural profession and its vocational education, are immense. The very nature of the problem is virtually uncharted. Hence there are no easy answers in terms of modest reforms within the existing system. We believe, however, that this history can help to provide an analysis of the crisis and to suggest how things might develop, first from the point of view of the self-interest of the architectural profession, and second from that of the public interest – they are by no means the same thing.

To comprehend the gravity of the crisis for architects we need briefly to cast our minds back over the stages by which their profession reached its present size and stature. First there was the pre-paradigmatic phase in which architects were responsible primarily for monuments, for grand buildings which were few in number and were the ornaments of their towns or regions. There was no organised profession and no specific training. The public interest was safeguarded, if at all, by by-laws and building regulations. This was followed by the establishment of the first paradigm, that of the professional architect in private practice with his small but highly visible corner in the total market for building. The profession was institutionalised under the RIBA which established its own examination for qualification and membership was based upon pupillage and increasingly upon university courses. Towards the end of this period the RIBA succeeded in establishing a quasi-monopoly through the Architects' Registration Acts. The public interest continued to be safeguarded by by-laws and building regulations.

Finally in the third phase, the modernist 'Official System', the architects made a highly ambitious bid for their profession to take overall charge of the built environment as a whole under the leadership of the Architect-Planner who was leader of the building team, government policy maker and self-appointed guardian of the public interest to boot. This was not a private practice, brass-plate profession but a public sector and salaried one which aimed at total penetration of the building market. The RIBA conceived of itself as an ex-officio Ministry of Architecture, even a Ministry of the Built Environment, enjoying the closest links and a two-way exchange of personnel with Whitehall. It was only appropriate that recruits for so powerful a profession should be educated exclusively in university courses under tight RIBA control. The vestiges of independent pupillage were terminated.

This is the hugely ambitious role for the architectural profession which has been in the process of collapse both before and during the writing of this book. Present-day planning policy increasingly favours the conservation of old buildings and areas as well as requiring new buildings to be in harmony with their surroundings, thus removing that license to reshape cities which was one of the major props of the RIBA's post-war policy. Planners, moreover, are now a profession of their own. In the 1980s public sector housebuilding was sharply reduced, removing much of the salaried architect's bread and butter. Although this was replaced by the boom in office building of the mid-1980s, this has now itself collapsed, leaving one third of all architects without work – many of them never to work again. Finally the Government announced early in 1993 its intention to repeal the provisions of the Architects' Registration Acts, on the recommendation of the Warne Report. Although this has now been withdrawn, the possibility of repeal allowed us to glimpse a situation where it would no longer be illegal for the architecturally unqualified to practise as 'architects'. In short two of the three pillars of the RIBA's post-war policy and of the modernist paradigm have collapsed, and the third is at least now open to question.

Architects, with rare exceptions, no longer administer the planning system, their role as leader of the building team has been supplanted by property developers and other professionals and they may soon lose any hope of certifying even as much as 50 per cent of new buildings. Where then does their narrow professional self-interest lie? The unheroic answer would be for them to accept what has been lost and concentrate upon those specialised areas of building design where they retain some competitive advantage such as office building, retail, public sector housing, as well as high profile buildings – signature buildings as they are called – where the stylistic stamp of a well-known architect is considered to be essential; for example, museums, opera houses, the headquarters of major international businesses and residential accommodation for Oxbridge colleges. This amounts to the narrow professional self-interest – for the profession to retrench to its core activity, the design of the more important building types. It represents a return to the brass-plate professionalism of the early twentieth century.

[181]

But putting the repeal of the Architects' Registration Acts back on the agenda could open up broader and more interesting possibilities. With the disappearance of the quasi-monopoly in architectural design other trades and professions such as traffic and civil engineers, surveyors, contractors, craftsmen, planners and developers will enjoy greater freedom to acquire and practise design skills. At present there is an extreme division of labour and over-specialisation in the building industry largely as a direct consequence of the architects' struggle to protect their expertise against competition in the early nineteenth century. This has had harmful consequences for the built environment. Both traffic engineers and civil engineers, for example, have a major influence upon towns and countryside through the design of roads, railways, bridges and other structures. Yet their education is altogether lacking in design. At present in this country the RIBA makes it impossible for a graduate engineer to go on to take a diploma in architecture and qualify as an architect-engineer without doing the full seven-year training. Even without the repeal of the Registration Acts there should be more cross-fertilisation between disciplines, and not only within the confines of college-based education but through a return to pupillage and possibly even to a modern form of the building lodge, for building, after all, is primarily a craft, a practical rather than an academic pursuit. Architectural schools may well reconsider the Arts and Crafts experiments, or the occasional practical building projects of the post-war period, or they might look abroad to the workshop-like ateliers run, for instance, by Christopher Alexander at the University of California at Berkeley. But the inescapable problem that they face is the academic framework itself, which has different protocols and tempos from those of the building process.

The built environment is inevitably the product of a collaboration of many different people. Part of the reason buildings today are so impoverished is that the expertise of each of these collaborators has itself become so impoverished. A practical response to this might be the establishment of more multi-disciplinary businesses and organisations. Architects fear the development of 'Design and Build', but firms offering a properly integrated service of design and construction could compete effectively. Similarly, there might be businesses offering an integrated service in urban regeneration and community architecture or in the rehabilitation and conversion of existing buildings, where architects have been overtaken by other professions. If the RIBA's response to their present crisis is to abide by the narrow professional protectionism which has guided it in the past then these new possibilities will be developed independently, some under the aegis of their own fledgling institutes, others as businesses in the market-place. That might be a good thing.

Before leaving this issue of specialisation it is important to note that we are all builders, instinctively, for building is a species-specific activity. It could be made easier for scientists, philosophers or poets, for instance, to enter the building professions. But even more important is to recognise that one does not need to be a professional builder to contribute to the built environment; we all have something invested in it.

Turning finally to the public interest, it is clear that the days when architects could assume the guardianship of the public interest have gone. At the same time the collapse of the modernist conception of town planning which aimed at reshaping the traditional city to accommodate modern patterns of activity, predominant for the greater part of this century, has left an ideological vacuum in our concept of urbanism, making it difficult to define the public interest. A return to the traditional city of corridor streets and squares enforced through conservation laws is merely a stop-gap measure, which leaves unsolved all the major problems such as suburbanisation, transport and the continued destruction of areas of mixed use. In this broadest field there are no easy answers either for the professionals or for the public and the body politic. It is the job of every citizen, however, irrespective of trade and profession, to contribute to the formulation of a new urban philosophy, a new *civis*. The depth and difficulty of the problem should not be underestimated.

Changes in the RIBA
examination syllabus

The RIBA voluntary examinations were initiated in 1861 and first sat in 1863. The examinations were voluntary in that they did not affect the existing system by which the submission of general evidence of qualification was the precondition for election to Associateship of the RIBA. They were split into two categories, a 'Class of Proficiency' and a 'Class of Distinction'. Both of these consisted of a number of exams taken after set preliminary or probationary work had been completed. The following is a breakdown of the syllabus in 1861:

1. Class of Proficiency.
Preliminary work – Measured sketch of existing building or portion of one; perspective sketch of existing building or portion of one; drawing of ornament from the round or relief; perspective view with working plan, section and elevation of a design by the candidate for some building with its whole specification and a portion of working details at full size.

Examinations:
    Drawing and Design – design for some building or portion in style named by candidate, subject given by examiners.   1,750
    Mathematics – arithmetic, algebra, Euclid books 1 and 2, mensuration.   500
    Physics – elements of mechanical philosophy, especially heat, light and ventilation; the composition and resolution of forces.   500
    Professional Practice – principles of estimating; law.   500
    Materials – natures and properties.   750
    Construction – Detail drawings and specifications for such branches of the work suggested in the above-named design as the examiners indicate.   750
    History and Literature – an outline of the characteristics of the principal styles of architecture in Europe; particular characteristics and history of one named style.   1,250
    Total   6,000

2. Class of Distinction.

Preliminary Work – Original details at full size of work for wood, stone, marble, mosaic, glass, iron, brass, precious metals, textiles etc.; sketches or measured drawings of existing buildings; drawing of the human figure from the round or from memory; a subject of landscape gardening; an architectural subject in colours; subject of decoration in colour or otherwise; some specimen of skill in modelling or in carving: specimens in four at least of these branches being necessary.

Examinations

Drawing and Design – designs, drawings and specimens of skill in style or styles named by the candidate with subjects given by examiners.   600

Mathematics – algebra, Euclid books 3, 4 and 6, plane trigonometry, conic sections.   600

Maths and Applied Physics – mechanics, statics, dynamics, hydrostatics, hydraulics, land-surveying, acoustics, chemistry, electricity, galvanism, geology, theory of colour.   400

Languages – Translation from Greek or Latin and from one or more living language.   300

Professional Practice – laws of property and arbitration.   500

Materials – natures and properties of materials including those not in everyday use.   400

Construction – complex construction in scaffolding, shoring, foundations, walls, roofs etc.   500

History and Literature – the structures, architects, writers on practice and theory, and works illustrating styles or structures, in any style or styles named by the candidate.   700

Total   4,000

The examinations in both classes were held over three days. Some modifications were made in the ensuing years. In 1862 drawing and design in the Class of Proficiency were given 1500 marks, while mathematics was raised to 750 marks. In 1870 the Class of Distinction marks were revised thus:

Drawing and design.	2,000
Drawing or modelling.	500
Mathematics.	1,250
Languages.	500
Professional practice.	1,000
Maths and applied physics.	1,000
Materials.	750
Construction.	1,250
History and Literature.	1,750
Total	10,000

In 1869 a Preliminary Examination was added which was not compulsory for sitting the voluntary examination; this was the seed for the three-tier system that was fully introduced in 1887. This Preliminary Examination was open to all who had spent at least a year in an architect's office. It consisted of

Drawing – free-hand from the round; free-hand from memory; drawing from memory of distinctive features of styles.	300
Mathematics.	300
Materials.	200
History.	100
Extra subjects.	100
Total	1,000

During twenty years (twelve examinations in total) of voluntary exams, forty-three candidates passed. The voluntary exams were ended in 1881 and obligatory exams started in 1882. These were obligatory in the sense that candidates for RIBA Associateship now had to pass them. They consisted of just one group of exams, together with set probationary work. Here is a breakdown of this examination in 1886–87.

Probationary work – plan, elevation and section of a building of the candidate's own design; with a perspective drawing, one sheet of details, and a drawing of some ornament from the round or relief.

Examination:	
History of architecture – characteristics and history of principal styles of architecture; candidate can chose one of five periods up to 1700.	100
Mouldings, features and ornaments – as characteristic of styles generally; as characteristic of the candidate's chosen style.	100
Sanitary science, strength of materials, shoring etc.	100
Plans, section and elevation of a building – detailed arrangement of a building for a given purpose with constructional and artistic details.	200
Materials, construction etc. – nature and properties of materials; principles of construction.	100
Specifications and methods of estimating cost – specification for the work designed earlier in the examination; specifying for other trades and estimating the cost of any building.	75
Professional practice – conditions appended to a specification and contract.	25
Total	700

In 1887, following the agreement at the General Conference of Architects in the same year that the RIBA should have responsibility for guiding and directing the education of architects, the RIBA instituted a progressive three-tiered system of examinations: Preliminary, Intermediate and Final. There follows a breakdown of this system as it functioned in 1902–03.

1. Preliminary.
This was to test knowledge 'in ordinary subjects of school education, and subjects of a technical character'. Applicants could be exempted from this if they submitted satisfactory drawings and certificates from 'well-known educational bodies'. The examination consisted of:

Short English composition.	40
Writing from dictation.	20
Arithmetic, algebra, and elements of plane geometry.	100
Geography and history.	60
One modern language.	80
Geometrical drawing.	80
Elementary mechanics and physics.	80
Freehand drawing from the round.	40
Total	100

2. Intermediate.
Intended to test progress while candidates were engaged in architectural offices. They had to prepare nine sheets of drawings with an illustrated memoir. After these 'Testimonies of Study' were approved they could take examinations. These were the subjects of the Testimonies of Study:
1 and 2. Two sheets on two of the Orders.
3. A sheet of deails of Classic Ornament.
4 and 5. Two sheets of examples (door, window etc.) from two periods of Gothic architecture.
6. A sheet of Medieval Ornament – freehand drawing from the round, in outline.
A short memoir on the building from which the above examples were taken.
7. A sheet with a diagram of a timber-framed roof truss with constructional details.
8. A sheet showing floor construction in various materials.
9. A sheet of details of joiner's work.
The examination consisted of the following:

Classic Ornament.	50
Characteristic English mouldings and ornament, 1000–1550.	75
The Orders – their origin, development and application.	50
History of European medieval and Renaissance architecture.	75
Theoretical construction.	75
Descriptive geometry.	50
Elementary applied construction.	125
Total	500

3. Final

This was to test further progress using more Testimonies of Study and examinations – together they should have taken three years. The required Testimonies were:

1. A study of ornament from the round, shaded.

2. A design of a building of moderate dimensions, with plans, elevations, and sections showing construction and ornament, with a perspective.

3. Drawings of a historical building made from actual measurement and showing jointing: plan, elevation, section and details.

4. A sheet of diagrams of arches or groined vaults in constructive masonry or brick-work.

5. A sheet of diagrams of a roof truss in iron or steel, with details and structural calculations.

Sketchbooks showing evidence of study and travel and of observation of building works.

The examination consisted of:

Design of a building of moderate dimensions or a portion of a larger edifice. Full drawings with details. Subject given some days before the examination.	350
Styles of architecture in general, and one chosen style.	200
Materials – nature and properties.	75
Drainage, water supply, ventilation, lighting, heating.	75
Specifications and estimating.	75
Construction – foundations, walls, floors etc.	100
Construction – iron and steel, shoring and underpinning	125
Total	1,000

British architectural education up to this time had been based on office work, with reading and lectures being supplementary. RIBA examinations were thus devised for these forms of learning. But they can also be seen as necessitating an extension of the minimal academic facilities then available.

In response to the growth of new schools in the 1890s and 1900s, the RIBA devised a system of 'recognition', by which if the school's syllabus was approved, if its examinations were conducted by an external examiner approved by the RIBA, and if its standards were checked by regular inspections and reports by Visitors, then the school could be listed as 'recognised' and its students would gain exemption from the RIBA Intermediate and, for some of the schools, the Final examinations. In 1902 Liverpool and the AA were recognised for exemption from the Intermediate, and by 1931 twenty British schools were recognised for one or both of the examinations (Mace 1986: 115). Other schools could also be recognised for exemption from the Testimonies of Study of one or both of these examinations.

The development of full-time and more part-time architectural schools also prompted the establishment of the RIBA Board of Architectural Education in 1904. This drew up a 'uniform scheme' of architectural education, worked to have this scheme adopted by the schools, and aimed to co-ordinate the various methods of training. The scheme was to be the framework both of an introductory course in the schools and of a more advanced course taken concurrently with office work. The syllabus was reduced to a simple list of five subjects 'governed by the principle that construction is the basis of architecture, and its correlative principle that architecture is the interpretation of construction into forms of aesthetic value' (*RIBA Kalendar*, 1905–06: x):

1 Building materials.
2 Construction, including (a) applied mechanics, and (b) the practical methods of the building trades.
3 Architectural drawing.
4 Design.
5 The history of architecture as explained by constructional, material and social conditions.

Professional practice and building legislation was to be left for study in the architect's office.

This outline syllabus, and later changes to it, was to be fostered amongst the schools and the Board was to be the 'central advisory body' which would initiate and administer the scheme. By 1908 (coming into effect in 1913) Associateship depended upon having passed through a course of study 'under or in accordance with such scheme or curriculum' (RIBA, *Clause 4, Supplemental Charter*, 1908). But the Board only gained control over the Board of Examiners in 1910, hence the RIBA examinations in these intermediate years remained independent of the 1904 scheme (Mace 1986: 115).

By 1912 the Board had made some adjustments to the examination 'in development of the changes already introduced in the Institute syllabus' (Blomfield 1911: 767). There were alterations in the Intermediate Testimonies of Study and examination, and, more significantly, an organised series of designs were required as Testimonies of Study to the Final examination, and a thesis was introduced. This is a complete breakdown of the new examination:

1. Preliminary exam – unaltered.
2. Intermediate.
Testimonies of Study – Nos. 1, 2, 7, 8 and 9 as already established. Now candidates could choose between No. 3 (details of classic ornament) and No. 6 (medieval ornament), and instead of Nos. 1 and 5, sheets of measured drawings of a building with the plottings and sketches.   100
Examination – in addition to history and construction, students could take a special paper either in history, mathematics and mechanics, or elementary design.   250
    Styles and history of architecture.   250
    Construction.   250
    Either – Historical architecture (one period).
       or Mathematics and mechanics.
       or Design.   200

                                                           Total   800

3. Final.

Testimonies of Study – Designs in answer to at least four of the Institute's problems.	200
Examination:	
Design (two days, with student submitting tracing of project after first day).	350
Construction.	150
Hygiene, drainage, ventilation, heating, lighting, water.	50
Building materials.	50
Professional practice.	50
Thesis – In the form of an illustrated essay or a design with a report, to choose from one of the following:	
a. Historical architecture.	
b. Science as applied to building.	
c. Design, including decoration.	
	350
Total	1,200

By 1921 the Design part of the Final paper had been extended to three days, and by 1925 it had been further extended to four days. Also by 1925 the Intermediate paper had been amended, so that it now took this form:

History of architecture – One general paper and one paper dealing with a chosen period.
Structures – calculation of simple structures.
Design – One day.
Construction and materials.

The basic form of the examinations initiated in 1912 thus remained, with few changes, until some time after the Second World War. In 1957 many alterations were made to the exams following the Report of the Architectural Education Joint Committee, and these came into effect in 1960 and 1962. The main changes were concerned with extending the coverage of building technologies, some adjustments to the Testimonies of Study, and the replacement of an Examination Testimony of Study, in effect an extended design project of the candidate's choosing, for the written thesis in the Final examination. Now, for the first time in RIBA exams, the term 'Building Science' was adopted to cover structures, materials and special requirements. Summing up these changes the RIBA's Memo stated, 'the emphasis is placed upon the primary function of the architect as a designer, using technological information as a means to design in an efficient and economic manner' (RIBA, *The Intermediate, Final and Special Final Examinations, Memo*, 1957).

The changes to the Intermediate examination can be shown like this:

Before 1960 – 3½ days	Hours	From 1960 – 5 days	Hours
General History of Architecture	3	History and Appreciation of Architecture: General	3
Special History of Architecture	3	History and Appreciation of Architecture: Appreciation	3
Design and Construction	12	Design and Construction	12
Mechanics and Structures	3	General Applied Construction	3
		Building Science – Structure	3
		Building Science – Special Requirement	3
		Building Science – Materials	3
	Total 21		*Total* 30

And those for the Final examination like this:

Before 1962	Hours	From 1962	Hours
Part I		Part I	
Design	27	Advanced Applied Construction	4
		Building Science – Structure	3
		– Special	
		Requirements of Buildings	3½
		– Materials	3½
Part II		Part II	
General Construction	3½	Examination Testimony Design	27
Theory of Structures	3		
Special Requirements	2½		
Materials	3		
	Total 39		*Total* 41

(N.B. This does not show Part III of the Final, on Professional Practice, which was simply divided into two papers)

The 1957 changes were an attempt to reinvigorate the examinations in the light of changes to building technology. Soon, however, a new desire to create a uniform academic system was to entail a different attitude towards the RIBA examinations.

The modernist reforms that culminated in the decisions taken at the 1958 Oxford Conference finally filtered through to the organisation of the RIBA examinations in the late 1960s. At Oxford it had been decided to abolish courses that supplied students for these examinations, but it also became clear that the examinations should be remodelled and that they should certainly not be used as a yardstick for the assessment of school curricula. Douglas Jones and William Allen, neither of whom were noted for their sympathy with non-university or part-time courses, were commissioned to suggest alteratins (*RIBAJ*, June 1965: 281–2). In their view the examinations were out of date and all of their content needed review. They particularly attacked the historical basis of many of the problems set for the Testimonies of Study, the content of the history examinations, and the separation of building science and construction, and they questioned whether design was even an examinable subject; for example, '[the exam] omits entirely the current emphasis on the well-studied brief' (*RIBAJ*, June 1965: 281–2). They suggested an outline syllabus of seven subjects, all of which were geared to their technicist vision of architecture.

After an Examinations Steering Committee had considered the issue from 1965 to 1967, far-reaching changes were agreed upon at the RIBA. In 1967 it was decided to end the Testimonies of Study, with effect from 1969 (acceptance was finally closed in 1979); design examinations were abolished and design projects put in their place; a further squeeze was put on part-time courses; and the written examinations were subject to further review. The result of this review was published in 1968 and can be represented by a comparative table:

Before 1968	After 1968
Intermediate	*Part 1*
1 History of Architecture	Subject A – Design Project
2A Design and Construction	Subject B – Building Technology:
2B General Applied Construction	B1 Principles of Building
2C1 Building Science: Structure	B2 Structure
2C2 Building Science: Special Reqs.	B3 Materials
2C3 Building Science: Materials	B4 Science of Environment
	B5 Services Engineering
	Subject C – History and Social Studies
Final Part I	*Part 2*
A Advanced Applied Construction	Subject A – Design Project
B1 Building Science: Structure	Subject D – Design Technology
B2 Building Science: Special Reqs.	Subject E – Planning and Economics
B3 Building Science: Materials	Subject F – Dissertation
Final Part II	
C Examination Testimony of Study	
D Design and Construction	
Final Part III	*Part 3*
Paper I Building Law	Subject G – Professional Practice
Paper II Contracts, Professional Conduct etc.	

(*RIBAJ* August 1968: 336)

The Intermediate and Final examinations were replaced by the RIBA Examination for Associateship, which was divided up into Part One, Part Two, and Part Three (this fully came into effect in 1973). The main intention was to raise the examinations to degree level, as had already happened to the school courses.

The most recent modifications of the syllabus have been accompanied by a reassertion of its role as the key guide for core studies in architecture schools (RIBA, 1992: 33).

BIBLIOGRAPHY

This is a selected bibliography arranged according to author. Good bibliographies arranged chronologically can be found in Barrington Kaye 1960 and Angela Mace 1986.

Abercrombie, M. L. J. and Hunt, S. M. (1977) *1960–1970: Ten Years of Development in a School of Architecture*, London.
Alexander, Christopher (1974) *Notes on the Synthesis of Form*, Cambridge, Mass.
Allen, William (1953) 'Science in Schools of Architecture', *RIBAJ*, August: 409–11.
Allen, William (1963) 'The Training and Education of Architects', *AR*: 173–6.
Allen, William (1964a) 'The AA School Today', *AA Journal*: 211–22.
Allen, William (1964b) 'The Education of Architects', *RIBAJ*, May: 210–19.
Allen, William (1966) 'Policies for Architectural Education', *Arena*, March: 223.
Allen, William and Mills, E. (1954) 'Building Materials and Techniques', *AJ*, 27 May: 628–31.
Allibone, Finch (1984–85) 'RIBA Medals Collection', *RIBA Transactions*: 90–5.
Allibone, Finch (1986) 'RIBA Prize Work of the Past', *RIBAJ*, December: 47–50.
Annals of the Fine Arts. 'On the Condition of the Architectural Students . . .', *Annals of the Fine Arts*, 1817: 19.
Ansom, Brian (1980) 'The Banner and the Question Mark', *AJ*, 12 November.
Anson, Brian (1983) 'Academic Debate', *AJ*, 16 November: 56–7.
AR (1983) 'AA Now', *AR*, October: 44–67.
Archigram (1965) 'Archigram Group, London', *AD*, November: 559–72.
Aslin, C. H. (1954) 'Inaugural Address of the President', *RIBAJ*, November: 3–4.

Backemeyer, Sylvia and Gronberg, Theresa (eds.) (1984) *W. R. Lethaby 1857–1931: Architecture, Design and Education*, London.
Banham, Reyner (1955) 'The New Brutalism', *AR*, December: 355–61.
Banham, Reyner (1960) *Theory and Design in the First Machine Age*, London.
Banham, Reyner (1962–63) 'Historical Studies and Architectural Criticism', *Transactions of the Bartlett Society*, 1: 35–51.
Banham, Reyner (1965) 'A clip-on architecture', *AD*, November: 534–5.
Banham, Reyner (1966) *The New Brutalism: Ethic or Aesthetic?*, London.
Banham, Reyner (1968a) 'The Bauhaus Gospel', *Listener*, 20 September: 390.
Banham, Reyner (1968b) 'Revenge of the Picturesque: English Architectural Polemics, 1945–1965', in John Summerson, *Concerning Architecture*, London.
Banham, Reyner, Pevsner, N., Summerson, J. and Voelcker, J. (1959) 'The Value of History to Students of Architecture', *AJ*, 23 April.
Banham, Reyner, Price, C., Hall, P. and Barker, P. (1969) 'Non-Plan: An Experiment in Freedom', *New Society*, 20 March.
Bannister, Turpin (ed.) (1954) *The Architect at Mid-Century*.
Barry, Alfred (1867) *Life and Works of Sir Charles Barry*, London.
Bartholomew, Alfred (1846) *Specifications for Practical Architecture*, London.
Baynes, Ken (1973) 'Henry Morris: Reform Through Architecture', *AR*, December: 369–70.

Bellot, Hale (1929) *University College, London 1826–1926*, London.

Benton, Tim (1975) 'The New Objectivity', Units 11–12 of Open University Course A305, *History of Architecture and Design 1890–1939*, Milton Keynes.

Berkeley, Bishop George (1721) *An Essay Towards Preventing the Ruine of Great Britain*, London.

Binney, Marcus (1984) *Sir Robert Taylor. From Rococo to Neoclassicism*, London.

Blomfield, Reginald (1908) *The Mistress Art*, London.

Blomfield, Reginald (1911) 'A Note on Recent Changes in the R.I.B.A. Examination', *RIBAJ*, 21 October: 767–70.

Boardman, Philip (1944) *Patrick Geddes*, Chapel Hill.

Bold, John (1989) *John Webb: Architectural Theory and Practice in the Seventeenth Century*, Oxford.

Bolton, Arthur (n.d.) *Architectural Education a Century Ago*, London.

Brandon-Jones, John (1952) 'The Education of Architects', *A & B N.*, 17 and 24 April and 8 and 15 May: 468–9, 490, 550–1, 583–4.

Brandon-Jones, John (1984) 'W. R. Lethaby and the Art-Workers' Guild', in Backemeyer and Gronberg.

Briggs, Martin (1949) 'History of Architectural Education', *Builder:* 104, 132, 162, 195.

Briggs, Martin (1951) 'Architectural Education', *RIBAJ*, June: 301–4.

British Architectural Students Association (1961) *An Interim Report on Architectural Education*, London?

British Architectural Students Association (1962) *Building for People*, London?

Broadbent, Geoffrey (1983) 'An Architect's Approach to Education', *Architectural Education:* 94–115.

Broadbent, Geoffrey and Ward, A. (eds.) (1969) *Design Methods in Architecture*, London.

Budden, L. B. (1932) *The Book of the Liverpool School of Architecture*, Liverpool.

Budden, L. B. (1945) 'The Future of Architectural Education', *RIBAJ*, July: 249–58.

Building (1972a) 'The AA Now', 16 June: 91–5.

Building (1972b) 'The AA Since the War', 20 October: 73–8.

Burnell, George (1864–65) 'On the Present Tendencies of Architecture and Architectural Education in France', *Sessional Papers of the RIBA*: 127–37.

Campbell, Louise (1984–85) 'The MARS Group, 1933–1939', *RIBA Transactions:* 68–79.

Campbell, Louise (1989) 'A Call to Order: The Rome Prize and Early Twentieth-Century British Architecture', *Architectural History.*

Campbell, Robert (1747) *The London Tradesman*, London.

Carlhian, Jean Paul (1979) 'The Ecole des Beaux-Arts: Modes and Manners', *Journal of Architectural Education*, November: 7–17.

Cates, Arthur (ed.) (1887) *Papers on Education*, London.

Chafee, Richard (1977) 'The Teaching of Architecture at the Ecole des Beaux-Arts', in Arthur Drexler (ed.), *The Architecture of the Ecole des Beaux-Arts*, New York.

CIAM (1951) *Report of the Hoddesdon Conference*, London.

Collins, Peter (1979) 'The Eighteenth Century Origins of Our System of Full-Time Architectural Schooling', *Journal of Architectural Education*, November: 2–6.

Colquhoun, Alan (1965) 'Some Ideas about Technical Training', *AA Journal*, November: 101–2.

Colvin, Howard (ed.) (1963–76) *The History of the King's Works*, London.

Colvin, Howard (1978) *A Biographical Dictionary of British Architects 1600–1840*, London

Conrads, U. (ed.) (1971) *Programs and Manifestoes on 20th Century Architecture*, Cambridge, Mass.

Conway, Dolan (ed.) (1969) 'Three London Schools of Architecture', *AD*, March: 129–62.

Cook, Peter (1967) 'Mirrors', *Arena*, May: 283–90.

Crafts, N. (1983) 'British Economic Growth', *Economic History Review*.

Crook, J. M. (1969) 'The Pre-Victorian Architect: Professionalism and Patronage', *Architectural History*, 12, 62–78.

Davies, Colin (1990) 'Developing the Network', *AJ*, 14 March: 14.

Davies, Paul (1974a) 'Students in Architecture – AA', *Architect*, January: 60–2.

Davies, Paul (1974b) 'Students in Architecture – Cambridge', *Architect*, June: 45–6.

Dean, David (1983) *Architecture of the 1930s*, London.

Dearstyne, Howard (1986) *Inside the Bauhaus*, London.

Dickens, Charles (1844) *Martin Chuzzlewit*, London.

Dix, Gerald (1981) 'Patrick Abercrombie 1879–1957', in Gordon E. Cherry (ed.), *Pioneers in British Planning*, London.

Donaldson, T. L. (1842) *Preliminary Discourse*, London.

Donaldson, T. L. (1847) *Architectural Maxims and Theorems*, London.

Downes, Kerry (1979) *Hawksmoor*, London.

Downes, Kerry (1987) *Sir John Vanbrugh*, London.

Downes, Kerry (1988) *The Architecture of Wren*, Reading.

Du Prey, Pierre de la Ruffinière (1977) *John Soane's Architectural Education*, New York and London.

Du Prey, Pierre de la Ruffinière (1982) *John Soane. The Making of an Architect*, Chicago and London.

Earle, P. (1989) *The Making of the English Middle Class, 1660–1730*, London.

Esher, Lionel (1983) *A Broken Wave: The Rebuilding of England, 1940–1980*, London.

Esher, Lionel (1985) *Our Selves Unknown*, London.

Esher, Lionel, and Llewelyn Davies, Richard (1968) 'The Architect in 1988', *RIBAJ*, October: 448–55.

European Association for Architectural Education (1985) *The Making of an Architect – Where do we go from here?*, Brussels.

Evelyn, John (1662) *Sculptura: or the History, and art of Chalcography*, London

Evelyn, John (1664) *A Parallel of the Ancient Architecture with the Modern*, London.

Ferrey, Benjamin (1861) *Recollections of A. Welby Pugin and his Father Augustus Pugin*, London.

First International Congress (1925) *The First International Congress on Architectural Education*, 1924, London.

Fisher, Robert (1984) *The Work of the RIBA Visiting Boards 1977–1983*, typescript.

Focus (1938–39).

Frampton, Kenneth (1985) *Modern Architecture – A Critical History*, London.

Gardner, R. (1974) 'The Development of Architectural Education in the UK', *AJ*, 9 October: 875–81.

Gardner Medwin, E. R. (1953) 'Inaugural Address', *AJ*, 2 April: 427.

Gerlernter, Mark (1988) 'Reconciling Lectures and Studios', *Journal of Architectural Education*, Winter.

Gelernter, Mark (1981) 'The Subject–Object Problem in Design Theory and Education', Ph.D. thesis, University of London.

Giedion, S. (ed.) (1951) *A Decade of New Architecture* (Proceedings of CIAM 6, held at Bridgewater, Somerset, 1947), Zurich.

Girouard, Mark (1966) 'English Art and the Rococo', *Country Life*, January-February: 58–61, 188–90, 224–7.

Goodhart-Rendel, H. S. (1940) 'Architectural Education', *Builder*, 3 and 17 May: 531–2, 585–6.

Goss, Anthony (1962) 'Realistic Projects at Birmingham', *AJ*, 4 April: 727–31.

Gotch, J. A. (ed.) (1934) *The Growth and Work of the RIBA, 1834–1934*, London.

Gowan, James (1959) 'Curriculum', *AR*, December: 315–23.

Gowan, James (1973) *Projects: Architectural Association, 1946–1971*, London.

Gowan, James (ed.) (1975) *A Continuing Experiment*, London.

Gronberg, Theresa (1984) 'William Richard Lethaby and the Central School of Arts and Crafts', in Backemeyer and Gronberg (eds.).

Gropius, W. (1935) *The New Architecture and the Bauhaus*, London.

Gropius, W. (1936) 'Architect in the Making' (address given at an exhibition of work by Liverpool students, Building Centre, 30 March), typescript in RIBA Archives.

Gropius, W. (1943) *The Scope of Total Architecture*, New York.

Gropius, W. (1951a) 'Architectural Education', in CIAM.

Gropius, W. (1951b) 'In Search of Better Architectural Education', in S. Giedion (ed.).

Gropius, W. and Bayer, H. (eds) (1938) *Bauhaus, 1919–1928*, Boston.

Gwynn, J. (1749) *An Essay in Design*, London.

Hanson, Brian (1987) 'Mind and Hand in Architecture: Ideas of the Artisan in English Architecture from William Chambers to John Ruskin', Ph.D. thesis, University of Essex.

Harris, John, Orgel, S., and Strong, R. (1973) *The King's Arcadia: Inigo Jones and the Stuart Court*, London.

Hellman, Louis (1986) 'Bartlett', *AJ*, 8 October: 26–31.

Hill, Christopher (1972) *Intellectual Origins of the English Revolution*, London.

Holford, William (1938) 'The Next Twenty Years', *RIBAJ*, 19 December: 165–74.

Holford, William (1962) 'Architectural Education', *RIBAJ*, July: 258–60.

Hosking, William (1841) *An Introductory Lecture Delivered at King's College, London*, London.

Hughes, Quentin (1981) 'Education and the Architectural Profession in Britain at the Turn of the Century', *Journal of Art and Design Education*, 1, 135–44.

Hughes, Quentin (1982) 'Before the Bauhaus. The Experiment at the Liverpool School of Architecture and Applied Arts', *Architectural History*: 102–13.

Itten, Johannes (1964) *Design and Form*, London

Jackson, Anthony (1970) *The Politics of Architecture*, London.

Jackson, T. G. (1950) *Recollections of Thomas Graham Jackson*, London.

Jencks, C. and Baird, G. (eds.) (1969) *Meaning in Architecture*, New York.

Jenkins, Frank (1961) *Architect and Patron*, Oxford.

Jenks, M. (1984) 'Birmingham Polytechnic', *AJ*, 17 October: 63–5.

Johnson, Peter (1987) *Architectural Education in the Commonwealth: A Survey of Schools*, London.

Johnson-Marshall, Percy (1944) *Introduction to Planning*, Assam.

Johnson-Marshall, Percy (1946) 'SATO and a Burma Plan', *AJ*, 7 November: 342–3.

Johnson-Marshall, Percy (1947) 'Architectural Education', *AJ*, 8 May: 388.

Johnson-Marshall, Percy (1957) 'From Schools of Architecture to a New University Faculty', *AJ*: 848–51.

Johnson-Marshall, Percy (1965) 'Education for Environmental Design', *RIBAJ*, March: 119–21.

Johnson-Marshall, Percy (n.d.) 'Stirrat – a Memoir', typescript in RIBA Archives.

Kaye, Barrington (1960) *The Development of the Architectural Profession in Britain: A Sociological Approach*, London.

Kerr, Robert (1846) *The Newleafe Discourses*, London.

Knowles, J. T. (1853) *On Architectural Education*, London.

Kostof, Spiro (ed.) (1977) *The Architect: Chapters in the History of the Profession*, New York.

Kretchmer, William (1965) 'Looking Back at 1924', *AJ*, 30 June: 1521–3.

Kuhn, Thomas S. (1970) *The Structure of Scientific Revolutions*, Chicago.

Kynaston, Francis (1636) *The Constitution of the Museum Minervae*, London.

Lakatos, Imrie and Musgrave, Alan (eds.) (1970) *Criticism and the Growth of Knowledge*, Cambridge.

Landau, Roy (1984) 'The Culture of Architecture: A Historiography of Current Discourse', *UIA-International Architect*, 5.

Latourell, Dean (1969) 'The Bartlett 1969', *AIA Journal*, October: 88–92.

Layton, Elizabeth (1962) *Report on the Practical Training of Architects*, London.

Layton, Elizabeth (1965) *Reflections on Architectural Education in the United States of America*, typescript.

Layton, Elizabeth (1970) 'The Lessons of Cambridge', *RIBAJ*, September: 403–5.

Lea, F. M. (1971) *Science and Building: A History of the Building Research Station*, London.

Leach, Peter (1988) *James Paine*, London.

Ledoyen, A. and Naddermier, O. (1976) 'Birmingham School of Architecture', *Architecture West Midlands*, April/May: 11–15.

Lees-Milne, James (1962) *Earls of Creation: Five Great Patrons of Eighteenth-Century Art*, London.

Lethaby, W. R. (1895) 'Modern Building Design', *Builder*, 9 November: 334–5.

Lethaby, W. R. (1901) 'Education in Building', *RIBAJ*, 8 June: 385–94.

Lethaby, W. R. (1904) 'Architectural Education. A Discussion – 1', *AR*: 157–62.

Lethaby, W. R. (1923) 'The Building Art: Theories and Discussions', *Builder*, 9 March: 405–6.

Lewis, Michael J. (1989) 'August Reichensperger (1808–1895) and the Gothic Revival', Ph.D. thesis, University of Pennsylvania.

Liverpool Architectural School (1910–20) *The Liverpool Architectural Sketchbook*, 1910, 1911, 1913, 1920.

Llewelyn Davies, Richard (1951) 'Endless Architecture', *AA Journal*, November: 106–13.

Llewelyn Davies, Richard (1955) 'On the Frontier of Knowledge', *AJ*, 14 April: 505–10.

Llewelyn Davies, Richard (1957) 'Deeper Knowledge: Better Design', *AJ*, 23 May: 769–72.

Llewelyn Davies, Richard (1961) *The Education of an Architect*, London (also published in *RIBAJ*, January 1961, 118–20).

Llewelyn Davies, Richard and Weeks, John (1962) 'Educating for Building', in British Architectural Students' Association.

Lloyd, John (1967) 'The Quality of Architectural Education', *Arena*, May: 275–9.

Lubbock, Jules (1984) 'Hull', *AJ*, 17 October: 72–4.
Luce, A. A. (1949) *The Life of George Berkeley Bishop of Cloyne*, London.

Mace, Angela (1986) *The RIBA: A Guide to its Archive and History*, London.
Macleod, Robert (1971) *Style and Society: Architectural Ideology in Britain 1835–1914*, London.
Macleod, Roy (1983) 'Whigs and Savants: reflections on the reform movement in the Royal
    Society, 1830–1848', in I. Inkster and J. Morrell, *Metropolis and Province: Science in British
    Culture 1780–1850*, London.
Macdonald, Stuart (1970) *The History and Philosophy of Art Education*, London.
Maclure, Stuart (1984) *Educational Development and School Building: Aspects of Public Policy,
    1945–1973*, Harlow.
MacMorran, Donald (1955) 'The McMorran Report', *AJ*, 10 February: 195.
Mairet, Philip (1957) *Pioneer of Sociology: The Life and Letters of Patrick Geddes*, London.
Martin, Leslie (1958) 'Conference on Architectural Education', *RIBAJ*, June: 279–82.
Martin, Leslie (1961) 'An Overall View of Architectural Training', in British Architectural
    Students Association (no pagination).
Martin, Leslie (1970) 'Education Around Architecture', *RIBAJ*, September: 398–402.
Martin, Leslie (1983) *Buildings and Ideas 1933–1983*, Cambridge.
Martin, Leslie, Nicholson, Ben and Gabo, Naum (eds.) (1937) *Circle*, London.
Matthew, Robert (1953) 'Inaugural Address', *AJ*, 26 November: 658–61.
Maxwell, Robert (1983) 'The Two Theories of Architecture', *Architectural Education*.
Meller, Helen (1981) 'Patrick Geddes 1854–1932', in Gordon E. Cherry (ed.), *Pioneers of British
    Planning*, London.
Meller, Helen (1990) *Patrick Geddes Social Evolutionist and City Planner*, London.
Mellor, David (1990) 'A "Glorious Techniculture" in Nineteen-Fifties Britain', in David
    Robbins (ed.), *The Independent Group*, London.
Mills, Edward (1945) *Architecture*, London.
Moholy-Nagy, L. (1934) *The New Vision*, London.
Muschenheim, W. (1964) 'Curricula in Schools of Architecture', *AIA Journal*, March: 74–80.
Musgrove, John (1983) 'Architectural Education: The Growth of a Discipline', *Architectural
    Education*: 105–12.

Naylor, Gillian (1984) 'Lethaby and the Myth of Modernism', in Backemeyer and Gronberg
    (eds.).
Newberry, F. H. (1887) *On the Training of Architectural Students*.
Nicholson, Peter (1828) *The School of Architecture and Engineering*, London.
Noble, James (1836) *The Professional Practice of Architects*, London.

Papworth, J. B. (1835–36) 'On the Benefits Resulting to the Manufacturers of a Country from
    a well directed cultivation of Architecture and the art of Ornamental Design', *RIBA
    Transactions*. 111–14.
Pattrick, Michael (1958) 'Architectural Aspirations', *AA Journal*, January: 147–61.
Paulson, Ronald (1971) *Hogarth: His Life, Art and Times*, New Haven and London.
Peacock, James (?) (1773) *An Essay on the Qualifications and Duties of an Architect*, London.
Pérez-Gómez, Alberto (1983) *Architecture and the Crisis of Modern Science*, Cambridge,
    Mass. and London.
Pevsner, Nikolaus (1936a) *Pioneers of the Modern Movement*, London.
Pevsner, Nikolaus (1936b) 'Postwar Tendencies in German Art Schools', *Journal of the Royal
    Society of Arts*, 84.

Pevsner, Nikolaus (1940) *Academies of Art Past and Present*, Cambridge.

Pevsner, Nikolaus (1950) 'The Training of Architects', *AR*, June: 367–73.

Port, M. H. (1967) 'The Office of Works and Building Contracts in Early Nineteenth-Century England', *Economic History Review*, 2nd Series, vol. 20, April: 94–110.

Power, M. J. (1967) 'Sir Bartholomew Gerbier's Academy at Bethnal Green', *East London Papers*, summer: 19–34.

Powers, Alan (1982) *Architectural Education in Britain 1880–1914*, Ph.D. thesis, Cambridge University.

Powers, Alan (1984a) 'Architectural Education and the Arts and Crafts Movement', *Architectural Education*: 42–70.

Powers, Alan (1984b) 'Edwardian Architectural Education: A Study of Three Schools of Architecture', *AA Files*, January: 49–59.

Price, R. (1980) *Masters, Unions and Men. Work Control in Building and the Rise of Labour, 1830–1914*, Cambridge.

Pugin, A. W. N. (1836) *Contrasts*, London.

Pugin, A. W. N. (1841) *The True Principles of Pointed or Christian Architecture*, London.

Pugin, A. W. N. (1843) *An Apology for the Revival of Christian Architecture in England*, London.

Read, Herbert (1934) *Art and Industry*, London.

Rée, Henry (1985) *Educator Extraordinary. The Life and Achievements of Henry Morris 1889–1961*, London.

Reilly, C. H. (1914) 'Architecture as an Academic Subject', in J. M. Mackay, *A Miscellany Presented to John Macdonald Mackay*, Liverpool.

Reilly, C. H. (1938) *Scaffolding in the Sky*, London.

Report of the RIBA Visiting Board (1968) *RIBAJ*, May: 204–10.

RIBA (1946) *Special Committee on Architectural Education*, London.

RIBA (1962) *The Architect and His Office*, London.

RIBA (1971) *The Charter, Supplemental Charter 1971 and Byelaws*, London.

RIBA (1992) *The Report of the Steering Group on Architectural Education*, (The Burton Report), London.

RIBAJ (1964) 'Higher Education. The Significance of Robbins', *RIBAJ*: 12–18.

RIBAJ (1970a) 'Education Year: The Cambridge Conference', *RIBAJ*, May: 203–10.

RIBAJ (1970b) 'RIBA Conference, Birmingham. Educating the Architect', *RIBAJ*, September: 393–408.

RIBAJ (1979) 'School Report', *RIBAJ*, August: 356–7.

Richardson, A. E. (1951) 'Papers Read at the Architectural Teachers Conference 1951', *RIBAJ*: 430–5.

Richardson, Margaret (1990) 'Working for Soane', *AJ*, 19 and 26 December: 48–53.

Ritter, Paul (1956) 'The New Approach', *AJ*, 22 November: 738–42.

Ritter, Paul (1962) 'Five Realities of Architectural Education', *AJ*, 2 May: 942–5.

Ritter, Paul (1966) *Educreation: Education for Creation, Growth and Change*, Oxford.

Robbins, David (ed.) (1990) *The Independent Group: Postwar Britain and the Aesthetics of Plenty*, Cambridge, Mass. and London.

Robertson, H. and Whittaker, C. R. (1952) 'Architects' Training and Efficiency in the Building Industry', *A & B N*, 6 March: 297–8.

Root-Bernstein, Robert (1984) 'On Paradigms and Revolutions in Science and Art', *Art Journal*, 44, summer: 109–18.

Rosenfeld, M. N. (1977) 'The Royal Building Administration in France From Charles V to Louis XIV', in S. Kostof (ed.).

Rosenthal, H. W. (1951) 'Architectural Education', *A & B N*, 26 July: 100–2.
Rosenthal, H. W. (1952a) 'Education for Architecture', *A & B N*, 24 January: 114–16.
Rosenthal, H. W. (1952b) 'Teaching Technique Reviewed', *A & B N*, 5 June: 662–5.
Rowse, E. A. A. (1939) 'The Planning of a City', *Journal of the Town Planning Institute*, 25, March.
Royal Academy of Art (1797) *Abstract of the Instrument of Institution and Laws of the Royal Academy of Art in London*, London.
Rubens, Godfrey (1984) 'The Practice and Theory of Architecture', in Backemeyer and Gronberg, 49–55.
Rubens, Godfrey (1986) *William Richard Lethaby His Life and Work 1857–1931*, London.
Ruedi, Katerina (1991) 'Radical Revision', *Building Design*, 15 March: 22–4.
Ruskin, John (1864–65) 'An Enquiry into Some of the Conditions at Present Affecting the Study of Architecture in Our Schools', *Sessional Papers of the RIBA*: 139–56.
Rykwert, Joseph (1982) 'The Dark Side of the Bauhaus', in J. Rykwert, *The Necessity of Artifice*, London.
Rykwert, Joseph (1983) *The First Moderns*, Cambridge, Mass. and London.

Saint, Andrew (1976) *Richard Norman Shaw*, New Haven and London.
Saint, Andrew (1983) *The Image of the Architect*, New Haven and London.
Saint, Andrew (1987) *Towards a Social Architecture: The Role of School-Building in Post-War England*, New Haven and London.
Sandeman, Robert (1846) *Remarks on the Proper Education of an Architectural Pupil*. MS in RIBA Archives.
Sandeman, Robert (1847) *On the State of our Profession and its Institutions*. MS in RIBA Archives.
Scott, George Gilbert (1864) *Thoughts and Suggestions on the Artistic Education of Architects*.
Scott, George Gilbert (1879) *Personal and Professional Recollections1*, London.
Shaftesbury, Anthony, Earl of (1732) *Characteristics of Men, Manners, Opinions, Times*, London.
Shaw, R. Norman and Jackson, T. G. (1892) *Architecture A Profession or an Art*, London.
Simpson, F. M. (1895) *The Scheme of Architectural Education Started at University College, Liverpool*, Liverpool.
Simpson, F. M. (1896) 'Architectural Education and a School of Architecture', *Builder*. 539.
Smith, John (1958a) 'The Bartlett Exhibition', *AJ*, 10 July: 47–50.
Smith, John (1958b) 'The Development of Architectural Education', *Architecture and Building*, May: 189–90.
Smith, John (1958c) 'The Schools', *Architecture and Building*, February: 43–72.
Smith, John (1961) 'Schools of Architecture – Birmingham', *A & B N*, 22 February: 257–63.
Smith, John (1962a) 'The Schools in Transition', *A & B N*, 14 February: 239–44.
Smith, John (1962b) 'Schools of Architecture – Cambridge', *A & B N*, 3 January: 17–24.
Smithson, Alison and Peter (1954) 'The New Brutalism', *AR*, April: 274–5.
Smithson, Alison and Peter (1965) 'The Heroic Period of Modern Architecture', *AD*, December: 587–637.
Spiers, R. Phené (1887a) *Architectural Drawing*, London.
Spiers, R. Phené (1887b) 'The Architectural School of the Royal Academy', in A. Cates (ed.).
Spiers, R. Phené (1890) *The Orders of Architecture*, London.
Sprat, Thomas (1667) *The History of the Royal Society*, London.
Startup, H. M. (1984) *Institutional Control of Architectural Education and Registration: 1834–1960*, M.Phil. thesis, Thames Polytechnic.

Steedman, Neil (1971) 'Student Magazines in British Architectural Schools', *AA Quarterly*, July–September: 36–40.

Stephenson, Gordon (1992) *On a Human Scale – A Life in Civic Design*, South Fremantle.

Street, A. E. (1888) *A Memoir of George Edmund Street, RA, 1824–1881*, London.

Summerson, John (1942) 'Bread and Butter and Architecture', *Horizon*, October: 233–43.

Summerson, John (1947) *The Architectural Association 1847–1947*, London.

Summerson, John (1983) *Architecture in Britain, 1530 to 1830*, Harmondsworth.

Swenarton, Mark (1989) *Artisans and Architects: The Ruskinian Tradition in Architectural Thought*, London.

Tarn, J. N. (1982) 'British Architectural Education for the Eighties', *European Association for Architectural Education*, February.

Tarn, J. N. (1983) 'The Education Debate', *RIBAJ*, September: 47–50.

Transbinary Architecture Group (1984) *Facing the Future: A Report on Advanced Courses in Architecture* (The Esher Report), London.

Trombley, S. (1983) 'The Oxford Conference and After', *Architectural Education*, 1: 90.

University Grants Committee (1987) *Report of the Architecture Review Working Group*, London.

Ventris, Lois (1967) 'The Bartlett School', *Arena*, May: 279.

Walker, Lynne (1984) 'British Women in Architecture (1671–1951)' in L. Walker (ed.), *Women Architects: Their Work*, London.

Walker, Lynne (1989) 'Women and Architecture', in J. Attfield and P. Kirkham (eds.), *A View from the Interior*, London.

Wates, N. and Knevitt, C. (1987) *Community Architecture*, Harmondsworth.

Weingarden, Lauren (1985) 'Aesthetics Politicized: William Morris to the Bauhaus', *Journal of Architectural Education*, Spring: 8–13.

Welcher, Jeanne K. (1972) *John Evelyn*, New York.

White, William (1885) *The Past, Present and Future of the Architectural Profession*, London.

Wightwick, George (1846) *Hints to Young Architects*, London.

Wilkinson, C. (1977) 'The New Professionalism in the Renaissance' in S. Kostof (ed.).

Wilson, Stuart (1969) 'Early Educational Reformers and Contemporary Architectural Education', *Architectural Science Review*, December: 99–104.

Wilton-Ely, John (1977) 'The Rise of the Professional Architect in England', in S. Kostof (ed.).

Wood, E. (1897) 'The School of Arts and Crafts', *AR*, 2: 243–4.

Woolley, Tom (1991) 'Why Studio', *AJ*, 20 March: 46–9.

Wren, Christopher (1710) *Parentalia*, London.

Wright, Gwendolyn and Parkes, Janet (eds.) (1990) *The History of History in American Schools of Architecture*, New York.

Wylde, Peter (1981) 'The First Exhibition: The Architectural Association and the Royal Architectural Museum', *AA Annual Review*.

Yates, Frances (1969) *Theatre of the World*, London.

Yates, Frances (1986) *The Rosicrucian Enlightenment*, London.

INDEX

Page numbers in **bold** indicate illustrations

Facadism p. 172

BLACKWELLS ART & POSTER SHOP
27 BROAD STREET
OXFORD OX1 3BQ
TEL. 01865 792792
VAT REG NO. GB 630 533 961

ATE: 17/02/95 12:11 NO: 21856

SHIER: DUTY MANAGER   TILL: 001

CRIPTION   QTY   PRICE   TOTAL

CHITECTURE ART OR PROFESSION
19041724   1 @ 10.99   10.99

AL SALE   10.99

          PAYMENT METHOD
BIT CARD   10.99

     TOTAL NO. OF ITEMS   1

ease retain your receipt as proof of
rchase will be required in the event
          of any query.

Jacobson p 172

1
2.
18
44
50
53
54
56
62
64
74-5
76-7
81
82
85
91
93
96-7
101
128-9
143
158
164.